BEYOND
THE HORIZON

Edited by
Julie Bomber

First published in Great Britain in 1997 by Poetry Today, an imprint of Penhaligon Page Ltd, Upper Dee Mill, Llangollen, Wales.

© Copyright Contributors 1997

A Catalogue record for this book is available from the British Library.

ISBN 1862260206

Typesetting and layout, Penhaligon Page Ltd, Wales.
Printed and bound by Forward Press Ltd, England

BEYOND
THE HORIZON

poetry *Pt* today

*'Past, present and future are all one timelessness
of truth ~ we are that truth.'*

Joyce Lee (Poem ~ When Love is Born)

Series Introduction

The Poetry Today series of anthologies was launched to provide a substantial showcase for today's poets. A permanent record of perception, concern and creativity in our late twentieth century lives.

Poetry is a coat of many colours. Today's poets write in a limitless array of styles: traditional rhyming poetry is as alive and kicking today as modern free-verse. Language ranges from easily accessible to intricate and elusive.

Poems have a lot to offer in our fast-paced 'instant' world. Reading poems gives us an opportunity to sit back and explore ourselves and the world around us.

Today's poetry readers have as varied tastes as the poets who write for them. The poems in this volume complement each other and provide insight into the real life of a society heading for the third millennium.

Foreword

Beyond the Horizon is a collection of poems which capture the mood of today and offer the reader a poet's view of the real world in which we all live.

No matter whether the poem be traditional or contemporary, they all invoke an insight into the wide range of human behaviour and emotion by their honest examination of the trails and joys of everyday living.

I have had a pleasurable, but difficult task of choosing ten of the people in this book as outright winners, my congratulations go to them and they are as follows:

Shirley Frances Winskill	*Travellers in Time*
Paul Chaney	*Move From my Vision*
Angela Tsang	*Mirror . . . Death*
Evelyn Wilkins	*Progress?*
Karl Mansfield	*Help*
Angela Cheveau	*Night in Winter*
Mary E Horsley	*Chapter and Verse*
Robert Gallant	*Alive*
Jane Hill	*The Pool of Ice*
Tracey Wadman	*The Maiden*

My thanks go to all the contributors to *Beyond the Horizon* - I hope you enjoy all the poems as much as I did.

Contents

The Poems

Fade to Black (and White)

Sat in the corner of the room,
There is a TV set,
From 'days when things were built to last',
It hasn't broken yet,

The screen is twisted to the right,
Towards my Grandad's chair,
The sofa gives an awkward view,
But no-one now sits there,

And when you flick the *POWER* switch,
The volume comes on loud,
And he'd admit it's turned too high,
But age made him too proud,

And when the screen illuminates,
It shows a grainy haze,
For now it's set on video,
To pass time in the days,

And no-one wipes the glass front now,
Since no-one thinks they must,
For once a gleam was on the screen,
But now it's turned to dust.

Kevin Matthews

Arthur

Notes

This Poem is in Memory of a Wonderful Father who died a few years ago. Herbert Arthur Ludkin

I was only two when dad went to war
He proudly belonging to the Tank Corps
Was blown up in a tank, the desert hot
Poor man beside him was killed on the spot
Blind - he was nursed by Nuns in Italy
Year later, Austrian doctor helped him see
The operation was a great success
Transfer German prison camp - what distress
'*Missing*' - telegram, mum thought he was dead
Pint of cabbage water - slice of brown bread
Saw lad of seventeen give up and lie
Lad succeeded - he willed himself to die
I nearly eight when this stranger came back
Rough khaki uniform - bulging ruck sack

Jenny Ambrose

The Jack in the Pack

Midnight leathers folded neatly,
on the casket, in the hall.
Ripe to take his final journey,
preaching lessons to them all.
Deep in shock, as deep as slumber
Mortified by loss and heartbreak.
Incense fired in the bowls
Murmured words from sinking souls.
Deep his life, with deeper passion.
Rhinestones fade as speed ensued.
Hungry for exhilaration,
throttled by his own submission.
Like a bullet from a rifle,
spun the thread to mulch the shale.
Disregarding jeopardy,
impetuous frivolity!
Whistling gasps that burnt the throat
Stronger than the hounds of hell,
into glory and it's trappings,
glory came and glory fell.
Deep the leathers on the casket.
Deep the mourning, deep the pride,
as they swung him in the cradle
Pillioned for the final ride.

S M Birkett

Pushed

Notes

Chingford, 1964, what a year!

You are to me what Debbie McGee is to he. I think Tony Blair should wear ribbons in his hair.

Cry and cry, then cry some more,
that's what you're doing,
and you really don't know why, or what for.

Just for attention,
a little bit of sympathy.
You keep whimpering on,
until those tears are all gone.

Your cry is now dry,
so you start to sob,
hoping that this time we pander,
because your sob did the job.

So you're centre to us all,
and we run back and forth,
for all your whims and desires.

But, not this time,
because we're all very tired,
of your tantrums and spoilers.

You can wallow on your own,
shout and moan all day long,
but no one will be home.

Because you pushed us too far,
that's why you're all alone,
wishing, just wishing, for someone to phone.

Steven Clements

Notes

Born in Barbados, lived in England since my teenage years. Nursing and other fields have not dimmed my vision of becoming a writer.

This is the fifth poem to be published in anthologies. I am also semi-finalist in competitions held by International Library of Poetry and Poetry Guild and won a prize for this poem (Poetry Today) which is reminiscent of my childhood.

My ultimate ambition - to see a book of poetry published in my name is paramount and I am determined to succeed.

Dedicated to my children Sandra and Michael. To Elizabeth whose faith in my ability remains steadfast.

The Angry Sea

Waves from the thrashing sea
Roll fiercely over the lovely white sand
Seem to disappear
Seaweed drift and float then land
Forming mountains of plant life with shells
Where living creatures also dwell

Amidst such chaos
Where trust outrules fear
Care of self the sublime
Sea dwellers care not about the loss
Knowledge of its depths over time

Mankind ignorant of this fact
Venture forth where sand and sea unite
The element of great tact
Allows, one can enjoy the right
To wallow in such pleasure
With good measure
The universe belongs to everyone
Its mysteries remain open to discovery

Cynthia Goddard

Notes

I am 43 and teach perform-
ing arts. I have had one poem
previously published in a
West Midlands Anthology
and won the Charterhouse
Poetry prize in 1993 with
*The Head Library of Anselm
Keiffer.*

My interests are closely intertwined with my work; I love
theatre, books and cinema.
Also, my garden - particularly the pond!

I cannot really recall a time
when I have not attempted to
write and my inspiration
nearly always comes from a
seemingly insignificant moment which leads me to ponder a greater truth.

Moving House

Up amongst the tipsy headstones, and the raised tombs
cracking open at the seams, their lids lifted and skewed,
a small figure makes a dash for the light as the trees
strain on invisible hinges in a wet, vegetable darkness,
clutching so hard on her St Christopher that he snaps
and falls like a gold seed in this plantation of the dead.
Frenzied now, she slips on the greasy stone of the path,
skittering across gravel where the memorial to the fallen
threatens to come to life, pausing only to catch her breath
beneath the portal, before swallowing the church's Norman comfort.

Thursday night and their voices are at full throttle as the
laudatory psalm for Sunday next is given a warm-through;
small chorister, being late, causes the master to turn and
transmit his most opprobrious of sneers, crumbs of snot
swinging and clinging to nose hairs, like parasite's eggs
threatening to hatch, and his cassock wafting a dead sheep stink.

Sunday morning, and the choir jostle in the frigid jungle
beneath the tower, where the bell topes dangle like creepers,
elbowing into their white cotton wings and fluted collars.
Small chorister turns away for a second and in that instant,
her starched white triumphs have gone, filched from the hook
by another, leaving no choice but to rag-pick from dusty flags,
and the vicar plucks disgusted at the shrivelled ruff,
muttering hot winey sanctimony into a little girl's ear, mote of
dirt as she appears to be on Mother Mary's pristine apron,
scabby brown blister on the bloom of Eve's apple.

So, abashed and mistrustful, she comes to the red-brick
Methodists, who do not deal in angels' wings and woollen worsted
and are all the fresher for it, seeming to a small child like
milk and biscuits after the sour stone of the Normans;
and a choir master here, who finds the songbird in her, who even if
not all to the good in other ways, at least has warm hands.

Lynn Miller

Notes

I was born 1 September 1918, my parents Mr and Mrs Betts, had a hard struggle, money was always scarce but we all became healthy, happy adults. I became Mrs Brown in 1941. I had 38 years of marriage, my husband died in 1979. I have two daughters, June and Rita, four grandchildren and five great grandchildren. I've always lived in Maidstone, I love my family, home and garden.

I enjoy music and have taught many children and adults, but now I'm retired from teaching organ and piano.

My other hobbies are writing, knitting and gardening.

We voted 1 May 1997, so I was inspired to write about Leadership. Where are the great leaders and writers of today?

I have had several poems published; I find inspiration from every day things and life in general.

Poetry Today is giving many people a chance to voice their ideas and opinions, it's a nice book, beautifully produced.

Leadership

Follow my leader was a childhood game,
we ran after someone and all did the same.
The leader stopped, jumped or did a sudden leap,
rolling - twisting or slow as a snake we'd creep -
in circle's, we all followed round and round
till the bell rang, then we trooped in a file from the playground
went back to the classroom till the clock struck four;
schooltime over, back to our homes once more.
Some children have parents from whom they can learn,
many find an empty house on their return,
others may run wild without motive or aim,
hooligans and vandals, who is to blame?

Character can begin in childhood days,
the poorest home can be rich in many ways
for the daily example is a constant monitor
giving from infancy the most valued and best tutor.
Patience is taught from a loving mother,
families have so much to give each other,
they share, tolerate, disagree and forgive,
protecting their good name and the way they live.

Unworthy and bad seed may be next door to the best
and they might contaminate, for good seed can die amongst tares,
and weakness is born in a world of unrest,
so much talent is wasted when nobody cares;
sagacious students are sometimes seduced by worldly wealth,
risking their assets and also good health,
for the long road to success can give heartache and pain,
rejection, frustration happens again and again.

A moment of truth comes when one rises from a bed of discontent,
freed from apathy, despair and unemployment,
they can firmly stamp on past mistakes when new hopes are found,
all those indiscretions of the past can be turned around for
sometimes suffering and hardship are lessons in disguise,
it takes more than good teachers of schooldays to make men wise.

Lavinia Brown

Notes

Now retired, I have two daughters and three grandchildren. I trained and studied to become an electrical engineer, but in early middle life, took up full-time social work. My health broke soon afterwards and I had to rebuild my life and career again.

I have always been interested in poetry from my early years, but it was only after I 'slipped' into a style of writing that it became a hobby and fulfilment.

But style and rhyme are only the means to an end: the mood created, the message stated, the vision projected is the poetry itself.

Land Mines

Twenty years or more of civil war,
had finally come to an exhausted end;
there really was no victory, no defeat in the event,
just a physical tiredness
With the destructive madness all spent.

The pen of peace could hardly be held,
dreary eyes half saw the document's word;
the reason for conflict in remembrance all blurred,
but sufficient the point had been made,
though what that was could not now be declared.

Both opposing leaders claimed their rewards,
staking their claim to the changing times;
Each said 'My peace I leave with you,
and so after the upheaval and strain
let the white flowers grow again.'

Yes!, let the white flowers grow again,
in a ground polluted with the land mine;
far and wide, uncharted, hidden and unseen,
a menace to the now and present
and future generations of descent.

Like a malignant destructive gene,
dormant through many a reproductive round;
but every now and then declaring its lease,
making mayhem and tragically to remind
of a legacy that cannot be unbequeathed.

Project the scene to the mind's eye,
of a loving child not yet born
wishing to give a mother flowers to arrange and show;
but she having to correct and scold with an inward cry,
'No!, you must leave the white flowers alone to grow.'

Is this the peace that was given,
the freedom that war did bestow?
a Garden of Eden out of bounds,
a present from God which dare not be taken;
where white flowers do sickeningly grow

E Ashwell

The Play is Over

Notes

In remembrance of my parents Will and Glady Waterman who dedicated their lives to bringing up us children the right way.

The wind whistles around the house
There's a cold chill in the air
Walls and gates shine with frost
In grey skies the sun is lost
But there's a peaceful silent scene
When the snow falls white and clean
In winter

Spring has come around again
The world wakes up to live anew
The earth puts on a fresh green coat
And drinks of the morning dew
Time to look forward to the light
Of sun and flowers birds in flight
On the spring scene

Summer next days lazy and hot
Fish are jumping in the pond
Flowers galore to bring indoors
A green lawn to have tea upon
A quiet meander through the trees
Shaded from the sun
An easy chair and a cool drink
When the day is done

Misty mornings and cooler days
The birds are flying on their way
Lights are shining in the windows
Dark nights here to stay
Falling leaves midst summer glory
Last of the flowers end of the play
The year has turned full circle
And winter is on the way

A Llewellyn

Travellers in Time

I'm Shirley Winskill from Ilkeston in Derbyshire. I'm married to Gerald and we have one daughter, Suzanne, who is at present living in Cambridge.

I became a poetry 'addict' at the age of seven, and composed my first poem when I was a first year child at our local primary school; so I've been writing poetry for practically most of my life, (with long intervals of course, due to family duties).

I became more prolific with my writing when Suzanne left home and became an undergraduate at the University of Birmingham. I've had forty-three poems published in various anthologies since 1991, many of which have been illustrated by my husband, Gerald. The reference section at the Ilkeston and district library keep copies of all my poems on file.

I was inspired to compose my poem, *Travellers in Time* after meeting John L Foster, who at the time was writing for MacMillan Education, published by Oxford University Press. I believe he also writes under the pen-name of Derek Stuart. I have signed copies of two of his books which I purchased after listening to one of his poetry readings. These books stand side by side with my four Poetry Today anthologies in a special place of honour in one of my many bookcases.

Have you held a hailstone
Machine-gunned from a storm?
A disappearing diamond.

Have you felt the sunbeams
Dancing on your face?
Warmth from the world-candle.

Have you felt the lick
Of a loving kitten's tongue?
Sandpaper in a good mood.

Have you touched a nettle
When wandering through the grass?
Poisonous snakes in disguise.

Have you held a baby
Sleeping in your arms?
A Traveller to the Land-of-yet-to-be.

Shirley Frances Winskill

The Best is Last

Notes

When one hits the bottom sometimes you are fortunate for someone to be there to lift you up.

Dedicated to my 'Saviour' friend Iris

When you hold each others' hand when one is sad,
Or laugh together at a secret joke:
When the other 's thoughts are known which make you glad,
And tiresome act no irate response provoke.
When the sight of loving lass with lad
tightens the bond when old as it did in youth;
when you love in friendship, not in lust,
and thrill together at a world that's not uncouth.
Then sharing passions which you thought were lost;
Like pets who treat you equally as one,
and dancing with good friends so happily,
Where nostalgia is a joy and not a yoke.
When one another leaves the other free
to do one's thing without a twinge,
then come together joyfully;
the green eyed monster left outside the fringe.

When either may for losses mourn,
be it friend, relative or sad twist of fate:
Being together makes you less forlorn,
Knowing that you're with a caring mate.

When you may voice a sudden thought
'bout something which disconnected springs to mind,
the other laughs obvious the mood is caught;
responding often 'So did I' What magic refined.
Lifting the other up when one falls down.
As tiresome joints alternately give way;
Looking to each other with laugh not frown,
whilst on your way proceeding with a life so gay.

When in old age the inevitable end to face:
Of one who's loved and not be scared;
because together you have grown with grace:
Best to have chosen, and been chosen your mate.
But above all as together you kneel in devotion,
aware always that your partner cares,
you will have in life achieved the ultimate;
To be known as an item by all enlightened folk.

Rees Thorley

Dennis

Notes

This particular poem is actually a song that I wrote in December 1994, with the chorus erased.

The inspiration behind this is my research and knowledge of one of Britain's most infamous mass killers, Dennis Nilsen, who strangled and decapitated his victims out of loneliness. Fifteen young men died at his hands to prevent them from leaving. He was a sad and lonely man but not fiendishly sadistic for his own pleasure like most would love to think.

You were just a lonely man with time on your hands
Some say you were a monster with no future plans
Did you really think that killing was the right thing to do
You just couldn't control the demons inside of you
Did you ever feel remorse or have any regrets
About those unfortunate to die when you met
Your killing spree lasted four long terrible years
No next of kin so there were never any tears

It was necessary to be extremely intoxicated
Necrophilia was on your mind that is why you're hated
You only destroyed members of an unloved society
That is how you committed your evil deeds in obscurity
How did you reside with such a rancid smell
Inside your habitation must have been like living in hell
All you had to do was make some friends
Its far too late now for you to make amends

You were just a lonely man with blood on your hands
Some say you were a beast with vicious butchers hands
Now your locked away has the compulsion disappeared?
Being surrounded by villains is the loneliness still feared?
Perhaps now you've had time to consider the crimes of your past
Has incarceration changed you, how long do you think you'll last?
Do you remember your victims, are you still obsessed with death?
Will you pray for forgiveness with your dying breath?

Trevor Andrew Vidamour

34

Notes

I have appeared in Auberon Waugh's Anthology of Real Poetry, won a certificate (2nd prize) in 1991 for a poem in the Scottish International Open Poetry competition.

I have also been featured in other anthologies, a few annuals and work in several country newspapers - having moved around quite a lot.

On Seeing a Painting of the Dead Poet

With the bright oriole of your hair
fallen on the pillow grey
They found you quietly sleeping there
at break of day.

Poor Chatterton! I pray your soul
shall from the death-pang that you braved
find peace and the felicity
your spirit craved.

Your gift, your labour and your youth
squandered in natural tendency
will rise in a continuum
and shine in its ascendancy.

Oh, the bright oriole of your hair!
Those heavy lids that hide your eyes
shall one day open in the sun
of your lost paradise.

Elizabeth Borland

To a Barn Owl

Notes

I am 54 years old, divorced with 3 grown-up children living in Cardiff, London and Scotland, and one grandchild Murren - she is 8 months old. I am a night care supervisor in an elderly person's home. I live in a small cottage situated by Washford river near Exmoor National Park.

I have written poetry all my life but have never submitted any for publication until 2 years ago.

I write mainly on rural themes taking my inspiration from the beautiful countryside surrounding my home and the Quantock and Brendon Hills where I love to walk my dogs, Winston and Tess.

Tyto, possessed of ghostly form,
Silently glide on wings of white;
Your myriad feathers keep you warm
When hunting in the depth of night.

Mystical owl; enchanted bird;
Fates harbinger of witchcraft's birth;
Your eerie call can oft be heard
as shadows fall upon the Earth.

Wise bird of mystery, swift of wing,
What evil omens you portray;
No harm can such a creature bring -
To live by darkness is your way.

Now, as the moon ascends its path,
You hunt for mice to feed your brood.
An innocent deed devoid of wrath -
Your only aim to search for food.

Nocturnal spirit, bird of prey;
Skilled hunter of perceptive sight;
So rarely seen by light of day;
Unique in beauty, eyes so bright.

To watch your graceful wings unfold
And marvel as you glide on high;
A magical spectre to behold
- Ethereal presence in the sky.

Mary Farrell

Notes

For the last 20 years I have earned my living working on or in the sea. Every now and again I write something worth keeping and that pleases me!

Most importantly, I am trying to do a good job as mother to my two teenage children.

The abuse of our planet and its natural inhabitants upsets me more than anything.

In My Back Yard

In the morning there was a thrush
Clear cold notes of dew upon the air
This dawn was very still
just withdrawn breath and listening.

Slanting sun shadows on the grass
touched the moss to gold,
the nodding snowdrops to new meaning.
A liquid inactivity, a waiting hush.

Velvet sea, a mirror calmness,
pastel pink with blue thrown against
the surface and tossed back
to meet the growing light.

Not quite a silent Spring,
no sign of death.
This is life, quiet but pulsing,
held but swelling'
here and compelling.

Not for me the palls of desert smoke
the sand held pain of destruction,
the oil death upon troubled waters
the wrong doing in the minds of men.

Not for me the fall and death of forests
by clamouring shrieking steel
or slow sour drip of acid,
dust to dust, death on death.

Not for me the wordy rattle of power,
the wrong decisions, for the wrong reasons.
There should have been a sense,
of awe, not economics.

Not for me, I'm not looking, not listening.
I see only this way,
in my small corner of infinity
I am hiding, both cynicism and eternity.

I'll help the suffering
If only to assuage my guilt,
as a member of the human race.
But I can't bear to look.

Tell me. How can I help?
A donation? I don't have much.
Tell me how I can change the minds of men,
and what will be their souls awakening.

Alice McKay

Journey to Heaven

Notes

Shuna Body is both farm worker and a farmer's wife and lives in the tiny village of Snargate on Romney Marsh. The poem was written on the day of her grandfather-in-law's death; and portrays the Christian hope that can be found in death.

This poem is dedicated to the late Dick Body.

I am standing on the windswept marsh,
Whilst a shepherd and his dog nudge the sheep along the lane,
and head for new pastures, where the grass is greener.
The man has an air of peace about him,
I stand and watch helplessly until at last his figure
fades in the distance
A farmer at the gate splutters He has gone
'Gone where?' his child asks
From our view, that is all
He is just as graceful and wise, as when he left our side,
His apparent small figure
is merely what our eyes behold . . .

And just at the moment when someone said 'He has gone'
The shepherd's wife and old friends sing 'At last, he is here.'

Shuna Body

What it was Like

Notes

What it was Like describes a period of nine months of my life, I took a job to save money in order to return to university. Last Christmas, I had to get up very early and for an instant I thought that I was still working at that job, it was then that I realised how unhappy I'd been during those nine months, the poems was written later that morning.

I used the poem to dump unwanted feelings, and to try and express what I'd felt like for nearly a year, to those close to me.

I remember what it was like
when my eyes ached and nothing felt right.
Being dragged from a beautiful sleep
to a cold harsh morning
saying hello to my parents while still yawning.

I remember saying it's 'only eight hours' to myself in my head.
Wearing thermals and gloves, switching on my torch
and bumping my bike out of the shed.

I remember the eight minute journey, knowing each bend in the road
timing it brilliantly, never wanting to arrive too early.
I also remember my optimism being marred, each time I slammed in my clock card
I remember the anger and the hate.
The work being, uninteresting and the machines supply unending.
With my friends and family at times with hollow voices saying, 'it's not forever, it will be all right, just you wait.'

I can remember it all only too well, if I think hard my eyes begin to swell.
The hate, the anger and the frustration all flood back so quickly with a little concentration.

My family were right, things have moved on and maybe my time has come.
But knowing an alternative which I detested, fills me with fear and haunts me with such might; that when I wake early with sore eyes and it's still dark, the memories hit me and I remember what it was like.

Phil Allen

Move From My Vision

Notes

This Manchester born street-wise Actor/Writer has lived in America and Japan and now shares a flat with Japanese friends in London. His other work includes stage-plays and a recent commission for a screenplay.

Interests include films, music (soul/blues/jazz), Japan and American comedian Bill Hicks.

What inspires him to write? 'Reading other writers work and realising that I could do that, or on some rare occasions . . . I wish I could do that.'

His inspirations are Alan Bleasdale - Charles Bukowski and Raymond Carver.

The poem *Move From My Vision* is autobiographical and deals with the conflict between a man's need for sex and his desire for love.

Move from my vision, you disturb my dreams,
my desire for what you could never be.
You soothe my loins, you satisfy a yearning,
but I also yearn to be understood.
Not having the strength of celibacy,
I search for she who is in my dreams.
How will she think of me, that I have
lay down with so many in our unknown years?

Such tenderness of thought,
but I seek only to step down from my horse,
an arrogant beast.
And even now alone on foot.
I still possess a confident stride.
Still the hunter, never the hunted
So then who is my prey? She is my prey,
she who must move from my vision.

Paul Chaney

Pause

Notes

Pause is a description of transition without a thought on life at present.

From whom do these feelings come?
To whom do these feelings go?
Why bury them deep within the earth's
of an unfair world?
Why drown them in a sea of hope?
Dreams with no eventual reality
leaves a meaningful mind
in hazy complex contemplation
The elements of time
will never decline
will eat away these dreams of mine.
These memories of mine
I shall define
as remaining with me
till the end of time.

Roseanne Butler

Notes

I'm 24 years old and live in Nottingham.

I have been writing poetry and short stories since my early teens, and this is my first published work. My inspiration comes from experiences involving people, dreams, animals, music (in particular I enjoy classical Indian music for its ability to transmit emotion and pictures intrinsic to each Raga or song.), natural wonders and natural hallucinogens, which all colour the mind in simple but sometimes dazzling ways.

This poem is about having visions, and exploring the changing landscape of the mind. It is an invitation that offers the reader a chance to share images from another imagination, but to look through their own minds eye. It is intended that the reader will perceive the poem in their own way, and in doing so change it. I see change as the basis of imagination because without it there are boundaries, and with boundaries there are limits.

This poem can put a picture in your mind, but I hope that every reader will get a different picture, or different meaning from it.

I would like to thank the many people in my life who have inspired me to write, and would like to dedicate this poem in particular to Paul Crisp, a trusted friend and fellow visionary, and dabbler in matters of self destructive hedonism. This is his birthday present. I should also like to mention a thank you to the Nottingham Posse for making sclerosis of the liver an ambition, and not a problem. You know who you are!

The Image

I shall conjure an image for your delectation,
from that we call our imagination,
and not what you'd call an hallucination,
so please, accept my invitation . . .

Picture through your mind's eye
ascending as ether in a golden sky,
and descending through ribbons of carmine clouds,
to lush green forests on mountains proud,

Weaving as wind through imposing towers,
where sorcerers once had learnt their powers,
and calculated to the dying hours,
secret spells where the fire glowers,

Upon Seas of glass, above emerald carp,
diamond eyes trained on the harp,
playing lucid melodious notes,
whilst drifting upon the silver boats,

And so on to the plains of tranquillity,
along the river from the undying sea,
following the ship of a thousand eyes,
attentive only to the golden skies,

Then on to the floating pyramids of night,
of the frozen pharaohs who dream of the light,
forever doomed to walk in the void,
their wealth and power long since destroyed.

Into the jungle of deep evergreens,
to the jade constructed temple of dreams,
where the crystal jaguars, vigilant and wise,
take in your features through sapphire eyes . . .

Alex Sinclair

Standing Tall

Notes

The year of Hale Bop - I hit 25. The year I wrote Standing Tall I was 24 and if I'm honest this poem was a sign of the times, which is about excepting who you are, no matter what other people tell you for whatever reasons. The time of my life when I finally let go of something.

I dedicate this poem to my lovely family and friends who were my strength when I had none and whose love is unconditional.

In my mind, I am me
I do not know what others see,
perceptions are subjective views
Executed by mindless fools
And Words tie me up at once in knots,
for when with others I am lost.

In my mind I'm, on my own
A stranger in another home,
my intelligence, I think is such
That I choose not to judge . . .
. . .
Instead I am the passive observer
ingesting surrounding infrastructure.
In my mind I am me
Tomorrow holds what others see.

If I had no eyes I would see the same,
if I had no tongue I would speak the same,
if I had no mind I would not be me
Then I would never know what others see.

Bettine Turner

An Athlete's Ode

Notes

I am a retired civil servant. As a professional technology officer I was responsible for the conceptual design of all new technical facilities at a large MOD establishment seeing the work through to completion.

For most of my life I have been a competitive athlete, running, jumping, throwing, race walking as well as rowing in coxed fours. I am also a AAA sprints coach and graded timekeeper.

The poem is based on observations made during a Sunday morning training run.

Whilst urban dwellers embalmed in early Sabbath sleep,
I an athlete prepare for a training schedule, I must keep.
An extra singlet donned, I'll soon be as warm as toast,
whilst sun's golden fingers dispels overnights white ghost.

'My', the air has a bite, but healthy tendons feel like silk,
an outstretched arm from a door ajar, seeks a pint of milk.
The common soon appears where Rush pond lies to circumnavigate,
and ducks in flotilla order around the island, expertly negotiate.

Out onto the road, and past the 'Bull',
whose revellers last night, drank to the full.
Then into the woods, whose wintry carpet hides many a snare,
but hare like it must be covered without being scared.

The ups and downs, are taken with consummate ease,
squirrels disappear into the camouflage of old oak trees.
A bold robin there in my path stands, checking my stride,
training like this, it's good to be alive.

Back home under the shower, I feel like doing it all over again,
but duty calls, baby would like to be pushed over the recreational terrain.
A few more miles, but this time with indulgent ease,
ah not so, I must step up a gear, or I will freeze.

Roy H Rudd

Daniel McGough's Cough

Notes

The poem is dedicated to my wife Sarah who I love dearly and who continues to give me the encouragement and advice that I need.

This is the tale of poor Daniel McGough,
Who found himself plagued by a terrible cough,
It tickled his tonsils, it made him feel weak,
His voice was reduced to the tiniest squeak,
His parents were frightened, they did what they could,
But red-faced young Daniel was not looking good,
A doctor was summoned, the best one in town,
But one look at Dan and he had to sit down,
His hands all a tremble, his face white as snow,
The doctor said nothing but got up to go,
A shrug of the shoulders then out through the door,
As Daniel lay coughing flat out on the floor.

With time running out it was all hands on deck,
So liquids and potions were poured down his neck,
Then Daniel began to feel rather uneasy,
The cocktail of drinks made his stomach go queasy,
With gurgles and gluggles his body rebelled,
The coughing fit ended, the tickle was quelled,
But just as wee Daniel was rubbing his throat,
A new sound was heard, quite a musical note,
And in place of the ailment that troubled him so,
Poor Dan now had hiccups that just would not go.

Simon Smailes

Notes

Una is a Reiki Master living in Limerick, who intends to move to the west coast of Ireland in autumn 1997. Although she has been writing poetry for a number of years, this poem represents a public acknowledgement to herself that she enjoys writing and this is her first poem to be published.

Listen was inspired by her growing awareness of the level of noise pollution created by people who fear silence, who shun nature, or who simply don't think about either.

She has written a series of poems about noise as she revels in natural silence herself. She believes that silence reveals personal truths and is rich and complex.

She enjoys walking on beaches and hills and feeling the wind on her face.

Listen

We do not hear each other speak
we're so wrapped in 'me'
Stop, For a moment and listen
Use your ears to see

The damage caused around us
why are we so afraid
of Listening to the silence
to the ache that we have made

In the earth around us
in our daily integration,
Please listen for a moment,
it could be our salvation

Una Flanagan

Notes

In the short time I have written/read poetry I have found it to mean a great deal of different things to different people, so all I can say is judge for yourself what poetry is and what it means to you.

I have.

Retribution

Here Zachariah comes,
hideous, distorted face,
is this retribution?
my niche turned to waste.
Abnormal, strange eerie feeling,
unusual, cold deadly silence,
is this retribution?
a prelude to violence.
That grass isn't green,
nebula? sky turned from blue,
is this retribution?
elite? chosen few.
Repetitive days,
stay dark like the nights,
is this retribution?
God's effectual rights.

Graham Blair

Love and War

Notes

Contrary to popular belief, not all budding poets and authors are middle-aged. I am sixteen and live in the north-east of Scotland.

I am in a loving foster family due to the abuse I suffered in my natural home. I have been diagnosed as depressed for a year and made several suicide attempts; the most recent being in April 1997.

I have written poems and short stories about my feelings of desperation as they have a therapeutic effect. I find I can express myself through writing, better than through direct speech.

This poem is about the immense guilt that I let my abuse continue and the bad feelings of not saying good-bye to my little sister.

This poem is dedicated, with love, to Maureen Johnston and to Christine and David Thomson.

The hurt I've caused, I can't explain,
The war's ongoing, so's the pain.
The wounds are open, gaping wide,
The mess I caused, I just can't hide.

The punches I've thrown come back again,
The love and hate corrupt my brain.
I've destroyed myself, I feel insane,
My heart's in pieces, and I'm in pain.

I pushed my parents so far away,
The bitterness, the hate, the price to pay.
I love them so, I did not realise,
The things I've said, I can't disguise.

Diana Barnard

Lost Love

Notes

A poem simply about unre-
quited love and optimism
about loneliness. The result
though is disappointment in
relationships.

We said goodbye
By a distant shore

That now seems so long ago
I would like to meet again
(The others, of them I know)
But to return to that far place
To hear you laugh
And see your face
That would be so fine for me
Worth the wait
But it will never come to be

Peter Firth

Whole Holes

Notes

Roy O Driscoll is an Irish poet heavily influenced by Ogden Nash and Charles Bukowski. With a far from extensive publication history, Roy continues to be prolific. The poem *Whole Holes* is from a collection called Agent Orange which as a whole deals mainly with the themes change, delusion and confusion (the collection has yet to be published).

Whole Holes itself is basically a statement echoing the sentiment everything you know is wrong!

The trees in the forest of life are dead.
The fish in the river of dreams are wide wake.
Clouds in my eyes. More rain, more pain.
The mud on my knees comes from my veins.
The holes in my head start and end with my mouth.
Solid waste. Disposal tastes like the mucus we swallow
like the icons we follow
Jesus Christ was disposed of.
Charles Manson is indisposed.

Roy O Driscoll

The Festive Season

Notes

I am a thirteen year old girl living in the outskirts of Dublin. I am in my first year at an all girl's secondary school. My hobbies include playing the violin, the Irish flute, hockey, art and of course reading and writing poetry.

I write poetry as a way of expressing my emotions freely. I have been writing poetry for the last two years and particularly for special occasions.

The things I regard important to me would have to be my friends, music, sport and poetry.

I would like to dedicate this poem to everyone I know but especially to my family and grandparents, who have inspired me so much.

It's that time of year again,
With the mulled wine and the Heineken beer,
With the giving and receiving of presents,
With Christmas past and Christmas present.

As the snow covers the ground,
And a sheet of white carpets all land around.

And soon you begin to think,
'I wish it could be like this every day,
I wish time would stop, would freeze, would stay'
But soon it shall all be over
And it will be back to life in Ireland with
The mythical four leaf clover.

Deva O'Doherty (13)

Celebration Day

Notes

I am 48 years old and was born in Sunderland. I have been married to Glynis Ann for 25 years in September 1997, we have two boys, Mark 23 and Gareth 17. I work as a checker in a cash and carry.

I have been writing poetry for a few years and have had over twelve poems published, my dream and ambition is to have my very own book published.

My inspiration comes from heaven above from my Lord and Saviour Jesus Christ, for he has blessed me with this talent to write my poems.

The churches in our village formed a choir known as Ryhope Churches Choir. The first concert they had started with a song 'Come on and Celebrate' and the inspiration just flowed to write *Celebration Day*. 'Praise the Lord'.

Come and celebrate the gift of his love,
The precious one sent from heaven above,
He came as a babe to this our earth,
At Christmastime we celebrate his birth.

He grew up and became a man,
To fulfil his fathers plan,
He was baptised in the Jordan by John,
His earthly ministry was only three and a half years long.

He said to the twelve follow me,
They saw him make the blind to see,
He made the deaf to hear and the lame to walk,
He even made the dumb to talk.

He turned the water into wine,
He is the true the living vine,
The tempest he stilled on Galilee,
He loves the world yes you and me.

One day they led him up the hill,
It was not his but his fathers will,
A crown of thorns pierced his brow,
He is crowned the King of Glory now.

Jesus bowed his head and died,
A soldier standing pierced his side,
He rose again on the third day,
And to heaven went on his way

And one day he will come again,
The bible makes it oh so plain,
And then we will be on our heavenly way,
On that *Great Celebration Day*.

David Reynoldson

Notes

The poem is about the confusion of a long distance relationship. It is hard to give all your love when you know they will be gone again soon.

I would like to dedicate this poem to Block 10, for all their help in coping with the distance. To my parents Mike and Yvonne, without whom I would not be where I am today. And to Ceri, who I know I do not show it very often, I love with all my heart.

Sort of Love

Sort of starting
Sort of staying
    Sort of parting
    Sort of playing
Sort of kissing
Sort of touch
    Sort of missing
    Sort of much

Angela James

Notes

Hailing from Liverpool but now living in South Wales, I first started writing about twenty years ago; though only intermittently. Then about three years ago the urge to write grew stronger, a sort of re-awakening you might say. Now at every opportunity I yearn to write.

I like to write satirical verse best as well as more conventional poetry.

Most of my poems are derived whilst driving my HGV where inspiration comes from different people I meet and generally seeing life go by from my windscreen; my 'window to the world'.

My hobbies include playing football, aerobics and gardening.

I would like to dedicate my poem to my beloved mother Frances.

Farewell to Summer

'Tis with a touch of sadness
I watch the summer bid farewell
No more constant rays of sunshine
Or fragrant flower's left to smell

The crinkled leaves of rustic
They teeter so slightly then fall
Then the wind it whip's them round and round
As they heed the winter's call

Telltale moisture on the window
Warns of frost not far away
Long gone the young and tender leaves
That promised much in May

Late night owl's proclaim the Autumn
As they hoot through moonlight tree's
There's a mist around the mountain
And a tingle in the breeze

The bird's they seem impatient
As they prepare their epic flight
Time to get the winter woolly's out
And central heating's on at night

Final petal's flutter to the ground
And pretty soon are washed away
As nature organises
Beneath cloud's of smoky grey

Heavy raindrop's never ceasing
Make puddle's in the soil
Pack away those summer T-shirts
And that bottled sun tan oil

So now it's time to store away the thing's
We only use in summertime
The hammock and sun lounger
For now the weather's not so fine

Yet I look forward to the winter
Snuggled up with lot's of snow
For even though it's cold outside
Within I'm all aglow.

Dave Mullin

War

Notes

My name is John Donald and I live in Watford, Hertfordshire. I am 18 years old but was 17 at the time of the competition.

War was the first poem I ever wrote and while looking through the Sunday paper I saw the competition and decided to enter.

I wanted to write a poem about war to show different opinions on such a destructive issue, how in today' high tech age people can still not sort out their differences with reasoning rather than with brute force, and how some people think its heroic to fight for your country even though you're losing so much.

War what an honourable thing;
To fight for your country, to fly your flag high.
To see such suffering to watch people die.

We must keep our country free at all expense.
Or the suffering and killing will be immense,
Would it be a sin to die away from home,
To poison their land and forever be known.

We must forget ourselves and fight as one,
Forget our wives daughters and sons,

Or should we stay at home and die a coward,
Or fight for freedom and be overpowered,
I know which choice I must, and will take,
I know its right,
And not a mistake

John K Donald

Notes

At the time of writing this poem, I was twenty-seven and studying English literature at Strathclyde University, Glasgow. I guess the main idea behind the poem stems from collective loneliness and how an individual relates to a mass society.

The reason I write poetry is that I like the way it can communicate large concepts in such an efficient manner. It is also a great release from everyday worries. I do not know where it comes from, but I guess that really does not matter. The best thing about poetry is that every interpretation is correct. There are no wrong answers.

Us

We are but one in a sea of stars.
A single poppy in a field of blood.
A grain of sand on an endless beach.
So why do I feel so alone?

Six billion people stuck like glue,
On a piece of rock, too much crew,
For a flightless craft without no aim.
So why do I feel so alone?

Problems mount surpass their weight,
Fill your mind with undue rate,
Round and round they will dance.
So why do you feel so alone?

I am one, we are many.
Collective us lost and weary.
No one cries for wasted lives.
So why are we all alone?

John Anglim

Notes

I dedicate this poem to my two children, my son John and my daughter Suan, with much love.

Untitled

'Go to bed', says daddy
'I'll be up when I can,
'You've got your favourite teddy
There is no bogey man,'

But parents just don't see him
They are so unaware.
My sister has and cousin Jim,
He's waiting up the stairs.

I put my fingers in my ears,
So I can't hear him breathe.
I scrunch my eyes up nice and tight,
Oh why don't they believe.

I run across the landing
And jump right into bed
Just in case his fingers
Grab me, from underneath the bed.

I peep my eyes out of bed,
To see if he's yet there.
The darkness swims about my head
But there's only my teddy bear.

Maybe there is more than one
In all the children's rooms
They fly around the night sky,
On stolen witches brooms.

On the wall instead of shadows,
There are pictures there instead
I can't hear him breathing,
My brother snores in bed.

I look up to the sky
And say his name out loud,
But it's not him, peeping round the moon.
It's only silver cloud.

The moon shines down inside my room,
The stars are large and bright.
It is a plane, I see, and not a witches broom,
That moves across the night.

Maybe daddy's right,
There is no bogey man,
I'll look again tomorrow night,
And catch him if I can.

Jayne C Griffiths

Notes

My name is Jody Partridge, I'm 17 years old and live in Kent and I'm studying media at Canterbury College.

I started writing poetry about two years ago, and I have over 100 of my own poems and songs (most unpublished). A couple of my poems are in anthologies and one was specially selected for a version on tape.

I base my poems on personal experiences of myself and others, then I extend them to the limits of my imagination.

I wrote this poem observing my surroundings while sunbathing on the beach, on holiday with my family in Portugal.

While Sunbathing I See

Souring gulls in this cloudless sky
of picture postcard blue,
Distant valleys and hazy mountains
creating a beautiful view,

People fishing waiting patiently for that innocent fish to bite,
mysterious dark caves inside eroded rocky coves
an enchanting sight.

Dips and ridges in the sizzling sand
washed by the tide,
Imprints of feet all sizes
side by side,

Oil tanned bodies lying relaxing
under the baking sun,
A cool sea breeze brings relief from the hot airs
for everyone,

Ice creams and lollies melting as they're eaten
under the beaming sun,
Many enjoy and savour as it cools and melts
on their tongue,

A powerful current of water as a speed boat rides
the oceans foaming waves,
People laughing and splashing under the suns
stretching rays,

A coastline of towering white cliffs so far
for my eyes to reach,
I saw these things today while sunbathing
on this beautiful Portuguese beach.

Jody Partridge

The Seasons

Notes

I am married with an eight year old son and after a twenty-two year career in a drawing office I became a redundancy statistic. We then moved from Chester to my husband's native Ireland and now I concentrate on being a Mum. I joined an English class two years ago and *The Seasons* was my first poem. It is also the first thing I have ever put forward for publication.

My inspiration came from the beautiful Irish countryside where I live.

I would like to dedicate this poem to my husband, a true countryman, and my son James.

Warm infant Spring follows a cold new-born year,
Announced by the primrose with her shy, pretty face;
While light fluffy clouds shed a fresh crystal tear
Over leaves reaching out for the Sun's warm embrace.

The hot youthful passion of long Summer days
Brings gossamer wings and a honey bee's bustle;
And swallows that soar on a warm lazy haze,
With the rich, sweet scent of the wild honeysuckle.

See the hedgerows and bushes with berries galore;
See bright crystal beads strung on spidery lace;
As mature Autumn's bounty is gathered in store,
See the harvest moon rise o'er the mists into space.

The bleak wind of Winter - a cruel, angry beast -
Kept at bay by the fire and a warm festive cheer,
While family and friends all join in the feast,
And reflect on the memories of an old passing year.

Mary Elizabeth Newsome

Notes

I was born in Birmingham on 25 August 1924 and educated at Moseley School of Art in Birmingham, I joined the WAAF in 1942 as a wireless operator. I have a son, Richard John Haines, now aged 52, and two grandchildren, Marianne and Alexander Haines.

I have been a resident of Melbourne since 1946. My father died in 1982 and my mother, Louisa Bishop, died in February 1997 aged 100 years and six months. They came to live with me in Australia in 1970.

My hobbies are reading and travelling overseas with my Scottish 2nd husband, we married in 1975. I love meeting people of all nationalities and listening to their problems, without giving advice. I am loving my retirement.

Heritage

The earth groans and creeks
Man ever fearful seeks
To run or hide, the elements cry
Aloud, eyes turned to the sky
We look, and hope for peace.

Man provokes, reasons, is defiled
Sets before each age his child
Born, in destiny, to run the race
To live with others, the human pace
He sets for himself, an upward climb
To knowledge, is shrouded by time.

We cannot live too long, we die,
Our minds transcend, wander, sigh
Sad facts are given, lie hidden
Along with earthly frame, forbidden
To burst too suddenly for man
His destiny is shaped by Divine plan.

Dorothy Ronald

International Negotiations

Notes

Carole Robertson has had poems published in a variety of magazines and anthologies.

She sat at a café table when it was Leningrad.
A sailor came and sat with her,
A sailor from the Baltic fleet.
He spoke some English and she spoke some Russian;
There was no difficulty about communication at all.

The table was varnished brown and shiny,
Round, covered with smaller rounds,
Rings from cups and mugs and glasses,
Tea and vodka and kvass.
A thousand conversations

Hung in the air like smoke.
They said nothing memorable. Constantly looked over
Their shoulders, or twitched with guilt
Less anyone should come up and say
You shouldn't have said that.

Foolishness. Whatever they said
Has long gone down the corridors of time,
Maybe filed on some celestial tape recorder
But lost in the files. Nobody knows
How long magnetic tapes keep.

They understood each other perfectly.
Looking over their shoulders into the nicotined smoke of suspicion
Clouding the café corners, making their eyes smart,
They said nothing and everything,
Remember only the stained circles, the lesser circles,
The deliberately circling words.

Carole Robertson

The Jazzcat

Notes

Michelle Hendricks, Vannes
27 July 1995

Roger J Gould wrote his first
play for a girl he was mad
about, when he was seven.
She promptly threw him
over, the first down of a
roller coaster life.

He loves music (grade 8
gramophone). He has had
short stories read on local
radio, several poems pub-
lished in anthologies, and
plays performed by young
people. Currently, he is
working on a novel set
around the east of Yorkshire,
from where he commutes
weekly to Hertfordshire.

Jazzcat, scatcat,
prowling the stage to sing her song,
her soulful voice, as good as Ella's,
needing the beat, deep and strong,
preening herself, scenting the fellas.
She winds herself between their stands,
stylishly, flirting with every player.
First her call, then she demands
that her mate should play her
coupling dance, with riffs or licks.
Each striving to exceed her best,
these musical toms who seek their kicks
in outperforming all the rest,
to sate this sliding, slinky, queen
as she smiles at each one's impro',
wrung from heart, soul, or libido.
Then, wantonly, she wails another solo.
Undulating to their sounds,
quivering, laughing, round she goes,
to cry out as they play, no bounds
to her passion, but each male knows,
he only matters who delivers.
In other sets she sings their tunes
of blues and love and smoky cellars,
but now the spotlights are her moons,
the stage her roof, and they fulfil her pleasures.

R J Gould

Lest We Forget

Notes

This poem was placed on the Canadian D-Day Memorial in the New Forest close to where I live.

I have written many poems including ones to commemorate the 50th Anniversaries of D-Day, VE Day and VJ Day. These I have framed together with letters from a very special lady who is endeared to all this Nation. I am also proud that these poems have been read out by a Padre in Canada.

The VJ Day poem was published by the local Burma Star Association which was a complete surprise. Apart from these I have had several poems published.

Two minutes silence is all we are asked to give,
to remember those who gave their lives so that
you and I might live.
Two minutes silence, not a lot to ask, to remember
those who years ago faced an awesome task,
To rid the world of tyranny, that we might live in peace,
To give our future generations a world where wars would cease.
Two minutes silence for all the lives that were lost,
Those who paid for our freedom at such a heavy cost.
So wear your scarlet poppy with gratitude and pride,
And remember that it was for our freedom that they fought and died.
The poppy is a symbol with its petals glowing red,
it reminds us of the price of freedom and all the blood that was shed.
Two minutes silence on this November day . . .
Two minutes silence to remember and to pray . . .

Betty Whitcher

Mirror . . . Death

Notes

I read many spine-chillers and horror books, which helps my imagination. I also enjoy other Arts (creative writing, drawing and painting). All these interests have inspired me to write poetry.

When I am lonely or depressed, all my feelings burst out and I write.

I have always wanted to publish my poems and to show my drawing to everyone.

My weary eyes slowly close into the darkness,
the beat begins to die and fade,
my body once tensed, now begins to relax,
sinking into Earth, like quick sand.

My fingers, held tightly close together,
with my fingertips in my palm,
slowly unravels like a lily flower,
till it touches the ground with an echo thump!

Gasping for air, I was,
but now . . . silence . . . not a sound . . .
. . . not a particle of dust touches the ground . . .
. . . still and frozen.

My life has departed from the real world,
into reflection.

Angela Tsang (17)

Still Life . . . Vibrant Life

In whitest shades of pale, the canvas glares
with tantalising challenge from the easel.
Creative juices urge me on as I prepare
the palette with its myriad of colours.
Excited, yet so panic-stricken like a weasel
I grab a dainty brush and carefully compare
the first stroke with the next and all that follow.

Last year's canvas stares bravely from the south
of the study, late sunlight softening stark Rembrandian shades.
Dark hues and lots of labour, sleepless nights
went into painting hollow eyes and trembling mouth.
I shiver as the mem'ry of it slowly fades
into the back recesses of my mind . . .
A cold breeze tries to blow the candle out.

I don't know yet exactly, I haven't got an inkling
how this year's picture will eventually turn out.
But the Creator of all Arts teases me on.
His Mouth is twitching. His eyes are twinkling.
His Sense of Humour infectiously catching on.
What has He got in mind, please let the secret out?
'All in My Time,' He says, leaving my backbone tingling.

Olga Allen

When Love is Born

Notes

This was my first inspired poem - A self-fulfilling Prophecy for a New World.

The Source of all Mankind is the Spirit of God within - our Eternal Soul.

This poem was written as a feeling response in America to what I perceived as hope for a loving world each by a personal example of truth.

Years later For the Present takes us Beyond the Horizon of joining Heaven and Earth!

Past, present and future are all one timelessness of truth - we are that truth.

My hope is for the child yet unborn -
Those who are now in faltering steps,
groping darkly in the abyss of our world
for a light by which to grow.

My dream is that those hearts unite
To see the folly of the age of man,
inspired with hope, they see the gloom
Of all our yesterday's of despair.

But tomorrow is dawning in these gentle hearts,
their days are being tossed in a helpless storm,
onward and upward they wish to go . . .
A spiral of love, shrouded in dreams.

That day will come in the tomorrow of their life,
when they will have known some bitter pills.
From the acid taste their feet will firmly stand.
In our world will right prevail.

A beacon will shine forth with light,
like moths will those inspired in love
Be beckoned to the very womb of life . . .
To bring Heaven to our hopeless Earth.

Joyce Lee

Notes

I live in Weston-Super-Mare with my partner and three teenage children. I am forty one and I work full-time as a secretary. I have written poetry since I was eighteen.

I have had one poem published in a book called The Other Side of the Mirror. Most of my poems have been inspired by people and their experiences.

I dedicate this poem to my mum.

Time to Let Go

When a loved one's body has become frail and stooped with age
They feel their life is over, they want to turn the final page
Their time is spent, they have had enough of life, enough of just living
They want you to let them go, to understand and to be forgiving

When there is no apparent reason for a body not to go on trying
How do you make the decision whilst you have a fear of death and dying
How do you know if you hold their hand today and say 'Okay'
That tomorrow they won't feel glad to be alive in what ever guise or way

How do you know that they are only hanging on because you will not let go
How can you be sure it's time for them to leave you for a place we cannot know
We think because we love them it's enough for them to be
Content with age and it's restrictions, but I wonder if we see

That they loathe their loss of independence and the things they cannot do
Without support from one of us, simple tasks taken for granted by me or you
Do we ask ourselves is it them or us who has the greater need
Do we will them to keep trying, are we blind to our selfishness and greed

They have given their whole lives to us, been there every single day
Yet now when they are asking us to listen our heart won't let them have their say
We know every day has become a struggle and so much harder to endure
Yet to give someone you love your blessing to give up the fight is the hardest test for sure.

Sara Angell

The Killer Among Us

Notes

People seem to think that poets are all middle-aged, have elbow patches and drive old bangers. So when people hear that I've written poetry and still only 23, their mouths seem to drop. I've only been writing for about 12 months and to be chosen for this book, for me is a great achievement, I feel that drugs are a great concern and should not be laughed at.

I hope the poem will affect some people if not a lot of them, hopefully people will realise that it's not just the older generation that worries about the effect of drugs but my generation as well, and if there is somebody out there who probably thinks I'm a bit of a fuddy duddy well wrong again, because I like nothing more than pubs and clubs, late nights and fast parties. So to everyone, I hope you enjoy my poem, and that you don't need drugs to enjoy yourself.

Drugs are so widespread,
That's what they said,
By the time you've read this sentence,
Another person dead.

The dealers will sell, to who ever they meet,
Their office is the playground, the clubs, and the street,
Just look at the needles, down by your feet.

Drugs come in many sizes, from smack , down to pills,
The people who do it, buy it for thrills.
After a while the drug takes hold,
Shattering your mind, to make you feel cold,

You loose all your perception, your feeling of time,
You get hooked on the drug, it turns you to crime.
After a while it takes hold of your soul,
And turns your heart black, black as coal.

So my final word is throw away that crud
Because drugs are the devils blood.

Paul Knight

Pipe Dream

Notes

I reside in the resort town of Eastbourne. I am a housewife and have been married for 35 years and have four children and one grandson.

I have always loved poetry. My father used to recite many poems to me when I was young, one of my favourites was 'Abou Ben Adhem.

My own poetry is based on my experiences and observations. I have written more than forty poems. I have had five printed and one put on audiotape. I also write short stories for children. Minerva Press would have printed them, but the cost involved for myself was too great.

I started writing when my children were young, but did not get too much time to concentrate, so really it has been the past couple of years that I have written the majority of my poems.

My hobbies are crosswords (I'm a fanatic), competitions, reading, cinema, theatre and listening to music. One of my twin sons is a very talented musician.

I love observing people and their situations. I was inspired to write *Pipe Dream* when I was watching the Edinburgh Military Tattoo. I am English, but there is something about a lone Scottish piper that I find very moving.

The poems I have had published so far include *Childhood Memories, Hair Raising, Beggar thy Neighbour, Life is not a Rehearsal* and *Intimidation.* I currently have two more poems in competitions and am awaiting the results.

Let me tell you the tale of the Piper,
he stood on the hill alone.
The skirl and whirl of his bagpipes
Thrilled folk to the bone.
He wore the Blackwatch tartan,
over his shoulder, a swathe of plaid.
His sporran and white gaiters
Had been handed down by his dad.

His name was Doogie Dougal,
and he was proud of his skill.
Folk knew they could always find him,
stood all alone on the hill.
They would gather at a distance,
then creep nearer to the sound.
The piping was so haunting,
it held the folk spellbound.

Throughout all the seasons
Doogie was always there.
In summer he felt light-hearted
And played without a care.
The long winter months depressed him,
he played very plaintively.
But the warming sun of Spring
Set Doogie Dougal free.

Let me tell you the tale of the Piper,
he died on the hill alone.
Folk said 'They could still see him.'
It chilled them to the bone.
They buried him with his bagpipes
In a deep deep grave on the hill.
But at times in the swirling mist,
you can see Doogie Dougal still.

Joan Enefer

Words From the Past

This poem is about remembering History. The first stage on the road to self-emancipation. Despair is our greatest weakness: it haunts us. As capitalism goes international, its irrationality and reliance upon exploitation intensifies. Crippled by reification, our hope is ground away to be replaced by the bitterness of the reactionary politics of the Right. But need only grows, social division and disintegration increases and the fundamental problem is never solved.

Don't go down this road please. Football is a competition - Nationalism isn't. One community or no community.

Recent History reveals that Capitalism is doing pretty badly, and we all suffer. So why the Right have faith in it I don't know. The collapse of the Soviet Union, and the move of the Labour Party to 'the centre' has not meant the defeat of Socialism; it has been its setting free to address society 'beyond the horizon'. Keep hope alive. All we have is each other, and we know where the problem lies . . .

They rush onto the page:
The tales of the age.
I thought I'd forgotten how to write,
but all the time I was just choking back
The fears of the memory.

The pain of the words,
straining to be heard
Above the echoes of the Right
That are bringing into tomorrow,
The tears of yesterday.

Peter James Warr

Dawn

I sat waiting, in the first rays of sun, to greet the dawn,
I sat waiting, I hear the sea and lone gull screeching, so forlorn.
Another day beginning, rising from it's sleep,
Another day for living, the memories to keep.
I sat waiting, quietly and patiently for the household to awake,
I sat waiting, listening to the sounds which hurried people make.
That golden hour each morning when the day is new and bright
Is by far a better warning to our senses, what is right.
I sat waiting, sipping tea in lonely state, such bliss,
The dawning for collecting thoughts, so few are times like this.

Patti Ryall

Mates

We are all but little pawns
Upon the Board of Life
Rank on Rank along the File
Danger lurks in every mile
For sin and shame are rife

Struggling on along life's way
Striving to reach our goal
Doing our best to help each other
Aiming to please our Father and Mother
And keeping our self-control

Father King and Mother Queen
She is the Matriarch
Will put her life upon the line
To save her King from oblivion
Never fails to make *Her* mark

One day we'll meet a Gallant Knight
He'll have our care at heart
Guarding us with buck and leap
We are safe within his keep
He knows how to play *His* part

The Bishop has a different role
We are often in his way
He loves to make the lighting dash
And though at times is rather rash
We let him have *His* say!

Rook keeps the straight and narrow path
But he also has to work
Castle; is his Nom-de-Plume
He will gladly meet his doom
His enemy to baulk

Although we are but little pawns
We are also very keen
To reach the end of this long road
And shed at last, our heavy load
So we too can be a *Queen.*

Joyce A Turner

72

Notes

I am 18 and live in Irvine-stown, County Fermanagh. I am a student in the final year of a BTEC in Leisure Studies. I hope to go to Sheffield Hallam University in September.

I have had 2 poems published with The International Society of Poets, entitled *Finding Hatred or Comfort* and *During Wind and Rain*.

I love tennis, reading, music, travel and writing.

Circumstances special to me inspire me to write, for example - beautiful places, different lands and soul mates who I have met and those I still have to meet.

Desolation

Go to the open ground
and wish
For you are not alone on a day
like this
When the fear and the pain
grips the heart with a clamp,
and leaves tears which fall
in derision.
Why here? You're not even there -
and you're going in the wrong direction.
A year without the one,
is like the land without the sun.
For this is not a child,
this is the heart of a woman -
falling, falling.
I must,
under the cornflower sky,
go to the open ground
and wish.

Deborah Johnston

Notes

The Northern Ireland conflict was the subject of my MSc dissertation at Bristol University. During the research I was struck by the intensity of the 'troubles' which infiltrate almost all aspects of people's lives in Northern Ireland, and by the palpable heartache, fear and mistrust which have been the legacy. Striving against the bitter animosity inherited by each new generation, recent years have witnessed a growing longing for peace. This was heightened by the ceasefire in 1994.

My inspiration for the poem was the deepening of the wish for peace which the majority of Northern Ireland's people continue to hold, despite the devastating breakdown of the ceasefire.

The Hope of Northern Ireland

The Newsreader speaks of another sectarian murder,
The power of Bomb and Bullet
Words heard too often in this divided land
The lack of surprise the listeners feel
fails to ease the sense of despair.

Among many, the passion for revenge is paramount
Dealing a further savage blow to hopes for peace
Their politics, tradition, history, their pride
must not be weakened by the 'other side'.

Centuries of hatred, fear and mistrust
cast a bitter shadow over this beautiful land
But a light also shines, brilliant and strong
From the people, joining together, who ache for peace.

After twenty five years, people felt the promise of peace
A warmth that many had never tasted
This was cruelly snatched away
But never before has there been a greater will to fight for it back.

Solutions will not be found immediately, there has been too much sorrow,
Bridges cannot be easily built to unite a segregated people
But we must continue to aspire to the time when
the flame of peace is stronger
Than the breath which fights to extinguish it.

Caroline Newell

I am but a Simple Soul

I have memorised millions of mysterious sounds
      - all clearly retained in my mind.
Collectively and individually they form elegant
      and intricate recalls
To me, the complexity is in my remembrance:
      not the content of the memories
In the loneliness of my self complication I can
      remember disconnecting the sexual deceit
from the honesty I hoped for.
      I often cry in my own separateness
Not because I am lonely for company
      but because I am lonely for kind.

I am but a simple soul. I want to have a sense
      of the unknown. I want all my memories
of meetings and loss to have been for a purpose
      I want that purpose to be thankfulness
for the lessons learned - not bitterness at it's continuation

I am but a simple soul. And I will easily understand
      you if you talk to me in ultrasound
and give me super human silence.

I am but a simple soul. And all I want is
      that you can take my exhaled breath and send it back
as sunlight.

I am but a simple soul. And my heart rumbles quietly
      and seriously like a generator
Purring in the depths of the mountains that it
      feels it has been locked under.

Anthony Sakofsky

Progress?

The minnow stream was a favourite place
lazily curling from arch to arch
below a pockstrewn boulder bridge.
Its sole worn banks curved muddily
down to where wild cress nodded
to kingcup shadows.

I waited, still, in the morning sun,
hunkered close to a crumbling bank,
watching intently for darting shapes
in shadowy depths, where willows bowed.
My net and jar, unheeded, lay
as yet unfilled.

The sun grew warm as I crouched unseen
by the old stone bridge, below the road
where horse and cart rattled by
from farm meadows where poppies laughed.
Cowslip and clover perfumed the air
as I dreamed alone.

But now, we see the stream's improved,
railroad straight, brickbuilt banks,
no willows, primrose, sourgrabs tree,
just iron bars and *Keep Out* signs
. . . Man's incision!

Evelyn Wilkins

The Oldest Profession in the World

There once was a man who money paid
To get himself, in bed, laid
And from this act an industry came
For the men who said 'same again'
The industries' name? Prostitution
Say some the oldest institution.

Now to be employed is to be respectful
But a prostitute! It's quite regretful
To think a woman could sink so low
To accept money from some Herbert or Joe

Now Joe and Herbert have a wife
And here they begin their double life
Mr Respectful and his spouse
Wouldn't have a tart inside their house
But a tart he'd gladly be inside
Excitement in an illicit ride

And the authorities' eyes don't want to see
Men using girls whatever age they may be
And so the profession continues today
But it's still the girls who've a price to pay

Rebecca Lynn

The Gardener

The man who loves his garden plot, is a
    happy man indeed.
He tends with love, each plant he grows and
    waters every seed.
For gardening's not an easy task, his back
    will ache with hoeing,
And back and forth across his lawn will tire
    his legs with mowing.

Though the frost and winds may do damage, and
    pests and diseases abound,
Nature knows how to cope with these things, as
    he sees the seasons come round.
On the day of the Horticultural Show, he's
    proud of his cabbage's size,
And every one claps when the judges announce, that
    his has won the first prize.

A gardener is a popular fellow, for, his cuttings he'll
    give, if you want,
And folk without gardens get many a gift, a
    lettuce, some flowers or pot-plant.
When winter comes, and tools put away, he'll sit
    by the fire with his dog,
And scan the pages for new seeds to try, in the
    latest Spring seed catalogue.

Joan Adams

Sign of the Times

Notes

I am married with two children and live in Cornwall, though I am a Yorkshire girl, born only a few miles from the Dales.

I have written poetry since a teenager, but love to write anything from letters to stories.

I have only recently started to show my work to other people and have had some published in local papers and four now in poetry books.

My inspiration comes from life, be it living things, or feelings and emotions. Anything that stirs me inside.

Through poetry I try and express my feelings in a way that other people can identify with.

What hateful monster lurks behind
Some peoples sick and troubled mind
What torturous, sadistic thought
To every murderous scene has brought
A multitude of pain and guilt
And lasting sorrow, grief, that's built
On ground prepared by evil minds
Who leave a wreck of lives behind.

He claimed 'twas voices in his head'
'It's time you made somebody dead.'
Premeditated thought more like
An insatiable need to strike
And hear the crunch of broken bones
The victims pleading, painful moans
Blood on his hands, but sated need
Completed now that awful deed
Murder - to take a life away
No goodbyes, no last words to say
And rob a family of it's son
Or daughter. In a moment, gone
Ruining another life
A child without a father now
A man without a wife

That place you felt was safe from harm
A rural village, peaceful, calm
No longer in this day and age
Can escape from the violent rage
That sweeps out streets, day in, day out
And no-one now, without a doubt
Can truly say they feel no fear
For daily, do we all not hear
Of murder, abduction and pain
From those whose lives will never be the same

Julie M Pinkus

Notes

Having had my beautiful son Danny Reay just over a year ago I am new to the joys of motherhood. Aged thirty I'm also beginning to enjoy being a published poet. This, just my third success.

Capri brings back many happy memories for me. It's a little piece of heaven. So beautiful and peaceful. The people are the kindest I've ever encountered. I now have many wonderful friends there. It's the only place that feels like home.

I dedicate Capri to someone very special to me. We discovered Italy together. My best friend, my mother Dorothy.

Capri

Although I'm here I'm far away
And the mandolins are playing
But sadly I am dreaming
So what are the mandolins saying

I can feel the sun it's beating down
Intensely on my face
I slowly open up my eyes
Oh what a beautiful place

The sky is of the deepest blue
Cliffs tumble to the sea
The land is green and luscious
Oh what a wondrous place to be

White villas cling to cliffsides
And blossoms dot the trees
It is so very clean here
Just for the eye to please

The sea is glistening turquoise
And white froth beats the shore
And when you close your eyes again
It leaves you wanting more

The yachts moored in the harbour
And the speedboats in the bay
Are lavish and appealing
Maybe I'll have one someday

I'm sipping cappuccino
And nibbling brioche
At Genoveffas' cafe bar
My dress is from La Roche

The men and women saunter by
They have amazing style
On this beautiful island of Capri
I think I'll stay a while

Cathy Melucci

Going Out with Jonathan

Notes

Noosha Mason was born in 1977 and lives in Chesterfield. She is a full-time mum to 10 week old Dylan Jay. This is the first time her work has been published. She is currently on a writers' course and spends her spare time reading, listening to music and writing short stories. She began writing two years ago and has no other ambition but to write. She hopes to become a successful writer in the near future.

The poem was written for and about her boyfriend of three years, Jonathan Gaunt.

Sixteen, pure and innocent,
Fourteen, a real lad.
When my sister dumped you
I had never been so glad!

The gig was so amazing,
I hugged you all the time
And though we took things slowly
How I wished that you were mine!

Our love blossomed on the telephone
After only just one week,
You'll never know how good it was
To simply hear you speak.

You took some getting used to,
I must admit at first.
You taught me to drink alcohol -
You seemed to have a thirst!

We'd go for walks at midnight,
You'd roll us up a joint.
We never looked at others,
We didn't see the point.

Noosha Mason

Notes

I live in Northampton, I'm a full-time housewife, have been married to Michael for eighteen years and have one daughter, Teresa who's studying to hopefully become a journalist.

My interest in poetry started at school as a subject I enjoyed. I started writing poetry about three years ago as a hobby and since have had several published. My poems range from true life experiences through to fantasy.

I was honoured to receive the prize book Successful Writing, by Teresa McCuaig for my poem Investigator.

When I wrote Investigator, I put myself in the shoes of the sleuth dictating the experiences.

Investigator

A mist is spiralling from underground
A stream of heated desire
Yet it's cold and clammy
Incredibly uncanny.

A stench that's musky almost rusty
Corroded dry and undusted
A fragrance that's back dated
An odour I really hated.

A sleuth on the case
Nothing I could trace
Everything seems erased
It leaves a really bad taste.

A wilting rose, a dying amber
All lie low when you enter
Night it never turns to day
O quintessence spirit stay away.

Sandra Boosey

Notes

I am a 26 year old Civil Servant, who currently works for the Child Support Agency in Longbenton in Newcastle.

Although I have always 'dabbled' at writing, it has always been a hobby and so I have never had anything published prior to this. I was once told that my father's family is related to Lord Byron - although I have never actually confirmed this for myself - so maybe this explains the poetry!

My interests include science fiction (both written and filmed), writing poetry and short stories, and all 'green' issues.

I have been married for almost two years, and keep a pet African Rock Python named Will!

Rose Tinted Life

A rose by any other name is velvety petals, and dewy soft rain
But only if you believe in the hype put about by romantics or those that
want to believe in romance.

A rose by any other name is actually thorns and aphids
With a deathly dose of *DDT* thrown in for good measure, just in case the
aphids get out of control.

A rose by any other name is street crime and depravity
The rape of women and children, and occasionally men - lets face it, rape
isn't particular in its choice of victims.

A rose by any other name is war and death
Destruction of the life of those who didn't start the damn war in the first
place - life that isn't political or religious.

A rose by any other name is illness and disease
Old people left to die of hypothermia in homes that are too cold because
the *NHS* didn't have a free bed that day.

A rose by any other name is the outbreak of hysteria
Martians have landed in New York in the US of A and the President hasn't
noticed the difference - you couldn't accuse him of being racist.

A rose by any other name is all this and more
A rose by any other name is famine and poverty
A rose by any other name is nothing of delicate beauty and fragrance.

Do you look at life through rose tinted spectacles?

Sam Barrett

Black Smoke

Notes

Why have this poem pub-
lished? What is Black Smoke?
What is the significance of
the two dolphins? Are they
irrelevant or are they some
kind of symbol? In what sort
of world does the narrator
live? Should one read or listen to poetry? Is it the narrator or the poet standing on
the pier? And finally, is this
poem humorous or bleak?

When I was young
I had a dream
Black smoke filled my sight
I learnt to laugh

One day, months later
Over a war-torn city
A pillar of black smoke I saw
Joy crept into my heart

Then I grew older
Black smoke disappeared
I prayed to my lord
Make it come back to me

Black smoke
Bring a smile to our faces
Lighten up our lives
Darken the world's skies
Blacken the earth's face

Now it comes
Every time I'm in desperation
I learnt it had to seek me
and not me it

Black smoke
Brighten up my day
Make me laugh again
Darken my vision
Blacken my perception
Come down from the skies
cover the ground and light

Stood there on the pier
Saw two dolphins jump out of the water

Martin De Vrind

Under Cover

Notes

At the tail end of the First
World War (1917) Henry
Moore was a private in the
15th London Regiment (Civil
Service Rifles). He was mus-
tard-gassed in the Battle of
Cambrai, France.

Between 1940-42 he was
Official War Artist and began
a series of 'shelter drawings'
depicting ordinary Londoners
taking shelter in the Underground system.

These graphic images not
only record a less obvious
and less sensational slice of
British War History, but also
evoke a strong, empathic
realisation of the effects of
war on the day-to-day lives
of ordinary men and women
on the home front.

These 'shelter drawings' inspired this poem.

Smudgy faces sleeping in the shadows.
Rustling wrappers discarded on the tracks.
Hearty tube mice hurry to investigate.

Shared flasks of tea between insomniacs.
An anonymously soft harmonica sings down the platform.
Quiet laughter.

Youngsters cuddle bears and blankets,
Oblivious to the sound of bombs above their heads.

Sirens. Fire engines. Bells.
Women listen anxiously.
What would they go home to?

A dozing dog growls low, roused briefly from slumber.
A caged bird chirrups resiliently under cover.

Clickety-click, clickety-click.
A beat of knitting needles keep double time.
A gossip of Grannies huddle in hushed chat.

Lovers hold hands, fingers intertwined.
Babies grizzle and whimper, soon soothed.
Murmurs, kisses and lullabies.

Drams consumed with ration-book sandwiches.
Old, toothless snores.
Coughing. Phlegm. Scratching.
Feet and cards shuffling.

Mankind chirrups resiliently under cover.

Audrey Tainsh

It's Time to Say Goodbye to Strawberries, Mincepies and Beans

we've come a long way today on this tired old road
frosted and ripped open
decay smell machine gun noise
what's left for us now until our death
echoes memories laboured breath

heaven appears as a snowdrop nears
a foot ahead has no eyes
as it's trampled into demise
a heaven shattered
all hope destroyed
nothing left hunger cries

time to leave one last goodbye
mother's kitchen that's a joke
delirium sets in
strawberries become my closest friend
then mincepies and finally beans

Rosemary Probert

The Irishman

Notes

I wrote this poem in 1974. I hope it simply highlights our ability to judge a people by the actions of its extremists.

It is also to the memory of Percy Ring, a shattering foreman on the Oxford ring road in the sixties. He was both a drinker and a theatre goer and grew up in Dublin early this century. He taught me much about Eire. He died tragically at work in the late sixties.

A fellow thumbed a lift the other morn.
I stopped the car and he, all travel worn
An Irishman, looked in.
   From mile-torn feet!
I thought of Ulster then - and men.
  Shot dead in any street:
  My kin, 'Get in,' I said.
'Thanks son,' said he, 'were you to Abingdon bound?'
'Yes' said I, 'I am' and then I frowned.
He had no bomb!

I looked ahead. All my kin dead - and his!
The road was wet, but sane
The sky had rained again.
'I knew it would,' said he.
'The clouds slip low you see'
I saw his eyes: They laughed.

In that quick glance aside.
I saw - unlike before.
It dawned upon my mind.
Not like last night - I did not want this fight
In fact I liked his kind.
We talked a lot and laughed.
We both enjoyed the ride.

I dropped him at the square
'Thanks boy', said he, to me.
Then offered me a fare.
'No thanks,' said I , no less.
'Goodbye, God Bless.'

Walter Waine

Destruction Earth

Notes

I am a student in Liverpool, Gloucester is my hometown, where I live with my mum, dad and sister. I am 21 years of age.

This is my first piece of published writing, although I have been writing for my own pleasure since childhood.

Most of my inspiration comes from my Christian faith, and I am driven by a desire to communicate that faith. My writing ranges from social issues to science fiction and fantasy, and is fed through a constant supply of books and magazines.

This poem was written at The Rock outreach café in Gloucester, in 20 minutes and was inspired by a discussion about environmental issues.

It is dedicated to Joe and Jemma who encouraged me to write it.

Jagged depths of earth's betrayal
Jolting evil to the core
Joining us in awful chaos
Jesting with the fatal one

Eating with the painful people
Ending anything left of happiness
Earth destroying itself inwards
Each of us bringing on the rot

Sinful passions of sinful people
Soaking up the people's deeds
Set to hasten the destruction
Souls that ravage and destroy

Unified in our ignorance
Unconcerned by result of greed
Uncovering the brutal truth
Unpeeling the skin of envy

Self-destruction continues apace
Sacrifices we will not make
Save us from our own destruction
Saviour deliver us your grace.

Neil Mitchell

Suffering in Silence

I sit here in this room,
All hunched up and withdrawn.
You're talking,
I'm crying.
I'm so confused, mixed up
Numb, depressed
Unhappy
I don't know how I really feel,
I can't explain it.
I can't talk about it.
You're still talking
Telling me how life goes on
And I'm not listening.
But I'm still crying.
I can hear you speaking,
but I'm not listening
The words sore straight through me,
without sinking in.
This isn't helping me
How would you know what I'm feeling like?
You don't understand,
It's never happened to you.
I want solutions
I want things how they used to be,
I want my happiness back.
But you're just talking
Telling me how life really is.
I get up and turn away.
Walking from the room through the door I came in.
You're still talking,
I'm still crying
And nothing changes.

Nichola Kinnersley

Notes

I am 31 years of age and have one son who is seven years old. I formerly trained as a chartered accountant and was employed as a senior manager in an NHS Trust. This resulted in boredom and depression and I am currently working as a carer, which I enjoy immensely.

I have had several poems published since 1994 in anthologies. A committed Christian I am inspired by God, nature, society and psychology.

This poem was written 10 years ago while studying for a degree at the London School of Economics. I was suffering from acute depression and somewhat frightened by a number of admirers. Depression has continued over the last 10 years and I started to receive effective treatment from May 1996. My depression still returns but is now controllable.

During the past year I have discovered God's strength and the love of good friends.

The Maiden

In that crowded, heated room,
there sat the beautiful woman-child,
all the world sought her bloom,
her soulful spirit growing wild

Every kind of man fought to possess her,
never seeing the anguish deep inside,
none conceived of the fight within her,
as all the while she cried and cried.

A poison took hold upon her mind,
It devoured her as she watched the fight outside,
but none, who fought for her, thought at all,
of the tormented soul that was struggling inside.

The world was fighting to have her beside him,
the most beautiful trophy that was had in a war,
hence they declined to support and be beside her,
to fight in her the worst war of all.

She fled that crowded, heated place,
and wrenched away from her dying heart,
her soul soared free, true to its fate,
and rested her mind at peace, alone.

Tracey Wadman

90

To Sleep and to Dream

As the sun falls
behind the world
the laughter rises above

Children lie to
sleep to dream
lie to dream to sleep

And as the sun rises
above the world
the pain,
it falls down below.

M L Davies

Notes

I am a 21 year old drama
student from Kent, studying
in Northampton where I first
began writing.

Masks is from a collection of
around 50 poems written in
the last two years. Masks is
the first to be published.

Masks is dedicated to Matt -
who showed me a love I could
only dream of, until I ended it.
This poem is also dedicated to
any women who finds herself
in a violent relationship, as I
did. The only way on, is out of
that relationship - It hurts and
that hurt never leaves you but
is becomes easier to deal
with. A heart-felt thank you
goes out to my family and
friends who helped me
through an extremely difficult
time. They all showed me that
life can still be full of so many
glorious experiences - thank
you!

Masks

My face smiles,
as I have fun
with my friends.

The dried out rivers
which once flowed
from my eyes,
are covered with make-up.

My heart which was
broken into a thousand pieces
is stuck together
with paper.

As I slowly rebuild
my life,
my life without
you!

It takes just one word,
one thought,
one yearn, from this
mending heart,
for the dried out
rivers to flow,
for the paper
keeping my heart together
to tear apart.

And all the while,
my face smiles,
when inside I
am screaming
with astounding intensity,
and, no one ever hears,
no one ever knows
that this smiling happy face
is in fact coming from,
a screaming, hurting,
yearning soul.

Tania Black

Thoughts on a Minoan Head

Notes

Some years ago I attended a poetry course run by the poetess, Anne Cluysenaar. An exercise she gave us was to bring some object to the class and construct a poem around it. I chose a small clay sculpture - a copy of a Minoan head - and this is the result.

Anne was so struck by the little artefact, that she subsequently composed her Cycladic Head Haiku (appearing in Timeslips, her latest published book of poems), dedicating the poem to me.

I should like to return the compliment, dedicating this poem to her.

From what fair cheek
Did the Minoan sculptor
Shape that clay?

In what far-off day
Did the clay
Take shape?

The potter throws his clay
His mud
And, from it,
Springs to life
His Galatea
Or, perhaps,
His Golem.

There, a long-gone Minoan state,
There, Atlanta, buried deep
In timeless, swirling seas.
Aztecs, Incas, all have gone,
Leaving shadows on the sun.

Who knows
What wondrous times have past
What wondrous states exist
In some long-gone, distant past?

What glories, come and gone,
What men's ambition fed
So that, betimes, on others dined
And then, dear God, all fled
To mud and dust returned,
Desire, lust, greed, interred.

And yet, O God, what else?

Anne Rubin

The Great Designer

Notes

The author of *The Great De-
signer* has written numerous
other poems, some rhyming,
some not. He has also written
a number of original nursery
rhymes for young children,
also several short stories for
children, with a poem to introduce each story.

He who designed the Universe,
had knowledge of the kind.
That they who are but mortals,
will never, ever, find.
The brain to plan, such vast expanse,
to scatter stars, so near, yet far.
To think of life, then think of death,
give everything that lives, the breath,
to live a span, and then expire,
must show to man, an awesome power.

It matters not, that men aspire,
to climbing, conquering, gaining power.
Their knowledge is forever less,
than that their *Maker,* does possess.
Whatever man achieves from Earth,
His Universe they'll never girth.
Man will live, his allotted span,
then become extinct, before he can.

No doubt on other worlds anew,
there may be men who'll think so too.
But none will ever live to see,
control of Universe, which only *He*
can make, espew, through endless skies,
that *He* alone can organise.

Why then, does man, forever dream,
that he alone, is so supreme.
For man, with all his cunning schemes,
will search forever more, but,
never will he gain the awesome power,
that *God Himself* does store..
It matters not, how much man strives,
he'll find one fact remains,
there is no way, that he'll take charge,
of what is, *God's Domain.*

Jack Blades

Notes

I am 65 years of age, a recently retired chartered accountant, married with one daughter, born in West London and now living in Berkshire.

My interests include football, cricket, music, concerts, theatre, gardening, real ale and bird watching.

I started writing humorous poems for friends two years ago and began a poetry writing course this year.

Down Dewy Bank was written for my wife as a Valentine's Day reminiscence of when we first met on the Isle of Wight in the 1950s. It is about love at first sight and the profound effect it can have on a young man of twenty-two.

Down Dewy Bank

Down dewy bank we ambled hand in hand.
In unison our hearts and minds inclined
to look for that elusive grain of sand
young lovers seek so rare a joy to find.
Near water's edge we reached that special place,
a secret cleft in Cupid's arbored realm;
our first sanguine al fresco close embrace
in darkling glade by moonbeam dappled elm.
As touching fingers sought the silken sheen
of burnished taffeta beneath the bough,
a sentient sigh swept round the sylvan scene,
as if the breeze had cast a spell somehow:
      The roving wolverine was stayed, eyes bright,
      held captive by your tender song of night.

George Puttock

Is it a Life?

Notes

I am 43 years of age living in
a village in Lincolnshire and
working in Cambridgeshire
as a senior library assistant.

I always wanted to write but
only started at the beginning
of this year when my hus-
band was ill. I needed to
write, I felt I had to.

This poem was inspired by
my life in Paris when I was
18.

From dawn to dusk,
life is the same everyday.
Every morning we get up
to go to work of course.
The afternoon is spent working away.
The evening brings some release.
Entertainment we need,
to push away the boredom,
to push away this useless life.
Excitement does not exist.
We carry on day after day regardless,
hoping one day something will change,
hoping one day a miracle will happen,
hoping one day our dreams will come true.
What sort of life is this?

P M Watson

Notes

I was widowed last year after 40-odd years of marriage. Still lonely, I go for walks with my little dog. Being alone, one notices things more acutely than when accompanied. So it was when I was struck by the damage caused by *The Storm*. The verses were composed in my head.

I have been composing poems for about 50 years - starting at school and have had several pieces published, including *Haunted*, composed on a lonely walk along a canal towpath, published in Simpson Publication's Book of British Short Poems and several poems in small society magazines.

Thoughts and feelings inspire my poetry - a trait inherited by my younger daughter. (The elder is too pragmatic!)

The Storm

The streets are with twigs bestrewn,
Branches too, lie torn away,
The wind has done its noisy prune,
By howling gale on a winter's day.

But now a weak and watery sun
Illuminates the litter strewn,
And the eye roams o'er the damage done,
Remembering the gentler days of June.

Yes, I recall those blossomed days,
When all those trees, with leaf,
Stood in summer's shimmering haze,
To cast their cooling shade beneath.

And Life itself's beset by storms,
Its shattered dreams lie all around,
And sorrow, in all its varied forms,
Like a cat, steals in, without a sound.

Remember the happier days now past
When all those dreams, just newly born,
In the golden days of Youth, once vast,
Promised such hope in Life's bright morn.

But memories fade - some are gone -
And Life will end, as end it must!
Though time and tide will flow on,
Must all one's dreams just lie in dust?

Joseph Cory Taylor

Notes

'Ancient Briton' had a career in overseas education. Countries like Kenya, Pakistan and Bahrain provided him with material for a number of short stories.

A keen walker and nature lover, he celebrated his retirement by walking the Appalachian Trail (Georgia to Maine) in 1993. This adventure inspired his early poetry, in which he finds echoes of Robert W Service and 'Banjo' Paterson. Appalachian Trail walkers traditionally adopt trail names; thus was born 'Ancient Briton'.

He has had several poems published, favours traditional styles but has tried others. He writes on many themes; *Stalker* is based on memories of youth.

Stalker

We owed to Richmal Crompton our hero, William Brown,
Of whom we learned the skills beloved of boys,
And one of these was stalking total strangers through the town,
Aged ten when we had long discarded toys.

Your Sixth Form swain, I followed you through crowded street and park
(For more mature passion now held sway)
Or sought the friendly willow in your garden after dark
Until your light went out at close of day.

Could anyone imagine that I ever wished you harm
In that innocent, romantic other time?
Why, all the months I sighed for you
And knew I would have died for you,
I never dreamed my conduct could be crime.

Ancient Briton

Notes

I'm twenty-nine and work for the Civil Service in London. I began writing as a teenager.

Guilty was inspired by a vivid dream in which I was walking through an almost deserted underground station in London. The people in my dream reached out to me with such desperation that it frightened me. Yet the last man looked so vulnerable and 'normal' that I pitied him more than I feared him.

The poem recognises the way in which we are often charitable only when it suits us and can be guilty of overlooking the people who most need our help.

Guilty

I saw a man without a face
he was crying out aloud,
but I pretended not to see him,
just a shadow, in a crowd.
    A junkie lay beside him,
    he could not face the day.
    he reached out to touch me
    but I ran away.
I saw a deaf and dumb man
he was looking for a friend,
he looked at me, but did not see,
somebody with a heart to lend.
    A tramp sat in the corner
    his body cold and thin,
    but when he looked me in the eye,
    I turned my back on him.
I saw a weak man crying
And I went to offer help
He told me he was dying
About to kill himself.
    His face was full or torment,
    I began to cry
    Then he got a gun and shot me, he said,
    'The guilty have to die.'

Sara McKenna

Notes

I am 43 years of age, married to Carol and have two children, Simon aged nine and Ellen aged two.

Brave Man was inspired by my father's death in May 1996. It was my first attempt at writing and I was very surprised it was chosen.

I wish to dedicate Brave Man to my father Ronald William James, known to his family and friends as Ron. It recalls his life and love of his family as accurately as a poem can, and for me it represents my great love and respect I had for him and all he did for me but probably neglected to tell him.

Brave Man

This was a brave man, brave till the end
as a young soldier he fought for his country
and fought till the end, returning home
triumphantly to family and friends.

This man was a husband, a father and friend so
loving and caring right till the end.
Forty years and more of struggle and strife,
this loving man cared for his family and wife.

This man worked hard each day of his life to
put food on the table for him and his wife.
Struggle came easy as so did his smile for
this man was no angel but he did have style.

Struck down by a cancer in the autumn of life
he fought once again this time for life.
The memories are strong for his family and wife
for this was a brave man for all of his life.

Michael James

Those We Love

Notes

My uncle Jackie McCulloch
wrote the poem to my
grandmother. He was born in
1911 and died in 1941.
When my gran died we
found the poem in her prayer
book. He was self taught as
owing to illness he never attended school.

They say the World is round and yet I often think it square,
So many little hurts, we get from corners here and there,
But there's one truth in life I've found while Journeying East and West
The only folks we really wound are those we love the best,
We flatter those we scarcely know,
We please the fleeting quest and deal full many a thoughtless blow
To those we love the best.

Jackie McCulloch

Growing Old Disgracefully

Notes

I am a retired Nursery Nurse with two grown-up daughters, Tara and Kirstine, who have 'fled the nest'.

Scotland is the country of my adoption. I was born in Derbyshire, spending the major part of my childhood in Wales.

I started to write poetry in my teens, returning to this pastime after my retirement. Since then, three of my poems have been published in various anthologies.

This particular poem is dedicated to All Women who sometimes feel past their 'sell by date.'

When Ginty was fifty life really began.
She travelled to Spain to acquire a tan.
Although she couldn't be described as teeny
She had the audacity to wear a lurex bikini.

She threw old caution to the wind.
In all her life she had never sinned.
She decided it was time she did
When she met a gentleman from Madrid.
The rest is not for publication,
She wants no further investigation.

On her return she felt rejuvenated.
It had been years since she had ever dated.
Her friends all asked her if she thought she'd been wise.
She said, 'Well ladies this is my advice,
Take a slice of life when ever you can
Even if it involves a man.
I'd really like to take a bet
There's love and laughter in you yet.'

Now, she walks jauntily down the street,
Bright pink trainers on her feet.
She wears drop earrings, just like boulders,
Which dingle dangle on her shoulders.
She disco dances to Tina Turner.
Old age is simmering on her back burner.

Valerie Duthie

Notes

I was born in Swansea, South Wales and am 49 years of age.

I have been writing poetry for 12 years and am inspired by a volume of two books entitled A Thousand Best Poems, which have been in the family for at least 50 years.

I was inspired to write *My Star of Comfort*, following the loss of a dear friend, Susan Matthews, who sadly passed away on 2 August, 1996 at the age of 48 years. Susan was married to Brian my friend; and both of them during a few troubled years of my life, gave me tremendous support and encouragement in saving me from despair. I feel greatly indebted to them both, and even though it may be a small return, I would like to pay tribute to them both.

I dedicate My Star of Comfort to Susan Matthews, formerly of 176 Middle Road, Cwmdu, Swansea, in memory of the loving and caring person she was to her family and friends. She will never be forgotten by me, and indeed by so many others who knew her.

My Star of Comfort

When you feel there's no tomorrow
When you have a broken heart
And all your joy has turned to sorrow
When you're feeling miles apart

When uncertain of the future
'Cause life's not as it was before
Does your path seem close to closure
Although you keep an open door
Does sadness strike and turn to tears
When you look upon the past
Does everything feel it's going to crumble
When you built it strong to last
Do you yearn to turn the clocks back
And wish you could relive again
Do you feel your prayers have failed you
And continue in your grief and pain
Do you ever search for reasons
Whilst holding on to faith and hope
When hurt and anger never ceases
Do you feel you'll never cope
It's only when you feel you've lost all
And depression clouds the day, you
Stop and think before you stumble
The 'Lord' will save you from more pain
For you'll be carried through your darkness
And guided forward into light
He'll point your head up unto heaven
Towards a star that shines so bright.
Don't fear, its your 'loved one' saying,
'Don't cry - you did your best
My love I would never leave you
I have simply gone to rest'

John Watkins

The Orchard, Lytes Carey

Notes

I live in Glasgow and have a husband, a daughter and two Siamese cats.

All apple trees are magic, but the orchard in this Somerset garden is thick with spells. You can visit and see for yourself - it belongs to the National Trust.

In the applegarth the paths criss-cross
and where they meet
four quince trees shed their golden fruit,
tumbled like lanterns in the autumn grass
about the sundial.

The paths run straight from tree to tree.
How straight is that? How far?
Further to walk than you can see,
further from here to there than there to here.

If you set forth upon these shifting roads,
venture your argosy, expect
that no direction will be what it seems.

Navigating by the star at the core,
you traverse all seasons, pearmain to pippin,
blossom and leaf and fruit,
make landfall by the sundial.

There the yellow fruit
casts other shadows on the leaning trees.
Who passed you on the path? Who did you hail?
What was the answer?

And when you leave
you must go by the path by which you came.
Beware. Never look back. Press on,
or you will find yourself, beyond the archway,
in any century but your own.

Pat McIntosh Spinnler

Childhood Memories

Notes

I am the mother of four grown children. I am 52 years old and live in Scotland where I am a carer.

I started writing about 18 months ago and have had three poems published and received an Editor's Choice award. I have always loved poetry. Nature, music and animals all played a part in my writing.

One daughter is handicapped which makes me look at life differently.

I write to people all over the world, like music and photography as well as reading.

I had a happy childhood, which is why this poem is dedicated to my late mother Catherine, who made me the person I am today.

I think back to when I was young,
Of happy days and lots of sun.
of holidays beside the sea,
harvest time, then home for tea.
Paddling in water ever so deep,
bursting tar bubbles with our bare feet.
Schooldays, and chewing gum,
puzzling over very hard sums.
Special days and happy hours,
memories that will always stay ours.
Now that we are adults grown,
how the years seen to have flown.
So children who are out to play,
they are your memories for another day.
It is so soon you will be a man,
enjoy the time now while you can.
Time goes so fast, come what may,
Oh! Childhood those halcyon days.

Isabella Muir-Ward

Notes

I'm the middle child of five
and I'm seventeen years old.
I've had nothing published
yet (apart from this) and
have won no awards.

I spend my time reading
comic books, playing com-
puter games and watching
television (mainly sit-coms). I
call this 'studying'. I also try
to spend as much time as
possible writing stories to
turn into graphic novels.
When Saturday comes I am a
keen footballer (and Liverpool fan).

I have been writing poetry
for at least seven years but
like every other aspect of my
life, it takes a back seat to my
art.

I recently met a poet and my
competitive streak insists that
I have to be better than everyone at everything so I had
to make time to prove to
myself I could do it. As the
first line suggests, I created
this poem as 'I drifted slowly,
though rain soaked streets'
(in Bristol), from there on in,
the poem virtually wrote itself.

Rain

I drifted slowly, through rain soaked streets
and pondered, on the way we are.
I asked myself: What's the worth
of being negative and finding fault
in all around us?

Water dripping from on high,
from dark grey clouds up in the sky.
It makes me think of a new time
when people look, and see the beauty around them:
A rose bush doesn't have thorns -
The thorn bush has a rose.

Why do so many people smile at other's
misfortune, yet not their own?

Thunder rumbles to remind me
that not all people as fortunate
as I am.
Not all have a room with a view of
the bright side of life.

Now I am warm and the
gentle patter of the rain
outside lulls me to sleep.

I dream of a rain
that will wash away the dreary
world
and leave us with only the bright
side.

Michael Flaherty

Notes

I am a 38 year old man from Plymouth. I consider myself a lyric writer more than anything else. I think I shall stop writing soon. The futility is all too apparent and the need is hopefully becoming redundant.

Moonstoned is merely a writer trying to drag himself out of melancholy and failing miserably.

Moonstoned

Drift away drift away
so high in the sky
moonstoned midnight madness
crying that silvery sigh
that moonstoned sadness
as night tiptoes silently by
no bed fellow no lovers
to find under the covers
Oh I have discovered
such darkness in flight
transfixed by God painting pictures
I am caught in the light
come away come away
I have found some new ground
sunstroked on mirage
as I trip over a sound
that unstroked visage
of a day soon to be drowned
no hand held believer
no honest deceiver
a shame I cannot leave her
where she fell by the way
come away drift away
along a fresh line of blood
let by this bitter quill
she abides in my moonstoned madness
she resides in me still.

C Neilson

Trial Run

Notes

This poem, Trial Run, is dedicated to my Dad, Thomas Griffiths, late of Gerallt, Tudweiliog on the Llyn Peninsula.

I wrote it for him while he was very ill in hospital during February 1997. He liked it a lot and was pleased when I told him it had been accepted for publishing.

Sadly on 20th May 1997 my Dad was taken from us aged 72. He had bravely fought ill health for a long time. We are all going to miss him, but we will always have our treasured memories of our times with him.

I would like this poem to be a lasting tribute to my Dad.

God said when he put us on this earth
This life it's just a trial run
When you successfully pass my test
I'll be calling you one by one.

I'll need to see what you can do
I'll be assessing you from birth
I want to see if you can cope
With the trials I give you on earth.

When I am happy and satisfied
And you've proved your ability
I'll ask you to leave your life on earth
And enter my kingdom with me.

No need to be nervous, don't be sad
Remember you've passed my test
Don't be scared to join me up here
I really do need all the best.

There's a lot of work for you to do
Once you have joined me above
There's a lot of people who'll miss you
But they'll still remember your love.

Meinir

Notes

Hi! I'm 22 years old and Scottish but have lived in England for the last 5 years; I currently reside in Leicester. I have nice parents, a brother and two sisters.

I've always loved writing and it's great therapy; less irritating than psychologists and cheaper than anti-depressants.

Reading is a passion of mine and inspires me to write. The poem started life as a short story of which I lost half to an infernal computer disc, so I adapted it.

I'd like to dedicate the poem to my husband Rob to commemorate our first anniversary together!

The Always Coming of Age

I had a beginning that was a conception,
Why? The old excuse,
He made my mother laugh.
Then the beginning of memory,
The tender age of three,
The breakage of my knee,
Caused by what?
The middle of childhood curiosity.
Another beginning,
Hatred directed at the joker,
Because he got in the way of a middle.
Where are all the endings then?
All but the first are endings too.
There is one I've forgotten,
Mum told and tells me about it,
I'm five years old,
The person I link arms with leaves,
She says I was upset and cried,
I can't remember,
I've seen a picture,
I don't recognise the face or arms.
Lots of middle,
Then a cruel ending, age fourteen,
Why? The old excuse,
People can't keep their hands to themselves,
I got into cult films
'Never be the same again.'
Said the rocky horror picture show,
I know what they mean.

Sarah Pascoe

Contradictions

Sweetened sugar, fat free lard
A well paid security guard
A void that's full, an inland seagull
A friendly bobby, a slim Mr Blobby
A night worker up with the lark
Environmentally friendly car parks
Military intelligence, friendly fire
Left-wing tabloids, silky soft wire

A straight priest, a celibate priest
An anorexic having a feast
A happy newsagent, a well dressed farmer
Being older than your father
An unopinionated taxi-driver
An insurance policy without a rider
A long distance journey without a hold-up
Manchester City win the European Cup

Zebras with spots, teenagers without
A tee-totalling lager lout
A Siberian heatwave, a huge microwave
Happy families, a wimp that's brave
Rich students, impotent gerbils
Any word that rhymes with gerbils
An animal that likes the vet
As for me - I haven't been born yet!

Silly phrases
Meaningless words
Or just contradictions
In terms!

Baggy

Notes

I am 17 years of age and live in Essex with my partner.

My parents are Linda and Ben. I have a sister Mandy and four brothers Jeremy, Gregory, Bradley and Phillip.

I have had another poem published entitled The Tree.

I started writing poetry at the age of nine and have done so ever since.

My main hobby is creative writing, as it gives me the choice of remaining as myself or becoming someone else.

I once reached a point where I lacked inspiration totally and came close to giving up, but with the love and support of Daniel, my partner, I found my way again.

This poem is dedicated to mum, with love.

Baby Blues

It's skin is smooth as silk,
it's hands are tiny and small,
it's silken mouth is perfectly set,
it's beauty amazes all.

It's tiny little body,
has just come onto earth,
now that it's been born,
we're filled with happiness and mirth.

When it was inside,
it didn't have a clue,
but now that it is here,
everything is new.

It's little lashes flicker,
it opens it's deep blue eyes,
they are the wondrous colour,
of the above winter skies.

They didn't all approve,
when the bairn was to be born,
some decided to disown us,
which made us feel forlorn.

We were happy and excited,
filled with hope for it's arrival,
but we were also worried,
for the strength of it's survival.

We started to prepare
for when it made it's way,
we were rushing around,
we made no delay.

Then came the day,
the bairn's to be born,
come on, hurry,
there's no time to yawn.

It's perfectly formed,
it's too good to be true,
it's so wonderful,
so soft and new.

We shouldn't really call it 'It',
for some that may annoy,
so after all this, the announcement is,
the baby is a
      Boy

Jodie Duchesne

Remembrance

Notes

I am twenty-six years of age and live with my girlfriend Jodie who gives me constant support and encouragement.

Life inspires me to write poetry which I have been doing for about sixteen years.

This particular poem was written a few years ago when I and my girlfriend at the time parted our ways. She gave me a pendant she had made and this is what the poem is about.

The stone of your heart lays cold
on my breast.
Truth hides in beauty and love
knows no rest.
The work of your hands calls
tears to my eyes.
The sighs of your body your soul
still denies.
The last words you spoke as you
left my home.
The memory remains with the gift
of a stone.

Daniel Duchesne

Intimate Strangers

Notes

Intimate Strangers is about short term escapism and how easy it is to fill our lives with shallow, often hedonistic, activities, objects and relationships. The poem expresses despair and hurt at my own escapism, and at that of many people around me. Living in this environment, attempts at something more meaningful can be 'trampled or unnoticed' (fifth verse, line two).

Intimate Strangers was written at a time in my life when great demands were being made of my time and I held several personal relationships largely through obligation rather than choice.

A soul full of nothing
is easy to fill;
A soul full of loving
is easy to spill.

I feel so lonely,
my heart turns to stone.
Everything's so phoney,
I can't feel the truth.

A world full of apparitions,
meaningless and cold.
Intimate with strangers,
selfish and bold.

The most delicate structure
to be understood or else destroyed
for possession or greed
are sterile and sold.

Effort spent falls by the wayside,
trampled or unnoticed.
Destroyed by the demands around me,
I can't give my love.

A soul full of nothing
is easy to fill;
A soul full of loving
is easy to spill.

Donald Houston

Seascope

Moonshine sands and shingle shamble,
barking dog and lovers amble.
Crusader cuts through murky glass
as gossamer sails sink into spindrift.

Sad siesta swell and sway,
sighing, scaring gulls away.
Heaving bow in twilight terrain
The watery wanderer takes to the sea again.

Charlotte Whitchurch

Notes

Ellsie Russell, married to Trevor, was born in Aldershot but now lives in Fleet, Hampshire.

She has no pets but receives visits from two cats, D'lou and Domino, whose antics inspired this particular poem.

Ellsie started writing poems and short stories as a child and has had several published. She has won cups and other prizes in literary competitions.

As a public speaker her favourite talk is 'Lillie Langtry'. Ellsie also enjoys tennis, swimming, photography, reading, and singing with a local group. She is also a member of Hartley Row WI and Fleet Morning Townswomen's Guild.

Ellsie is widely travelled and loves Australia where she has climbed Ayers Rock. She hopes someday to write 'That Book'.

Cat Trap

The cat with ever watchful eye
dozes in the noonday heat,
mouse dinnered, replete.
But let a shiny beetle scuttle by
and she'll unwind in a Dervish whirl,
claws unfurl
to razor her surplus prey.

Ellsie Russell

Notes

I have been writing and reading poetry since I was a child but have only recently gained the confidence to send in items for consideration. This is my third published poem.

My writing is private and personal, often letting me express my negative thoughts and feelings. It is a source of self-disclosure, helping me to realise what is really going on for me. I also enjoy using language for self expression.

This poem stems from the realisation that my marriage was falling apart and I didn't know what to do about it. We have since separated.

I Need to Talk Again

There is no time
I am not making time
I am wasting time

What do I want?
Is it worth fighting for?
If not, why do I want it?

What must I change?
Is it my expectations?
Is it my outlook?

Blotting out with alcohol
Filling the void with food
Sleeping for escapism

But haunted by dreams
Taunted with self-loathing
Shaken with anger

Wanting to hit out
Wanting to show I hurt
Wanting to be comforted

Afraid of the future
Sentimental of the past
Trapped in the present

With no way out
Except
Through

Kate Hamson

November

November can be the gloomiest month
With the sun slinking across the sky,
skulking on the lip of the horizon
- If not obscured by thick dirty clouds;
a month that often sees
The rain and frost in an unholy alliance
Chilling deeply, cutting down to the bone;
yet after this comes
The sure and certain return to a world
Of golden light and silvered heat.

George B Burns

Help

I'm here, I shout,
No one notices except the dancing
Shadow behind the flickering
Candle light.

The shadows dance around me.

I wait.

Not knowing where to go.
I'm lost in my own mind.
Scared of my own thoughts
Not aware that the darkness is
Getting smaller and smaller
Suffocating my thoughts and mind

Help!

Karl Mansfield (17)

Of Course You Could

Pass me the bottle,
so I may relax,
and watch the pink elephants,
crawl out of the cracks . . .
in the floorboards, the walls,
and out of the ceiling,
pass me the bottle,
for my head is reeling.

Too much . . . not enough!,
I can always drink more,
and I'm only happy,
spark out on the floor,
I'm not in a stupor,
Just resting my spine,
due to the influx, of cider and wine.

I've not got a problem,
 I could stop tomorrow,
But please be a friend,
for I'd like to borrow . . .
some money from you,
'cause my heart is aching,
for cider and wine,
and that's why I'm shaking.

My dignity's gone,
and the future looks bleak,
my words come out slurred,
when I try to speak,
but I've got the bottle,
I don't need your sorrow,
I'll admit I've a problem,
But say it tomorrow.

Pete Nash

The Exciting Rhythm

Notes

I am 74 years of age, born in Wales and have been retired for 10 years. I am married to Gwladys with a son Calvin, daughter-in-law Gwenda, and grandson Steven Rhys.

I have had poems published in 23 anthologies since 1990, many based on 6 years army experience. I served in a Tank Crew with 3rd Royal Tank Regiment from Normandy to the Baltic, as part of 11th Armoured Division, which overran Belsen. I was wounded in April 1945.

I am active in the Royal British Legion and am currently branch president.

I wish to dedicate this poem to a special ex-comrade, Walter Sale, from Bolton, who survived the war, but nevertheless was a victim of war, dying very young, at 43, in 1963.

The strains of the tango,
spanned the wartime years,
la Cumparsita, over and over just one tune,
thrillingly frantic, then haltingly slow,
that strange sad harmony permeates times' mist,
brings back memories, and hints of tears.

I see again a canvas tent,
and the music, over and over, the same,
la Cumparsita, one record, one record, that's all.
The melody followed wherever I went;
hauntingly the music, pervading, enticing,
surrounded the loneliness whence it came.

Smoke filled cafés, overfull with khaki,
accordion strains vibrating, abound;
that tune again, la Cumparsita,
a resonance, over and over, so eerily;
dum dum dum dum, da dum dum dum dum,
the musicians skill submerged by the sound.

The dingy dark dives underground, resound,
floorboards bouncing from nail studded boots.
Dum dum dum dum, da dum dum dum dum,
that's it again, the sad sexy sound,
Britons, Poles, French, Belgians, Russians,
dancing, and torn from far away roots.

That Latin sound, compulsive, exciting,
followed me too often to mention,
dum dum dum dum, da dum, dum dum dum,
helped block the visions of harrowing fighting,
yet why does that sorrowful sound,
relight the past to perfection?

Iolo Lewis

Coalesce

There is light on every horizon
There is a dream in every child's heart
There is a person in every family
Willing to play a part

There is a pot of gold at the end of a rainbow
Whether it's real or fantasy
There is ache from every person with sadness
And a smile from those who are happy

There's guilt inside of everyone
Even the innocent
There's a cloud in every sky
And success in those who are patient

There is water in every desert
But not for us to find
We can build anything we want to
But the hands are slower than the mind

It's in our nature to be quiet
It's in our imagination to be loud
But remember the sky is the limit
Although we can reach through the clouds.

Daniel Elsey

I was born in Fulham, London, January 1932. I am married to Barbara with two sons Karl and Curt.

I served with the English and American Airforce at home and abroad and later with the Army Engineers specialising in explosives. I have now left military service and my most recent civilian occupation has been government enforcement officer.

My hobbies are playing jazz on the piano, photography and DIY (I am currently renovating a 50 foot patrol boat).

I wrote my first poem in 1968 called *Epitaph for those in the 5th Column*, about the fear and loneliness experienced by those personnel involved in hazardous intelligence undercover operations.

Reflections is a poem which recognises the significant changes in personality brought about by long service in extremely stressful situations in hostile terrain, classic example - Vietnam.

I recently had a poem published entitled Predator, which recognises the incompetence, exploitation and corruption seemingly the norm in civilian activities.

My ambition is to have the dedication and discipline to finish a war novel I have been writing for a few years too many.

Reflections

When I look in the mirror a stranger looks at me,
I often wonder who he is and what it is I see

His eyes are cold and watchful, his constant smile is false
and despite his friendly aura, I sense no pity or remorse

What spawned this dreadful creature, this nightmare of my dreams
My malevolent companion who's hoarse from silent screams

Perhaps one kill too many, another village blown to hell
When your soul had died inside you, it's difficult to tell

One day I'll smash that mirror and maybe change what I can see
and think back to the good days and the way I used to be

R J James

Innocence Abhorred

Newsprint forecasts what is true,
as it has done, what it will do.
Scrambled messages across our land,
a nation sighs over print-stained hands.

It's Christmas in June now, or so they say,
but they are subtle as they tease out the lie,
tomorrow it will be Christmas in July.

Wars challenge what we see as right,
screening out words for our delight.
There was a person who trespassed on truth,
but he was silenced at the end of his youth.

There is a statement they like to show,
that, 'the public has a right to know.'
It seems untruths are no longer lies.
We will be innocent until we die.

Ian Little

Notes

I am in my mid thirties and have always written poetry.

I decide on the subject, then the rhythm takes over. This rhythm determines the wording and style of the poem; it is everything.

As well as writing, I like reading, painting and music.

I am fascinated by the power of memory and believe it is the sixth sense. It is not tangible yet, few of us can question its existence. It is our past, our present and our future and is the solution you find when you add time in motion and energy in motion together.

I have an MA in English Literature, concentrating on Modernist writing, which often raises the subject above.

Echoes

I am the recollection you have had before
Of something you heard or someone you saw.
You know I have meaning, but can not say what;
I am the imprint your conscious forgot.

My shadow is silver, my brilliance is gold;
bend yet closer, watch my petals unfold.
Try to catch me, I will move away,
I long for tomorrow, you belong to today.

I am the total of everything past,
of the endless summers that did not last;
Life is fleeting but echoes linger,
I can trace your memories with an icy finger.

You have been here before, and you have seen this place
And the voice is familiar and you know the face;
I brought it back to you for you to recall,
and I am just memory but memory is all.

J Martin

Song

Notes

This poem is dedicated to those who live in the shadow of their mediocrity. Rejection is nothing compared to hollow, unrequited love. You cannot lose what you do not have.

How hopeless are my whims and wishes,
which strum laments upon my soul.
How wonderful this wistful dream,
to draw her near, to have, to hold.

How shy am I to have my time,
to risk my sorrow and make so bold.
How salvaged is my aching heart,
overflowing with love untold.

Neil Coe

Notes

I am a 24 year old student at Liverpool Hope University College.

This poem is dedicated to my good friend Collette Brooks who made me realise dreams are worth fighting for.

Night in Winter

Night shoots down the day.
The sun falls
bleeding
below the horizon.
Blood stains the sky violent red
As the pulse of day slackens.
Moonlight slices the night
Piercing darkness with brutal light,
stars glint in the darkening skies.
Day exhales,
and closes it's eyes.

Angela Cheveau

Job

Coloured person wanted
White on top
Black on bottom
Blue in the middle
With a tinge of yellow
Non-coloured persons considered
Providing you can show evidence of transparency.

Is this discrimination against the invisible people?

D Colgan

A Paradise of False Heavens

Written in a state of idle boredom, the poem symbolises how a brief sadness or grief has such power to take over our lives and the way in which we magnify the sadness ten times when in reality its significance is inconsequential. It is also this ignorance and weakness of our more selfish selves that allows the grief to take hold of our meagre existence. And as the title suggests we do live in an assumed paradise that is moulded into perfection and safeness, only when this mould is broken or disturbed do we realise how false this heaven is.

Who are our saviours
Making these troubled minds,
the talisman of our failures
In the depths of one's horrors,
beneath silent corners that binds
Ten million pixels of unlived tomorrows.

Whose are these blemishes
Favouring the solitary hour,
a tomb of their weaknesses
Ourselves encased in foreign vaults,
and held cradled in the ignorance of power
The miniature of our ten thousand faults.

Hamida Bhatia

Old 'Killie'

Notes

I am married with a daughter, son and two grandchildren. I am retired and live in Haydock, St Helens. I love to read history.

I am not prolific in writing and only do so when some thought appeals to me.

This poem is of the town where I was born. I was on a visit to Kilmarnock and just felt nostalgic memories.

'Killie' is a well known nickname for the town. Tam Samson was a local seed merchant and great friend of Robert Burns. (The printing house was wherethe works of Robert Burns were first published in the 'Kilmarnock Edition').

I am of Celtic origin, one of Scotia's sons
In Kilmarnock town I lived, where the river Irvine runs
It nestles deep in Ayrshire, where fields are lush and green
And yonder in the distance, the Kilbirne hills are seen
If you look to the horizon, and the day is fine and clear
You may see the Isle of Arran, in its majesty appear

I recall Kilmarnock, some forty years ago
The river swelled by falling rain, rushing past full flow
It was its wont to do that, a very awesome sight
And made what was a tributary, a snarling wall of might
The streets that were so narrow they told of older days
When the sound of iron wagon wheels, filled those cobbled ways

I recall Tam Samsons house, where Rabbie Burns oft stayed
Pulled down because of progress, it made me feel dismayed
The printing house has also gone, that showed the world the bard
We must be realistic, but to understand is hard
Burns advocated better life, for all, not just a few
And probably would understand, the old makes way for new

I've lived away for many years, thirty six in all
I have been back from time to time, and made a fleeting call
But all has changed from what I knew, as is the way of things
We must move on and not look back, as it only sorrow brings
But in my quieter moments, my memories I cherish
Of happy times in a town that was, they shall never perish

George Lyons

Nature 1, 2 and 3

I stand so tall, so proud upon the horizon where I watch
the sky meet with the hills, the lovely green hills;
my weathered branches spread about me, touching, reaching,
swaying amongst the breeze where I stand so still.

The blossom falls all around me, birds rest upon my brow
from flight,
some take shelter of me, deep into the night.

The gentle wind talks to me, it whispers as my leaves
cascade down to the floor;
seasons change, and so with it does my age, but I'll
remain for more.

I run so freely, sometimes calm, but often wild
as my waves get angry then return to mild;
a ripple descends as nature talks to me -
slowly, wondrously, flowing back into the sea.

Drops of rain fall gently from the sky -
each one as individual as you, or I;
It lands upon anything, everything, in it's path,
nature enveloping the moistures in great demand -
no aftermath.

Jo Barton

Market Day

Notes

I wrote this poem for my sister and her husband, they have a stall on the Portobello Market.

This is my first publication and I would like to dedicate it to my dad who passed away last October.

Market Traders, we're all the same,
we buy, we sell, it's a hard old game.
Saturday morning its 4.00 am,
packing the car it's bloody mayhem.
Still we make it, and we've set up the stall,
people start looking, but they're buying sod-all.
It's starting to rain, it can't get any worse,
hang on Jill, look 'ere, she's going for her purse.
She's bought it, we've cracked it, we've made our first sale,
good start to the morning, we surely can't fail.
It's three o'clock and were doing quite well.
What's that mate? Take two fifty, no go to hell.
Three pounds is the price, your getting a bargain.
I can't sell it for less mate, or theirs no profit margin.
Here comes a del boy, he's gonna try it on,
what's that Del, you want two shirts for the price of one!
Yeah! Love to Geeza you know the score.
It's two for a fiver, need I say anymore?
It's turned six o'clock, and we're packing away.
We've done really well, it's been a good market day!

P Judge

Poetry Poem

Notes

I was born in London to parents who immigrated from Jamaica, I am 24 years of age and have five sister and six brothers and still live in London where I work as a chef.

I grew up listening to music and fell in love with lyrics and rhyme. I became a born again Christian in 1993 and most of my poems are religion based.

Poetry Poem, as the title outlines is simply about poetry, my definition of poetry is contained in the last line Shakespeare is regarded as the greatest poet and I borrowed probably his best known verse to begin the poem. The message is everyone can read and enjoy poetry.

If music be the food of love, play on
Feed your appetite with a song
If poetry be the drink of love, rhyme on
Take a drink of rhythmical expression

Psalms are the perfection of poetry
Shakespeare's works are admired greatly
Pam Ayres and Roger McGough are often witty
Linton Kwesi Johnson and Gil Scott Heron are known for their social
commentary

Poetry is not for the elitist, educated or aristocracy
Of course not all poems are of great literacy
Poetry is not about rhyming, even though it is considered so by many

Poetry is the inner self crying out his hopes, longings and spirituality

Carlisle Clarke

Notes

I was born in South Africa in 1973 and grew up near the town of Duivelskloof (translated means Devil's Gorge). In this place conflicting opposites co-exist in a witches cauldron of cultures, languages, legends and beliefs and this forms the backdrop to the poem Countdown. This explosive situation does not only exist in the journalist's conviction but also in the heart of the individual who weighs up good and evil, black and white. This meaningless task only widens the gorge.

Countdown

After thunder and pain
happened more rain
yesterday forever
thought I was clever
clearly you're Cain

Sweet promises spoken
with foul breath broken
you're the sequel
to 'All men are equal'
the gates of hell open

Spread out flat
on the cross of matter
you are crucified for your sins
you croak thrice
and journey to St Peter
only to be told:
'management holds the right
to refuse admission,
now piss off and forgive.

'And, oi! . . . while you're at it:
for Christ's sake make up your fucking mind
whether you want to be Jesus or Lucifer.'

I give because I was given
I receive what I deserve
to reach nirvana
you have to kill yourself first

K Fleischmann

Notes

I am a 76 year old Londoner, married with two daughters,and for the past 27 years I have lived in the West Country.

I have had poems, short stories and advertising copy printed over a number of years, with one item being translated into Russian. I have also won prizes here and there for my work.

I live a quiet, confined life - mainly looking after my wife.

I have written since childhood. When I was quite young I won a League of Nations essay competition, (That dates me!).

Poetry is my favourite form of expression, I look at life and ideas occur. My favourite poet is Robert Burns - by a mile, the master of suspension.

The Door

Out there it's chip and chafe
In here it's snug and safe.

Out there I wear the mask
In here - the natural task.

Out there the arrows dart
In here the better part.

Out there the strife and care
In here - beyond compare.

Out there the razor's edge
In here the loving pledge.

Out there the empty pew
In here the heart is true.

Out there - despairing cries
In here your blue-grey eyes.

Out there the pompous band
In here - I take your hand.

Out there the world's alarms
In here - you're in my arms.

Out there the nations fight
In here - turn out the light!

Jack Lane

Old Lime Trees

I had not seen
How tall the Limes had grown
While you who knew them too,
Slept in your grave.

Until today, I had not seen
How high into the sky
They reached with green
And ancient splendour.

I had not heard your sighs
Until today, because,
Perhaps, that moment of your being,
Waited for me.

Marie Schendler

Cheese

Events created for the sake of photographs
Bearing teeth and upturned edges
Smiles of pretend joy, created by 'cheese'
People together, pretending to be close
People apart, in reality.
As if a photograph of you could replace
A hug, a word, a genuine smile.
Instead we live for photographs
Things so temporary, always in mind
Urgency, a need to preserve something
A time, an age, a feeling.
Instead we capture a silent moment
That we know in truth is not what it seems
But we take it anyway
So that memory can betray us
And we think that those smiles are true.

Kerrie Jackson

136

Avenue Habit Bougiba ~ Sousse

Notes

I must have given the poor
old man a good long look,
because a French-speaking
Arab came and asked me ~
very politely, 'He wants to
know if you are married, because he'd like to marry you.'
I was about 65 at the time.
But compassion knows no
barriers.

Poor old man in tattered rags,
where do you belong?
Daily begging in the street
Piteously forlorn.

Dirty rags to cover you
Dirty calloused feet,
traffic whirring ceaselessly,
you stand in the street.

Do you lay your filthy head
Down on rag and bone?
Do you love in your dark hovel?
Or are you alone?

How can you know that I care?
Language keeps apart.
Human sympathy must hover
Though we're worlds apart.

Jane Phillipson

At That Moment

If I had spoken at that moment
Told you what I thought you knew
Touched your sleeve as you were leaving
Shown you how my heart was grieving
Would you still have left me there
To live in regret and despair
Or could that instant - thrown away -
Have begun eternity with you?

Beryl Laithwaite

Always be Yourself

Notes

My name is Maureen. I am married to Ian and we have four children, Mark, Kim, Scott and Gary. We live in Poole, Dorset.

My hobbies include writing poetry, reading, music and gardening.

I get my inspiration for writing simply from life itself and people. I enjoy writing poetry very much as it is my way of releasing all my thoughts and feelings.

Special Moments Shared on Mother's Day is soon to be published in Jewels of the Imagination by the International Library of Poetry.

Always be Yourself is dedicated to anyone who like myself is shy and lacks confidence.

Always be yourself and never try to be
Somebody else, just for wanting to please.
Speak and be heard if you have something to say
Explain how you feel and never be afraid.
Hold your head high and don't be put down
Let your strength show and stand firm on your ground.
Believe in yourself and understand too
The person you are and always be you.

M Barber

Soldiers' Lament

As night falls and the battle fades,
we prepare our tactics for the coming days,
the gunsmoke blurs, the smoke fires burn,
the stench of death lies at every turn,
some pray for peace, some for home,
but the bitter hour is yet to come.
Our bodies are weary, some hot in fever,
our clothes are ragged and food is meagre,
but we fight on because life is dear,
we'll march to the front and hide our fear,
come morning light, Oh let dignity rear,
and we will die for our country, we hold most dear.

R Roberts

Romantic Thoughts

Notes

I was born 26 July 1950, I have been married to Kathy for 19 years and we have two children, Ben aged 12 and Lucy aged 8½. I am employed as a postmaster/shopkeeper. I was born and have lived almost all my life in rural Tewkesbury, Gloucestershire.

I have had no other works published previously and have won no prizes.

My interests include sports in general and cryptic crosswords.

English language and the use of words fascinate me, odd phrases, mispronunciations, mis-use of words often spark off ideas for 'amusing' lines.

My children have inspired me to write some children's stories and my wife inspired *Romantic Thoughts*.

When words of love are proudly written
We read of music, flowers and bliss.
Of misty mornings and moonlit meadows
And the magic of a kiss.

Of far away places in far away lands
Where far away beaches run down to the sea.
Of candlelit dinners in far away corners
Where far away poets are longing to be.

Let them dream of this romance, and let it come true
The world would be better for happiness shared.
Yes I'll drink to their health, these modern day lovers
We would all feel much better if somebody cared.

But I am much different, though often I dream
Of a subject which seldom, if ever is told.
With you by my side through life's ups and downs
I will ever be happy when together we're old.

Paul Keicher

Notes

Chapter and Verse

I am 49 years of age, divorced and I live in the Cotswolds where I work from a converted cattle barn at the end of the garden as an Acupuncturist. My two children work abroad.

When my husband left 18 months ago I started to write my way out of my rage, grief and pain, journalising and recording dreams and poems. It kept me clear to be able to support patients through their own challenges. This poem is a middle-of-the-night outpouring of those emotions. I wrote the last two lines in the morning. Things always seem better in the morning!

I am a Buddhist and fanatical gardener and my main love is travelling and writing as I go. The 'grand plan' is to take off for a year, buy an old van and go round the National Parks of America taking photographs and writing about my process as I go.

Opening the book
At breakfast you
Shut me out.
Opening the paper
At dinner you
Closed the conversation.
Talking only to friends
Silent with me you
Closed our marriage and
Opened a new chapter
For me.

Mary E Horsley

Ourselves Unknown

Does there ever come a time
When we know who we might be
To pick a few choice words
Say 'That's definitely me'
Do others really know themselves
Or am I on my own
Is it really healthy
To be yourself unknown?
Should we try to label
The way we think and act
No two people are the same
That we know is fact
I do not have the answers
The questions are not known
We should be open minded
We should be ourselves unknown.

Sharon Tipper

Song of a Hopeless Love

Notes

Lucio is a 28 year old graduate , with a degree in foreign
languages and literature. The
enchanting   Baudelairean
rhyming verses and the dra-
matic passion of Lorca's poetry led him to appreciate the
beauty of the written word
when he was twenty-one.
Since then he has been writing poems in Italian and
English.

*This poem is dedicated to a
person for whom the author
has felt the most intense emotions and pains love might
ever give him. They may
never meet again but, during
the night, something will always speak of this person.*

Two eyes within the space of a dream
Twice dreamt under a moonless sky.
Two icy glances caused my stream
Of words to freeze. My spirit ran dry.
With an evil laughter,
like that of the potent in the face of the weak,
reality threw its doors wide the morning after.
I could no longer speak.
I ran to the horizon where a summer dawn I embraced
 - to which I'm still laced -
And the ice melted inside
And my spirit shook and cried.
Within the time of a dream, two eyes,
like two lonely stars hanging from a moonlit sky,
your wintry blue eyes.
. . . And of any strength I'm left bereft. Goodbye.

Lucio Daniele

Money-tide

First, privilege uncoiled itself
And with cold eyes started to gulp.
And then a swarm of blue, voracious flies
Settled upon a carrion of pelf.
Spiders in fur began to spin
Derivative cocoons of purest gold
And every issue of true moment then
Resolved to a transaction, bought or sold.
Weevils devoured the charitable spirit,
Eating its core till it was scrawny hide,
While all mankind tightly engaged itself
Fashioning chimes to ring in money-tide

Dean Juniper

Notes

I was born in Birmingham, 16 December 1975. I am a history graduate from the University of Teesside, embarking on post graduate research at the University of Sheffield.

I have had numerous poems and some short stories published and am currently attempting to break into scriptwriting for television.

I am an avid supporter of Walsall Football Club.

I am interested primarily in ideas, the poem reflects my deep rooted concern over abortion, which I feel is a grave social injustice and is part of the erosion of traditional values in our society.

Innocent Ghosts

We are dying. We are dead,
permeating dreams with guilty red.
We cry and hope you hear
pitiful whispers in your ear.
We ask one question. Why?
Oh why did you let us die?
Do you recall a night of lustful fun
Which spawned a daughter and a son.
Infants who should have been
to you are just a dream. Our dream.
We want to live. We want to be whole
We want to live. We want a soul.

Paul Williams

Kite

Kite, kite flying high
Take me with you through the sky,
Take me with you far away
Where there is no night or day,
Holding tightly to your line
Between the arches of my mind,
Into a world of mystery
The walled garden of inner me,
And set me down there for a while
So I may try to unravel,
The bindweed choking the sighing rose,
She began to bloom there while I dozed,
I think I came too just in time
She needs transplanting to a warmer clime,
Somewhere where the frost can't touch her
So that all around may see her.
Kite, kite flying high
Take me with you through the sky,
Take me with you far away
Where there is no night or day,
Beyond the arches of my mind
Show me the secrets there to find.

Myrt Bradley

Fear

The smothering darkness closes like a tomb
All sounds are muffled. Black dust in a shroud
Seals every quivering pore. Grimed pit-props crowd -
My red-rimmed eyes descry them in the gloom.
They jostle with grey phantoms for some room
To watch me die. They creak - I cry aloud;
The frightened whimper's swallowed in a cloud
Of suffocating coal, that spells my doom.
The cavern ceiling groans, as if it strains
To thunder down and crush this cowering mole.
The leering rock-face drips with mocking tear
Derisive of the bursting in my veins.
Each day I sample death in this grim hole,
For every day, Fear whispers in my ear.

Mair Price

Instructions

Notes

I am the father of two grown-up children who have turned out pretty well and now, alarmingly, I find myself a grandfather as well, even though no one asked me first . . .

I always write about what I can see and feel - hopefully make you think and laugh at the same time. My greatest reward has been when people have said how much they've liked what I've done, without realising I was the man behind the pseudonym!

In real life, I am a socialist who is lucky to be able to fight for my beliefs, as a trade union organiser.

Children come without
Instructions
A confusing situation
Made worse
By helpful friends
And relatives
Telling you how
They operate different models
Whose controls
Seem to work
The opposite way
To yours.

And every time
You seem
To nearly get
The hang of it
They disappear
In the night
To be replaced
By another one
The same
But different
With strange pedals
And wobbly steering.

In the end
We would despair
Were it not
For the knowledge
Hidden deep
In our being
That one fine day
(Sunny or not)
We will be
Smug
With the duff
Instructions   To be continued

Mike Scott

Notes

I live with my family in Battersea, London. I have three brothers and one sister - I am the 2nd youngest.

I like basketball and rollerblading.

I wrote this poem in my English class at school. It is an extended metaphor comparing fireflies and stars.

Fireflies

In the evening
They fly through the night,
Lighting the sky.
What a wonderful sight.

Humming and buzzing
They hover in the sky,
Shining brightly
But quiet they fly.

Up in the sky,
You see the stars.
Shining so bright
From miles afar,

Along with the moon,
Twinkling so bright.
Calm in the sky.
Shining all night.

Peter Oyediran (14)

Notes

Thanks to all those who helped get me through it and continue to do so.

Pain

I live with pain
Every day

Pain is tiring

It stifles, numbs and consumes,
Colours and warps experience

Pain is part of me - my habitual companion
Defining personality

Pain is a constant, ever-fresh source of tension, frustration

But what is pain?

We determine others' pain in relation to ours
By their relative reactions:
Screams, shouts, winces, groans
But words?
Burning, splitting, crushing, bursting
Yes, we know what it does! It hurts . . .

Is it then simply a verb? It does but is not.
Maybe it's a process -
Stimulus, neurones, current, nerves, synapses, chemicals

Is it just a frame of mind?
Men have undergone surgery without anaesthetic and
Without pain
What is the difference between their state of mind and mine?

Could I think away my pain?

But my pain is real
It's real and it doesn't go away
One day, though, one day I know I will be rid of it
And then I will forget
Just as easily as taking a walk
My pain will have shrivelled up and gone
Leaving only its shrunken form in my memory.

Mandy Sasia

Marigolds

Notes

I am a widow and have been so for 20 years. I loved my husband dearly; and have written many poems for him. I have four children, all grown-up and married, two sons and two daughters - all lovely people!

I have been writing poems since I was 10 years old and it has given me a lot of pleasure from so doing!

We found the marigolds again,
Tho' we had not been there for years,
They were by the same brook,
And down the same lane,
And I found myself . . . in tears.

By the moorhens nest.
Beneath the willow, . . . forget . . .
Forget we were ever apart.
Weep not again on a pillow so wet,
For here . . . in this place
is my heart.

Mary Rankin

Precious Lives

Old songs and hymns in a sweet sad voice,
Warmest of smiles and kindest of eyes,
Serene self-effacement, generous soul,
Strong steadfast spirit, heart-wise.

Does truth only reach us in memory's recall
Of treasured times, taken for granted before?
My mother's life, gift to us all,
In sweet retrospect I view it with awe.

Precious the lives of those we love long,
Pay them attention in their present stay.
Tomorrow their journey may take them too far.
Value their mystery and beauty today.

K Bradbury

Dreamtime - Walkabout

Aborigines - now they have the right idea,
Go out on walkabout and disappear,
They call it dreamtime, it sounds good to me,
Lost in the bush, all alone and so free,
Back to the roots, ancestors to find,
Away from stress - get things off my mind,
Eat off the land, dig for grubs and the worms,
Not very tasty, I suppose I could learn,
Dreamtime sounds great, I think I might go,
How nice not to meet somebody you know,
On reflection I don't think I've got what it takes,
Couldn't stand all those crawlies and slippery snakes,
Dreamtime sounds lovely - I don't think I will roam,
Instead I'll go walkabout in the woods at home.

Winifred Curran

The Judas Touch (Exert)

All that separates my lonely mind from pain,
Is a cold, white corridor of numbness
Where silence deafens with unspoken words
And feelings rise like tombstones out of the emptiness.
Like headstones of a cold silent graveyard
Where fear stalks, over dark ground
Seeping upwards in a white and swirling mist.
    Ashes to Ashes!
But here nothing is certain and silent numbness lurks
Everything is suspended, like death, while the hand tightens
Squeezing the joy and love from the heart
In painful, pitiful drops
The same hand that prodded it to life
Fingers reaching from the dark expanse of nothingness
The touch oozes warmth and tenderness -
    Fanning it into life -
    False life!
    The Judas touch!
    He giveth and he taketh away!
Through the numbing ache I feel the irony
The sorry sadness of it all.

Wendy P Frost

The Ultimate Question

The day when I die,
Will the earth fall beneath me?
Will heaven's gates open?
And God come to greet me?
May I come in, or not?

Annie Dibben

Jacqueline

Notes

This poem, dedicated to Jac-queline du Pré, was written while I was listening to her playing a short cello piece called Silent Woods composed by Dvorak.

'Silent woods' that gave up their secrets
when your cello sang its song,
a hundred shades of green lit up by the sun
and the magic of your playing,
stately oaks and ageing elms
bending with your arm in perfect harmony.
You were the breeze and the storm
that breathed life into the old masters,
before your legs abandoned you
and your fertile hands had to ride
that rough wheeled chair.
The crying in the night belongs to Elgar,
for you and he were surely lovers of the mind;
your fingers plucking out his soul
and feeding it to the strings through your golden bow.

The silence that followed crippling disease
echoed around the world in graceless concert halls,
and silent woods that gathered in their secrets.

Phil Mirams

A Friendship Lost

Notes

I was born in 1978 in Dublin, Ireland. For the best part of my childhood, I was brought up in a small town outside Limerick city. In 1988, I moved to Leixlip in County Kildare and have lived there ever since. I am currently studying Journalism in college and have just completed year one. For the duration of the summer months, I am working in a local newspaper, as a Journalist. I have always had a strong desire to become a successful writer and hopefully some day, my dream will become reality.

This poem was written about a friend who died tragically when I was eight years old. Fiona, nine, was everything a friend could hope for. I realise everyone says this about those who were taken from this earth at both a young and old age, and maybe it is true. The fact is that Fiona will never be replaced. I feel that maybe because I was so young when I had to deal with her death that it was harder for me to come to terms with it in the long run. It was only when I wrote this poem that I am now able to talk about her openly. All that knew her should count themselves lucky as she was - and still is - one in a million and will never be forgotten.

This poem is ode to Fiona . . .

Head held high, a walk of grace,
Amorphous smile upon your face.
Always laughing, they used to say
All of a sudden it faded . . . away.

Friends forever, I liked to think
Tragedy struck, hearts did sink.
What once was happy, now is sad
A twist too soon makes many mad.

Plenty suffered: who would've thought
What may seem small is one great loss.
It always happens, one wonders why
But life goes on and memories don't die

They live forever in hearts that care
Although hard to accept - it's just not fair.

After all these years not a day goes by
When I wish those memories ceased my mind
For fear of forgetting the good times we had -
Not all were good, yet none were bad.

The fact is no one recovers
For in their own way, everyone suffers.

The world would not be, if thoughts could kill
Miss you forever, always will.

Anita Mullen

Ode to My Father

Notes

I am 22 years of age and have recently finished a degree at Worcester College of Higher Education (English and Sociology). Having said this, I was born and bred in Wales.

This being the first poem that I've written seriously, I now hope to take up poetry, as you have given me the confidence to do so. For this poem though, it was the upbringing which my own father gave to me and my realisation and appreciation of this in later life, which inspired me to put pen to paper.

The poem is dedicated to my father, Robert Naylor under the title For Love, Education and Trust.

Enemy, murderer, demon or beast,
Drinking my soul for your own blessed feast.
Fiery breath and intoxicated shames,
Your damnation of me, is your claim to fame.
Saturated spittings soak my salvation,
As you condemn matters of fruition.
Yet, now I see your obsessiveness,
As a key for my succession.

The child I've seen,
Has shattered my dream of escaping you.
Yet his innocent eyes,
Made me realise that I am you.
My new understanding,
Has dampened my hatred, which was cramming,
My thoughts, my hope, my love,
For the attention you gave me.

Now, I play enemy, murderer demon and beast,
Drinking his soul for my blessed feast.
Hoping, praying, that this obsessiveness
Will be the key for my boy's succession.

Virgil Hilts

Exile

Notes

The focus of this poem is on the strains of the human condition; in particular the secret - and sometimes dangerous - territories a person can find themselves drifting into when they lose sight of their life's path.

Although the poem is ultimately a whole, the three partitions, or fragments, are important because each illustrates the separate trajectory of an abstract action as represented by a physical/environmental reaction. This, in its essence, sees the inner world removing a person from the outer world and placing them, in a state of exile.

I   Boxed in.
The window pane to him
as a dream is;
all encumbering.

Soused in daylight,
every genuine hour reframes him,
blooming his features
with the sun's indolent ascent.

Reaching its peak,
it bleaches the glass white,
wiping away his definition
in a visible combustion.

II   Everything sealed.
Beneath a skin of dust
the television transposes
one image after another.

Soundless images,
that flicker out in silence -
as he concentrates on
the air-conditioner's whining trill.

A single sounds monotony,
which settles his centre,
anchoring him
to its aural mooring.

III   Sleeping diagonally across the bed.
She touches corner to corner,
bridges post to post;
offering him the choice of triangles.

In need of his attention,
her skin flexes the light
with melamine semblance -
yet he turns on himself.

Trapped alone in the mirror,
his reflection like a sombre cenotaph
bereaves all hope
of ever finding himself here.

T D Curphey

The Thunderstorm

The skies are darkening,
Birds are strangely silent.
Air is heavy and oppressive,
A storm is coming.

Trees stand lank and listless
In the humid weather.
They await refreshment
From the coming rain.

A distant flash of lightning
Lights the southern sky.
A warning roll of thunder
The storm is nearly here.

Soon the sky is forked with brightness,
And loud thunder booms.
Raindrops start to trickle
And soon become a torrent.

When the storm has passed by
The earth is sweetly fresh.
Grass and leaves are cleansed.
Brightening skies appear.

A thunderstorm is much like life.
We struggle through the black times
And think we'll never bear it.
But these times do pass
Happiness comes again.
We need God's help, have faith
And ride the storms of life.

E D Evans

Who Would Be Saved?

(A Fictional Conversation With God)

Sitting in my garden one glorious day in May
I had the inclination to close my eyes and pray
The feeling came upon me because there was no doubt
That in that peaceful garden the Lord was round about

After I had thanked him for what he'd done for me
I asked for his permission to speak quite openly
I said, 'Lord please excuse me, but curious I am to know
The destiny of mankind from what your records show'

The Lord said men are sinners an abomination all
And not like he intended before our tragic fall
But he was understanding about our earthly sin
And that is why he sent his son a victory to win

'Lord now may I please question,' I asked appearing bold
'My present situation from what I have been told
Is it true that when I die I can in heaven dwell
And be with you for evermore not tormented in hell?'

The Lord said yes he promised if I was born anew
Then he would surely raise me up with the other chosen few
I said, 'So it is true then not all will leave the grave?'
'My word is clear,' the Lord said, 'The righteous will I save'

'And Lord what do you say now about the damage done
To this our earthly dwelling that Satan sought and won?'
He answered, 'This I tell you his days are soon to end
Then I will put all things to right all this I do intend'

'And what about creation?' I then put to the Lord
'Your book and that of science are not in one accord
These men say it all happened without help I recall
Whereas your book says clearly that you created all'

The Lord replied, 'There are some things mankind will never know
But all will be revealed in heaven to those I elect should go
One thing you can be sure of whatever is said of me
It's true that in just six clear days I created all you see'

My conversation ended, the Lord had spoken plain
It's clear that those who love him have everything to gain
And so my eyes were opened to glimpse part of his plan
That God would have the righteous saved, every woman and every man

Harold Eley

Moon Tears on Polurrian Beach, Cornwall

Married to Leonard I have two children and four grand-children. I live above Polurrian beach.

I started writing poetry about 15 years ago and have had 103 poems published (unfortunately not in one book! But with different publishers), came 3rd in a United Kingdom National competition and won The Cornwall Federation of Women's Institutes Blaikley Salver for Poetry in 1996.

My hobbies are quilling (paper filigree) and belong to the quilling guild, photography, reading and several other crafts.

Inspiration comes from various sources but often poems just 'arrive!'

The silver sequin softly glows within jet velvet folds
And sheds its glistening strands to weep across the dimpled silk
Which undulates and pulses in the softness of the night.

Around its edge curved honeycombs of ruffled lace-like milk
Spread lazily to ebb and flow within the span of light
As though to probe the mysteries surrounding darkness holds.

When breached, the milky liquid stretches out and quickly moulds
Around the feet of brooding cliffs as black as pitch and stark.
Caressing, stroking, wrenching at their solid stony hearts
It reaches where I am content to sit here in the dark.
Then creeping round my boulder comes the dawn on golden darts
As peace and quiet and solitude my aching soul enfolds.

Paddy Jupp

Let's be Practical

It's good when you're messy and dirty,
When there's paint on your jeans and your hands,
It's better than reading and writing,
Or learning of faraway lands.

It's good when you're running and jumping,
When there's mud on your feet and your knees,
It's better than adding up numbers,
Or learning to measure degrees.

It's good when you're working with wire,
And lighting up bulbs in a row,
It's better than tests on a Friday,
Or learning to spell threw and throw.

It's good when you're playing a bugle,
And sounds have a life of their own,
It's better than dates learnt in history,
Or learning who sat on the throne.

It's good when you're making an omelette,
And mixing up eggs in a pan,
It's better than mapping and graphing,
Or measuring the school for a plan.

It's good when you're acting in drama,
And speaking the words of the bard,
It's better than sitting up quietly,
Or learning to write from the board.

It's good when the day is over,
When the work is complete, fully done,
It's then that I really start living,
Doing more of the things I find fun.

N D Ifould

Heaven's Silver Glow

Notes

My name is Ronald Gregson Smith, I was born in Crewe Cheshire. I am 43 years old, married with three children. I am invalided. I have just qualified for my DHPC, Dip Hyp Dip Psycho Dip Coun Dip SUBPICT. I live in Kinmel Bay North Wales. I was given the Honourable status of the Hon Lord by Prince Kevin of The Hutt River Province Principality in Australia.

This poem is my very first poem that I have entered for publication or a competition and I am truly amazed that it was even excepted, as poetry being out of my formal caricature, getting a poem published has made me very proud of my first accomplishment in life.

My interests in life are that of the Psychic World and its practice also the practice of my faith that being the Pagan Faith of White Witchcraft.

This poem is I hope the beginning of a new hobby, who knows, maybe even more than a hobby? My inspiration comes from the moon, the sun, the night and the environment but of all my faith, because as I look at these things, words just flood into my mind.

I wish to dedicate this poem to my loving wife Alison and my children and all Pagans throughout the world.

As light grows dark and night comes to day,
My ladies silver glow doth shineth the way,
Her calming glow, her love she doth show,
The tears she shed for those gone before,
Her warm cares we must adore.

The Goddess brings life's own rewards,
As she brings forth the seas to our shores,
With her life the heavens sing,
As from her love all life begins,
A time of love, a time of sleep, a time of dreams.

Her bewitching smile, her pleasing touch,
Gives her the look we adore so much,
Her darkness reminds us of death's sweet dream,
From where we came and where we have been,
From this earth to the heavens her glow is seen.

From the beginning of time our lady did shine,
Her light and power is yours and mine,
As day turns to night she shines to our delight,
No fear in our hearts as she departs,
As her love remains forever in our hearts.

Ronald Smith

Moth to a Flame

Notes

This poem is based on Blanche from the play 'A Streetcar Named Desire' by Tennessee Williams.

Pure white, fragile and vulnerable.
Ghost-like you flit through this world.
Like a child in a candy store.
The things you discover terrify you.
But, soon you are addicted to the high.
You need more of these sweet, terrible things.

The flame now looms above you. Menacing.
Everything hurled into a realm of shadows.
Nothing is real any more.
Still you crave the warmth.
But, the light exposes your soul.

The beautiful flame burns your wings.
You crash back to earth. Broken.

J Garnham

Notes

Although I have always enjoyed reading poetry I only
started writing about seven
years ago.

I write mainly about my love
of nature or Arthurian Legend which has fascinated me
since childhood.

I often write a poem after a
holiday, especially if the place
has a 'magic feel' about it like
Tintagel has.

Or seeing nature's beauty
unfold through the changing
seasons whilst walking in the
park with my Old English
Sheepdog, Emma.

I have had a few other poems
published but this is one of
my favourites.

Tintagel

Out of the mists of time and tides
With Britain near vanquished, torn,
Out of the West Pendragon strides
Thus here was the legend born.

On these far flung shrouded hills
A Brotherhood was planned
To quell all evil Saxon Spills
On this fair and precious land.

Under Dragon Banner Britain unites
Who would fight to make men free,
A table round to seat all knights
Flower of youth and chivalry.

If you walk these ancient hills alone
When the moon is on the run,
Stars shimmer down on sea, gorse, stone
All time merges into one.

You hear horses thundering along
Fierce clash swift sword on shield
True Comrades in triumphant song
Victors on bloody battlefield.

From Eastern heights here comes the sun
All things remain just as before,
Tonight if the moon is on the run
Arthur's Knights will ride once more.

Margaret Austin

Notes

I was born in 1948 in Hillgate, Stockport. My wife's name is Frances, and we've been married for 28 years and have three children; Stephen, Ray and Hannah. Our family home is in Stockport, Cheshire.

My hobbies are reading, writing children's storybooks and poetry.

My inspiration to write comes from observation and imagination.

I have had work published previously which includes *Ode to the First Days of Spring, This Summers Day, My Life Will Have to Do* and *To While . . . Awhile.*

The inspiration behind *Into the Linn* came from my daughter Hannah, while walking together by the side of the river Goyte in Reddish Vale woodlands.

I would therefore like to dedicated the poem to Hannah with thanks.

Into the Linn

Looking out at the top of crag fall
does the view she afford leave you breathless,
there nature flows like some full-blooded vein
onwards, ever onwards . . . relentless.

Falling into the Linn, she cascades to a spume
flowing in lustrous splendour, and might,
and how many before have marvelled her beauty
kissing the air with such vigorous delight.

Each flitting the moment with muted tenure
a swarm of gnats gather to dance on her spray,
an enduring sight, and with purpose I'm sure
perhaps in such doings they withstand the day.

Once at this spot, some battle was fought
and leaping for freedom across aged stones,
an unfortunate creature did stumble and fall
into the Linn . . . to claim his still bones.

Leslie Sheridan

The Bloke on the Bus

It was just an ordinary average day
When I first fell into lust.
My calendar read the 15th of May,
When this bloke sat on my bus.

He was the big type, you know,
Quite tall with plenty of shouldering.
He wore his hair like a halo,
And his eyes were best described as smouldering.

I would sneak a peek, every now and again
Behind the safety of my thick book.
My neck would ache due to the strain,
As I pleaded, please take a look.

Susan L Williams

Case Dismissed

Notes

I gave up pharmacy to write in 1987. When working on a television script two or three years later, a poem came out of the blue and then a succession over many months. Although the interruption was not welcome I felt compelled to go along with the poetry until it dried up a year or so later.

God, sure I'm hooked on publication
Adulation
And laureation
But there's no way I cooked up the ego

God, sure I lust after sex education
Porno-elation
And fornication
But just who invented sex, Amigo?

God, sure I'm chasing material things
Braques and blue Mings
East and west wings
But remember, avarice came from the Deo

God, sure I'd swap my soul for Cruise's looks
My portrait on books
World tours by Cook's
But it was you who made me a Leo

Ray Sturgess

Notes

All of us at different times
suffer the burden of keeping
a secret, it may be a simple
birthday surprise or the difference between life and
death. I am sure that many of
us at some time have wished
we could unburden the se-
crets of a lifetime, enabling
us to continue the rest of our
lives with a clean slate.

I am a forty-five year old wife
and mother of three grown-
up children who lives in west
Yorkshire. I have had several
poems published in books
and magazines in the last two
years and a short story
judged to be worthy of high
recommendation.

Naked

If only we could tell all the secrets we hold,
Let them pour out, watch them unfold,
Relieve the burden of holding them in,
Mop up sadness, wipe away sin,
Bleach the stain of crimson red,
That lies like truth upon our beds,
Cut up the pain, chop up the guilt,
Wash it all out to dry like silt,
Blow it away on a hurricane,
That will never touch this land again,
Take from our shoulders, all we can't share,
Leave us stark naked, without a care.

Linda Bedford

Dartmoor

Notes

I have always been struck with a sense of awe when visiting Dartmoor, or any ancient stone-age site, and this poem is an attempt to express that awe. It is the same sensation I get when visiting an art gallery and gazing at a Rembrandt, Turner or Goya. It reminds me we are part of a continuum and that art is a corner stone that says, you have been here before. Poetry is another reminder of that continuum and I'd like to leave my mark.

We walk the landscape and we see
The neat hut circles, standing stones;
The land is bare, there is no tree
To cast a shadow with man's own.
We wonder at the maker's hand
That shaped each stone into its form;
He had no iron and worked with sand
To smooth a surface, bevel quern.
What do we share with those gone by
Who gathered honey, tended kine,
Who read their seasons in the sky
And turned their honey into wine?
They must have had a common tongue
And must have travelled from afar
Was Greece the cradle whence they sprung
To follow up the northern star?
This we know; they placed their stones
To read the moon and know her tides
To make a shelter for the bones
Of those they honoured who had died.
The dolmens stand in place today
Time has stolen their bones away,
Has stolen arts and skill and speech
And made a gap no man can breach.

Martin Green

Notes

I am a 24 year old for the Maryhill area of Glasgow.

The inspiration for this poem came of my 22nd birthday upon realising just how fleeting time is (yesterday I was 13, tomorrow 90!) and how bizarre to reach a point in life where you are to some extent discarded with little more than your precious memories remaining.

Twighlight

Hair white by the passing of ninety winters,
cherished memories hidden behind watery blue eyes,
oh what tales they could tell.
How terribly strange to be ninety?

Twilight years, rivers of tears,
with her woollen shawl conceals her fears.
Dismissed as no longer valid,
starving for a little recognition,
in the isolated loneliness of old age.
How terribly strange to be ninety?

Once she had been beautiful and sought after,
engaging everyone with her infectious laughter.
Landmarks she remembers that are no longer there,
family around her that don't really care.
How terribly strange to be ninety?

Four score years and ten,
her brittle old photographs appear to whisper in the silence.
Confused and bewildered by technology and science,
like sand through the hour-glass her time ticks away,
she thanks *God* for his mercies and every new day.
Oh how terribly strange to be ninety?

Scot Crone

Notes

I have been enjoying writing for many years and I have had eight poems published in various anthologies. My aim is to have my own book of poetry published.

Apart from writing poetry and short stories, I also have many hobbies, these include drawing and painting, cross-stitch and music.

My inspiration for writing comes from many sources, but mainly from people; my son, my family and friends, and my favourite singer, José Carreras. I have followed his life and career for many years and his character and spirit have been inspirational in some of my work.

Unrequited Love

My heart waits patiently for you
and welcomes all you start;
a warm embrace, a tender face,
a voice to melt my heart.

My heart, it listens for your voice,
it makes me smile within.
Your voice, it warms and calms the storms
that certain days can bring.

The feelings that you bring me
with eyes that melt my heart.
A smile that can't be beaten
that makes me fall apart.

My heart, it longs to reach you
with the gift of silent speech.
With wishes steeped in passion,
is your heart within my reach?

If I could have a wish come true
these feelings would be free.
And in return, your heart would feel
the very same for me.

Susan Fleming

Notes

I am 28 years old and presently unemployed but I have trained as an actor.

In this poem I wanted to capture the feeling that for me, September is the one month of the year that one can actually feel the season change with the flip of the calendar.

Words for September

September I see has made its way here
That month that begins the decline of the year
There's a scent in the air that I just can't explain
It's the wintry whiff of a year on the wane

The first shades of night, they fall around eight
And the leaves on the ground are a sure autumn trait
There's a chill in the morning that hangs soft and cool
On the uniformed children returning to school

The coalman's back out, doing his rounds
His horses' hooves trotting, new seasonal sounds
Warm coats and sweaters they make a return
At the heart of each home a glowing fire burns

In the quiet early evening, the sky is still bright
As the swallows pass over on their southerly flight
The flower that was summer, sadly now wilts
As away from the sun our hemisphere tilts

This month can still hold the most glorious days
Unique to the years autumnal phase
Nature's pure colours they put on a show
Reds, golds and yellows just glitter and glow

But these thirty days can vanish so fast
So I must try and catch them before they can pass
For when that cold winter is upon us again
Oh sweetest September, your a memory then

Damien Muldoon

Notes

I wrote this poem for Ben, who has poor eyesight, and longed to see dawn. So I painted dawn in words for Ben.

I have always enjoyed poetry and I am moved to write when I see the beauty of dawn and sunset, and the realisation of my own mortality. I try to capture fleeting moments of beauty forever in poetry.

I have one daughter, three sons, and three granddaughters. I run a ladies fashion shop and also a large garden. I enjoy painting and writing.

My age is more than I care to be!

Dawn From My Balcony

On my balcony, above the sea
No clock ticks, a refuge
Enchanted, I watch
Sunrise, drive the purple night away
The sun, newborn again
The sea, new painted
By dawn's light
Horizon's purple, lined with gold
Nature's theatre before me
Clouds build castles in the sky
Distant islands float
On veils of grey mist
Ships drift by, mysterious
Gulls first flight
And I am drenched
By dawn's golden light
My soul now quiet.

Constance Fox

Could it Be?

A new millennium,
or the end of time.
Could it be?
Our time has passed,
and this century,
our very last.
Could it be,
that time will end,
or could it be,
that time will lend,
itself to us for as long as it can,
and then take it away,
and destroy our land.

Alexis Burke

Notes

I am a 22 year old female
bank clerk. I have worked as
a bank clerk since leaving
school in 1990. I live and
work in Watford.

I have not yet had any other
work published but I am
working hard toward having
one of my short stories published one day! I love both
reading and writing. I read
all sorts of different types of
fiction and I especially enjoy
thrillers. I have been writing
both poetry and short stories
for as long as I can remember.

Impossible

How could you be so cruel to me?
And worse, so very kind
I wish back my summer winterland
With its first hopes and promises
Sitting in isolated company was I
Feeling small and young and vulnerable
Calling back those first days now
With my own cherished smile
And I would not write since then
I have saved this for the hurt
And I thought that I was waiting
Now admitting there is nothing to wait for
I long to stay far, far away
But I cannot stay away from everything
Images of ambitions filter through my mind
As I wake to my daily routine
And you, you're there
In my imaginary future
Standing behind the door of 'impossible'
Whilst all my other fantasies
Swirl around, each waiting to be caught
And all I'll need is deep determination
But you, you would need more,
More than I have got.

Michele Reeves

When Time Stood Still

Notes

I am 31 years of age, married with two young children, Arthur and Alice; a part-time lecturer and trainer I live near Malvern.

I have had work previously published, a short story entitled Time to Change and a non-fiction book about spreadsheets.

I started writing poetry many years ago, but I destroyed a lot of my poems as I didn't like people reading them; they are too personal.

Feelings inspire me to write, usually when I feel strongly about something.

This poem is about the way I felt just after my dad died. I was 21 at the time and my dad was 46, he committed suicide after a long period of depression because he and my mum had split up. The poem is very sad and it was hard to write, even 10 years after my dad's death. I miss him and I wish he was still alive today. Despite the way that he died I will always remember him as the sociable, happy and loving father that he was. He gave me so much, and his love is still alive.

The poem is dedicated to my dad, Jim Griffith.

When time stood still
my world stopped turning
the day that would not end.
People carried on around me
as though nothing had happened.
How could they?

The sun shone down
on the green grass
and the beautiful trees,
the blue sky, white wispy clouds;
he'd never see them again.

Such pain inside me
I couldn't see for tears
He'd always been there, but not anymore.
So this was how it was
when people die.

I went to see him, in the morgue
hoping it was a mistake
For a moment I thought it was,
he looked so old, like granddad.
But it was him.

I tried to speak, to tell them;
but nothing came out.
I wanted to kiss him goodbye,
but when I touched him he was cold.
The coldest thing on earth.
I drew my hand away.

Goodbye, dad.

For all your love I want to thank you
for everything you were, when you were warm.
You made me what I am today.

Deborah Thompson

Pain

To the memory of Sapper Lee Glyn Thomas.

My lonely heart is broken but my mind is oh so clear,
And memories come flooding back of times that were so dear.
This natural reaction to our pain of life's events
Is obvious to everyone that speaks with good intent,
But what the hell do they know of my inner sense of grief,
Of my constant need for comfort and of feeling no relief?
There are many friends and family who share my sense of pain,
But inside I still feel empty, as if sentenced to remain
Alone with simply photographs to remind me of a love
That once was shared by two, but now is only shared by one.

Self-pity can consume a mind until destruction comes
A life of guilt and loneliness that leaves one all alone.
'Tis easy to believe that all your feelings are unique,
'How can they comprehend the salvation that I seek?'
But only you are asking for the answer to 'Why me?'
For as the rest of life continues something inside starts to see
That a far much larger scheme of things is planned out just for you,
And that in the end acceptance will resolve all life's revue.
However, at the moment the unfairness of it all
Is all that lingers in your mind with feelings of remorse.

A learned man once wrote 'To thine own self be true,
So it must follow as night the day that life is true to you.'
Provided that what guides your way is coming from the heart,
No person or event will shape your decisions to depart
From your own self-expression to be honest 'til the end,
And to hell with what the others say, I don't have to defend
Myself to them or any man who tries to change my path
As long as my intentions do not harm or hurt in wrath.
So now I have decided to accept my sense of pain
And in so doing, rest awhile then start my life again.

R W Matthews

Progress

She stood on the cliff-top, naked, looking out to sea.
Her father watched her
'She's like a young Amazon,' he thought as she ran by.

She stood on the cliff-top, costume-clad, looking out to sea.
A young boy gazed up at her.
'She's like a young Amazon,' he thought, as she ran by.

She stood on the cliff-top, a woman now, looking out to sea.
A handsome lover stared at her.
'She's like a young Amazon,' he thought as she ran by.

She stood on the cliff-top, a baby in her arms, looking out to sea.
Her husband gazed towards her.
'She's like a young Amazon,' he thought as she sauntered by.

She stood on the cliff-top, her arms tight about her, looking out to sea.
No eyes sought her this time.
'I am like an Amazon,' she thought, as she walked slowly towards the sea.

Rosaleen Rutherford

This Other Me

Transport me to another place
This one is all wrong.
It is stifling and strained
And I want to be gone.

This world is dark and alien to me
Yet here I exist
But how can this be?
When every step I take
Feels inappropriate
The image is correct
Yet I feel like a fake.

Who am I fooling?
None so much as myself
Never fulfilled
Until I gain the freedom
That will be my wealth.

Take me to a planet where I can survive
Where I effervesce, ignite
And freely take flight.
Where I can run, play and truly live.
Where my heart is open
Sharing all the love I have to give.

Sacha Pierre

Autumn

The howling wind finds all the cracks
Like a tormented soul not finding rest
Trees relinquish leaves in a carpet of hues
Feet tread like some unwelcome guest.

Autumn displays a hunter's moon
Season of mist eerie and bleak
Non-migrating birds search for food
Feathers tousled as shelter they seek.

Another cycle heralding change
Earth prepares, hibernation now here
Flowers flaunting their perfumes now gone
Cessation as the soil rests for next year.

Clare Whitaker

Genetically-bound

I live in the South of England.
'Animal Songs and Vegan
Verses' was printed in a limited first edition in 1993. I
have written some poems and
articles mostly in animal
welfare literature and recently I have been fortunate
in being selected for four
anthologies, besides being a
future participant on the Internet, with a book prize.

I was much prompted by the
title I chose for my book. I
can never forget the terrible
cruelties that have been involved for animals in this
century: the ecological truth
that has been so unwisely cir-
cumvented.

Monster to monstrosity bred.
To human-kind an heart of lead.
From swift-flight bird
To this specie too absurd.

From fast-hooved horse to
Strength bred rhino,
Machine-bred man
Cogged in to brain insane.

Will synthesise the Genesis
Science now proclaims, persists
In moving cog or factory-fit
Even forget of a beginning or an end.
A race elite.

John Amsden

Guilty or Innocent

Presumed guilty
Or am I innocent
Found beyond doubt
Sentence without a cause
Cast to a cell
Damned for all hell

The light has gone
Only dark remains
Space is only limited
Scared to speak out
In case I'm found out

Truth would be heard
But not believed
Or taken in
Or matter to anyone
But to one's self

G Mitchell

Notes

I am 18 years of age and live in Street, Somerset. I started writing in January 1995 and have been writing ever since.

I have had poems entitled *Smile* and *Love Is* published previously.

I write poetry because it expresses my own emotions and experiences in my life. It's a way of making sense of things that only I understand.

My inspiration to write this poem came from the fact my boyfriend proposed to me and I wanted to express how I felt.

I would very much like to dedicate this poem to my fiancé Mathew Watts.

Thinking of You

While I'm lying on my bed
I'm getting these thoughts in my head
I've been with you so long
and it seems like forever's been and gone
I love you and I know that
this is the real thing
I never thought I'd settle but I know
this isn't a fling
I can't imagine my life without you
as we've been through so much it's untrue
All those little things you
helped me with
And all the nasty things I did
you've stood by me through the
good and bad
Even though you must of
been mad
I can't begin to tell you how much
you mean to me
All I know is you and me were
meant to be
There's just one thing I'd like to say
Which is I will never leave or hurt
you ever
'cos I know I will love you and be
here always and forever.

Clare Woodey (18)

A Gypsy Girl and Friend

Notes

I am a retired florist, seventy two years of age. My hobbies include flower arranging, embroidery and poetry.

The inspiration to write poetry, was all around me, in this world.

I have had several poems published previously which include *Sometime to Pray, Memories of Sound, Crooning Lullaby, Youth, Seasons, Generations* and *Bethlehem,* published by Anchor Books. *Our Heritage this England,* published by the Poetry Guild, *A Blind Sailor* and *Songs of the Earth,* published by the International Library of Poetry. I also had some made into tapes, ten were selected out of three thousand.

Glancing out at the distant view
early the morning touched with dew,
though those hills once so near
so familiar, now look queer.

Head held high you cheated the cold,
each line you seek need not be told
travelled those roads over those hills,
and travel them now, thou feet are still.

You sought each valley, every nook,
found your water from a babbling brook,
made your fire, had a brew,
washed your kids and clothes too.

As you played, once long ago,
walked so brisk in sun or snow,
toiled the land sowed the seed,
ate the fruit and drank mead.

Once with the family and friends
knowing the farmer around every bend,
welcomes you to toil his land,
pick his fruit, with gentle hand.

Travelling now has come to an end,
for my gypsy pal and friend,
God blessed you with creation,
how he loved his gypsy nation.

Naomi Ruth Whiting

Notes

I am a 69 year old retired engineer who is married.

I have been writing for ten years and have had poetry published in Head Over Heels by Arrival Press and in church magazines. I have had technical articles on solar panels published by Link House Magazines Ltd and Motor Caravan Magazine and a technical paper on The Use of Solar Energy published by Wales Junior Gas Association for which I won a silver medal.

Taking Stock

If you can take your own advice
And act upon it in a thrice.
If you can pay the price that life
Demands of you with all its strife.

If you can show compassion live
While also trying to survive.
If you can take time off a while
To be happy and maybe smile.

If you still cheer to nature's sound
And hear it, above all around.
If you are loved by those *You* love
And watched over from above.

Then your cup is full my friend
May you enjoy it, until the end.

Jeff Jones

A Poem - To Dorothy With Love

Notes

A Poem - To Dorothy With
Love, is the first poem I have
written.

My neighbour Dorothy, has
been a passionate gardener
all her life. Sadly, recently she
has had to leave her beloved
garden behind. She is now 87
and has been put into a
nursing home.

Dorothy's garden was always
there to greet me when I
opened my back door. This
tiny haven has given me so
much pleasure.

It was very painful moving
everything, but at least the
garden will live on with me.
Afterwards I felt so sad - I
wanted to write my feelings
down. My poem is written
from the heart.

I've desecrated your garden
And it nearly broke my heart.
But I did if for the right reasons
To conserve your life long work.

I know how much it meant to you,
And it meant as much to me.
I've taken your rocks and pots and plants,
They must survive you see.

When I remember your beautiful garden
It makes me want to weep.
I'm so sorry for the destruction
Treasured memories I wish to keep.

I miss you so much, my dearest friend -
More than words will let me say.
I couldn't risk folk might not care,
So your garden could not stay.

I will love every plant I have taken
I will cherish each beautiful flower.
Fond memories of you with your roses
Will be with me for ever and ever.

Lin Gonzales

Notes

I was born in a little village in North Wales called Bagillt. In the 70's I moved with my family to Tralee, County Kerry.

Both my parents are dead now but I live with my teenage son Gary. I have two brothers and one sister.

I love reading, writing and enjoy meeting people.

My first poem was published in January 1997 in a preview book of poetry. I wrote the poem especially for children in need and it was entitled 'Child Born Poor of Birth.

Old Soldier to Young Centurion

You stand before me, a man of war - You a mere mortal.
Flesh that burns by the rays of the sun.
That freezes by the night till numb,
And drowned by the seas of the earth.
I too have faced battle,
Steel armour, which crushed my body.
A cold sword, which gave me false courage,
To take life, to face another fellow man.
It is not honour, nor courage. It bears the mark of hatred.
Love will flee a battle. When this day is over,
You will not render to sleep.
For your soul will invade your eyes,
You will relive death.
Those whom you have slain, clearly as day,
Will face you once again.
Those you called foe, once laughed
Whose hearts beated with the blood of life,
Lay empty.
Aged before their time.
Mere carcasses of flesh and bone.
Now decaying on the earth.
Deprived of life . . .

Helen Dineer

Raging Calm

Notes

I am a civil servant, married with two teenagers.

I love reading, nature, and aromatherapy and am fascinated by people.

I have had four other poems published and am inspired by intense emotion.

I like to be different, when the kids let me!

I feel the rage that's mounting
That rises black and dark,
Emotions like a fountain
All rough and bare and stark.

There is so much needing saying,
And so much left unsaid,
What's the price that we are paying?
Hearts broken and full of lead.

The path that I must travel
Is a climbing, twisting way,
And my thoughts I must unravel
Just so I survive the day.

You only see the blankness
That you draw across my face,
You won't ever see the frankness
That I've hid back in a space.

And so, to spare your feelings,
I pretend that all is fine,
And I sit and stare at ceilings,
While I sit here drinking wine.

C Kelly

Blindness

I am twelve years old and attend Halliford School in
Shepperton Middlesex. I live
in a Victorian house in Kew
Gardens. I have one sister and
two brother, one of whom is
my twin.

This is my first poem and I
wrote it when I was eleven
years old and had to do
homework on blindness. I
was at boarding school then
but have since changed to a
day school, which I much
prefer. I tried to imagine
what it would feel like to be
blind.

I love art and am doing a
water colour course pres-
ently. I enjoy rollerblading,
sailing, learning the electric
guitar and am very interested
in Army life and its connections.

Don't take the mick,
Because we're not thick,
When we cross the road,
We get crushed like a toad,
If we fall in a lake,
We're forsake,
It's all dark and black,
It's like I'm in a sack,
I turn my back
I'm still in the black,
I'm blind,
Nothing wrong with my mind,
I can talk, walk, speak, smell and hear,
But I can't see, it's no 'He-He,'
It can't be, it can't be,
You laughed because you're daft,
I'm pale, I'm a blind male,
I can't see - it's not great,
It's like being behind an iron gate,
It's just what I hate,
If I could see I'd laugh, I'd be happy,
I'd even change a nappy,
It's not so bad and I'm not mad,
When they say,
'So you see what I mean'
I feel like a bean - not all clean,
I have a white cane,
No! I'm not insane,
I use my brain,
I picked up a picture, I could not see it,
I could not see it because I'm blind,
So don't be tight, unless you want a fight.

Giles Chester (12)

Notes

This poem is dedicated to the memory of my lovely dog Ebony, (a black Labrador/Border Collie crossbred bitch

I lost both my mum and Ebony at the same time. Mum used to bring me a cup of tea in the mornings and Ebony would come too, and sit beside my bed.

They are still alive in spirit, and have both been to comfort me. I hope that this poem will comfort others, as I now know that death is not the end.

I now have a rescued Jack Russell and many other pets.

I have just started writing poetry and have had one other poem published entitled *As I Sit and . . .* in the book Gone but not Forgotten.

).

Remembering Ebony

I remember a black velvet head
Cold wet button nose
Warm brown eyes searching my face.

I love you, you're my best friend
I want to be beside you,
Beside you at the end.

And, in my mind we'll take one last stroll together
Watching your tail wag with pleasure
This is one walk I wish would last forever.

Whilst your body has gone,
You're here in spirit still
As I walk through the door
I see the shadow of your image once more.

And, in the morning,
I hear your soft paws padding down the hallway,
A soft bump as you sit by my bed,
I reach down one last time,
And touch your ebony head.

N J Brocks

Notes

I have been writing poetry since 1995 and have had poems published previously, these include *The Black Cat, Four Score and Three Years* and *The Number One*, in The New Voices Anthology II by Minerva Press 1996.

This poem is loosely based upon an article in the Daily Mail of August 1994 under the heading 'In Praise of the Unbeatable Fox'.

The poem is an attempt to convey the basic essentials of a fox's existence, ie his need to hunt to survive, for himself and 'his family'. An animal misunderstood and persecuted but in point of fact one with appealing individual characteristics. Its natural 'guile and cunning' is necessary to ensure its survival. It is essentially a survivor.

Survival

Through the meadow's long lush grass he passed and his gait was certain
               and bold
The white tip of his brush was hidden from view but the red of his coat
               shone like burnished gold
Suddenly he paused with keen pricked up ears eyes searching about
               everything on hold

Reassured that all was safe he commenced again his stately tread
On the relentless essential search for food
Insects, worms, mice, carrion birds, fruit and particularly rabbit yes a fine
               spread
For his family waiting at home in the earth.
A vixen with five cubs a month old; as important to them as man's daily
               bread.

Through the temporary shade of trees and shrubs that the copse did
               provide on his way he went
To the Farmer's fields beyond where times before he had found
               nourishment indeed heaven sent
Slowly cautiously; eyes ranging and examining.
Then muzzle lowered with sensitive nose sniffing; to his work he bent

The task over twenty minutes did take as his sharp featured face
               manoeuvred that and this way
When a slight movement he spied; a rabbit taken unawares
And with eyes fastened upon it never leaving his prey
He stalked and then stalled the main food for that day

His forepaws tight into his body were pressed
But his hind legs had risen as high as could be
And from them he leaped with deadly intent
A high arc like curve breathtaking to see
Down onto the rabbit his victim thus seized
Clutched with his forepaws then dispatched by only he

Swiftly now the fox did move the rabbit from his mouth a-dangling
His trot was brisk as his steps he retraced homeward bounding
Back to his waiting family he hurried
Over fields through copse and meadow; he requires no hounding
Of animal guile and cunning to the full but not of human deceit and
               betrayal
Our perspicacious friend could be seen. In image resounding

Foster Humphrey

A Show of Magic

Notes

I am a retired police officer, aged 40 years. I am married to Ruth and we have two teenage children, Claire and Barry. We live in the town of Denbigh, North Wales.

I am only able to write poetry when I am emotionally moved by something, particularly visual. I have had a number of other poems published on such diverse subjects as the Bosnian conflict and the transportation of live calves abroad in crates.

Having seen the Riverdance show on video and television on numerous occasions, I was moved to write this poem, by its sheer beguiling brilliance.

There's truly some magic in this mundane world,
That allows for the sense to become unfurled,
Possessing grace, beauty and a haunting style,
It's Celtic-ness my sensations, it does beguile,
I listen, I watch, I'm sensually transported,
My heart speeds fast, as my feet, they are courted,
Every note, with each tap and step are so individual,
With feelings of passion and longing, being the residual,
What are the ingredients in this vibrant potion?
That can so tantalise and tease my every emotion,
I speak not of an elixir, or of some miracle cure,
But of Riverdance the show, unique and pure,
A concoction to force tingles to flow down the spine,
Its contents as intoxicating, as finely matured wine,
All its performers display such delightful ability,
That to not feel total pleasure in their artistry,
                                  Would be sheer futility.

Robert H Griffiths

Notes

Born in Salford I have lived in Lancaster since 1990. My previously published work has been mainly academic papers and articles.

This poem arose from the simultaneous fear and hope I felt in meeting 'her' someday, or not.

It's dedicated to someone I love, and someone I hope will come along. And she'll know this poem's here for her, just in case she's looking!

Just in Case She's Looking

For some time now, when I get home,
And twilight hours are passing,
In the window I place a candle, lit,
Just in case she's looking.

I've had no calls, no notes, no signs,
To end my anxious waiting;
Still, I light the candle as I always have,
Just in case she's looking.

I know some day she'll be close by,
For just like me she's searching;
And she'll know the candle's there for her,
Just in case she's looking.

It doesn't matter if she doesn't call,
Though a shame to waste these feelings;
But I hope the candle stays when I'm gone,
Just in case she's looking.

Michael O'Donoghue

Vita Nuova

Notes

The author of this poem has endeavoured to express in words the wonder and beauty of the natural world with the coming of spring. There is a sense of loss in the draining of the bold colours of autumn in the grey, soundless landscape of a long winter, but the signs of spring at last revive hopes and expectations which emerge from the darkness into the sunshine of a new life.

Living in the unique setting of the New Forest is a source of inspiration in the writing of verses, some of which are set to music by the author, who also directs a group of Madrigal singers.

Grey robes of winter clothe the earth,
Faded autumn's splendour.
The swallows fly to lands of sun and ease
Over the lonely seas.
The leafless hedgerow, bare of summer's richness,
Braves the icy blast,
The woodland creatures in their fastness
Slumber deep. The night-black crow
Is toss'd in darkling skies by the frolic winds.

And when the sun appears,
All nature wakes to warmth and light.
The seeded wheat in the fields springing green,
A smiling primrose peeps from leafy crown,
The flickering sunlight spreads a warm caress
As people dream, in hope of summer days.
Drifts of snowdrops shine in woodland ways
And dawn brings in the birdsongs with their praise.
Welcome to the bright new year! New life has begun.

Beryl Louise Penny

Notes

I am a nineteen year old student from Medford, Massachusetts. My biggest inspiration comes from periods of great emotion such as sadness, anger, and love and I am greatly influenced by nature, dreams, and the unknown.

I started writing poetry about two years ago when I began to read the works of the legendary Jim Morrison, my greatest influence and my favourite poet. Aside from poetry I also write songs and music.

I would like to dedicate this poem to Stephanie Visconti, a good friend of mine who passed away recently. May she never be forgotten.

Alive

broken dreams crash the landscape
chanting in foreign tongues
lashing out like flames,
they devour in a rage
of insatiable hunger,
feeding on the souls of young fools
'The time has come'
the lowly voice announces
'There is no rest for the wicked'
feel the life seep out slowly,
trickling,
dripping down deeper
into the Abyss . . .

Robert Gallant

Slumbering Insomnia

I dreamed of a grey sky -But no clouds to be seen.
I saw in the darkness the bright yellow ball.
But even the sun cast no light at all.

I dreamed I was walking by a fast flowing stream.
It was shrouded by lilies but even although
Life was within them they appeared not to grow.

I dreamed I was chasing myself in a rage.
But the calmness within me forced me to crawl.
And I searched for a stranger - It wasn't me after all.

I dreamed that the mountains were deep awesome pits.
And the tree-line was vague and the snow-caps were black.
And the only way forward was a road leading back.

I dreamed of a circle - It had gates on four sides.
But the path was a maze and no progress was found.
By the pilgrims in purple who wandered around.

I dreamed I saw grasslands where the deserts once stood.
And the water was dry in the bed of the sea.
And the price of the water was totally free.

I dreamed I was dreaming and when I awoke.
My dreams were still with me as clear as before.
So I drifted back off and I dreamed a bit more.

Gerald Morgan

Memories and the Sands of Time

Notes

I am an American, who has lived in Britain for over twenty years, married, forty-something and presently working with American university students studying in London.

My biggest hobby is travelling, but I also enjoy reading, dancing, swimming, horseback riding and writing. Life is my inspiration.

This poem was written in memory of the old folks at my grandfather's nursing home, sitting in their wheelchairs, staring vacantly at nothing, with dead eyes.

I would like to dedicate this poem to Sally and Lenard Clayton, and Sandi Clayton-Emmerson, without whose encouragement this poem would never have been written.

Here I sit dribbling down my chin
Dependent on another being
Bruises from the wheelchair
running down my shin

Useless limbs, now wasted appendages
My eyes no longer seeing
A memory of lace
and a pretty face

A life of fun and wicked sin
like viewing a movie reel
as I am fed my meal

Oh how I yearn to play
like a frisky child enjoying the day

But all I have left are memories
and soon the sands of time
will take even these away

Christine Clayton-Owen

Notes

Lynne Wallace is 25 and is originally from Lancashire. She moved to Edinburgh seven years ago to undertake a degree in Communication Studies and remained there after completing her degree.

Monolithic Persona is her first published poem.

The poem is dedicated to Jason with thanks.

Monolithic Persona

A grain of sand upon the shore
Indistinguishable from the rest,
A face amongst the millions more,
A leaf blown east and west.

Blending in like sea and sky
Lost within the crowd,
A single drop that falls from high
An ever changing cloud.

One second lost within the years
Replaced as soon as gone,
The first of sad and lonely tears,
That ends as they began.

A penny of a thousand pounds,
The same as many more,
Strange footsteps fall on unknown ground
The next like all before.

A blade of grass deep in a field
Soon lost without a trace,
Memories that are soon to yield
To another nameless face.

L D Wallace

Reward for the Patient

Today is similar to the rest,
but today's undoubtedly the best.
For today she arrived with a glassy crest,
to wash away an unwelcome guest.

Will she still be here next week,
or am I witnessing a freak?
I sit and watch her uncrowded peak,
longing to meet her, hear her speak.

I skim the surface on my way,
devoured by her salty spray.
Inside her is where I want to stay.
Today's undoubtedly the best day.

James Allen

Notes

I've been writing short stories and poetry for as long as I can remember. I love to write - for me it's a form of relaxation.

I get my inspirations from many places, personal experience and life in general.

This poem could have several meanings, depending on a person's point of view. In my opinion it's about someone who is different or feels different from other people and society ignores or laughs at them. It's about individuality and having a point of view - which is the only thing that a person truly owns.

Painful

A kick in the mouth slows you down.
A punch in the stomach makes you frown.
These words that hurt will bruise your pride.
The pain will burn you from inside.
The damage in your soul is hard to mend.
You look around - seeking a friend.
They ignore your pleas, your screams and shouts.
All you receive is a kick from these louts.
All you desire is an opinion of your own.
Nobody understands how it feels to be alone.
A change of direction fulfils all your needs.
But still you whimper and lick your wound as it bleeds.

Clair Knight

Prince

Never again will eyes be so large and brown
So trusting of nature with innocence shine
That gait that's so bouncy, the laugh of a clown
This is what we will remember when we think back in time

A four-legged puppy that never grew up
With thoughts of greed and food galore
In dreams the legs chase cats, and they try to get up
In play the tail is pursued and the toys chewed from the floor

'My cheeks blow up, a gaze full of naughty,
Then looks of pleading, for hungry am I,
Upon my begging unsuccessful my actions run haughty,
Forgotten the next moment, so joyful am I'

These thoughts and many more will last in our minds,
Many fleeting glimpses of you in golden moments,
Your spirit is free, abounding and kind,
You are always remembered with fondness and endearments.

Shirley-Joan Collie

Notes

I met my husband when we were both students at Oxford in 1950. We have lived in the same house in west London for forty years and brought up a family of five (now variously in teaching, music, television and design). I have taught English, and creative writing, in local colleges.

I now write prose mostly and, very occasionally (and privately), a poem, when a thought presents itself strongly in terms of images. I have published articles, a short story, and recently a handbook/anthology of prose and poetry for religious study, entitled Ways of God (publisher James House.)

I started writing poetry at the age of seven, and have wanted to be a writer ever since. (I remember my mother 'borrowing' them, typing them up . . . inaccurately . . . and producing a hand-made booklet.) This particular poem was written while attending a course at London Colney on the philosophy of Teilhard de Chardin.

I am starting a second degree course shortly in philosophy and religion. My other interests include the theatre and flamenco dancing.

Three-in-One

It is good to vegetate,
Apparently motionless
But growing very slowly under the sun,
Reflecting light, sharing existence
With stones, plantains, trees . . . We all do it
After lunch, on the beach, in the bath,
But the very new and the very old
Vegetate more.

Animal is good too:
Functions we enjoy
Half abashed (but what is life without 'em?)
Eating and drinking, digesting and lusting,
Enjoying the rich bad smells,
Flesh and blood freemasonry,
Frigging nimbly like the monkey,
Running strongly like the horse.

We boast a higher life
Still, goodness knows,
Unfolding heavens beyond
Our little orb: the depth and height, and breath
Of love-fire fusing one to one, both to many
And all, all together,
Into a Supreme . . .
Something.

I'd be sad to lose
The monkey life.
The sharpest joy of all.
It seems, doesn't it, the likeliest to go?
Nor am I wholly sure what will be left.
Slow sun-warmed being
Or the gaze widening
To vistas?

Both in their way universal,
Either would be good . . .
All three,
The blessed jackpot.

Ann Smith

The Last Great True Wilderness

Notes

I was born in 1973 in Matlock, Derbyshire. At present, I am working in science research for Unilever on the Wirral.

My hobbies include playing guitar and writing music and lyrics. From this grew an interest in poetry.

The Last Great True Wilderness was written whilst I was at Loughborough University in 1992. It is one of my earliest poems and is the first poem I have had published. The poem was originally the final verse of a three verse poem on the subject of the environment.

At the ends of the earth;
Where icebergs furnish the seas;
Mountains and castles of ice,
Break up the horizon;
Colours of purple, blue and green.
A nomadic polar bear,
A solitary whale;
Picture it in your mind;
'Cause tomorrow it might not be there.
When the tourists start tramplin';
And they start drilling for oil;
The last great true wilderness;
We want to stain and soil.

Peter Lake

London

Notes

I am currently working in London for a marketing company, though following my creative instinct I am looking to pursue a career in the design field.

Although I have always enjoyed writing, my interest for poetry emerged during recent times.

I studied illustration at University, and I feel my artwork is a useful accompaniment to my poetry. My writing, which is based on personal experiences, reflects my outlook on life. I know that with self belief and hard work invested you will succeed.

Passing by without a mutter,
Unhealthy traffic, a cough and a splutter
Hurried echoes in deep concrete,
The silent warrior with marching feet
Another contender in the biggest rat race,
The deepest scar on the urban face
The business man in lunch-time drinking,
A golden cure to aid his thinking
Familiar cries, 'Help the homeless please!'
An empty shell that no one sees
Commuter patience fading fast,
The passenger trains choking their last
In all its glory and all its pity,
The busy graveyard of London City.

Robert Morton

Fear of Darkness

Fallen stars in what we found
Eternal night-time came.
After all the sun has no soul,
Reality is to blame.
Open your eyes and look around,
Fear everyone you see.
Darkness is here, we can't escape,
All we have is you and me.
Re-assess the trust you've laid,
Kind words and friendship lost,
Never believe the lies of a day,
Even a smile can cost.
So what happens now, what do we do?
Shadows are screaming, are they afraid too?

Angela Bevin (18)

La Verita me fa Male (The Truth Hurts)

Notes

I am fifty-two years old, the mother of four children and six grandchildren. I was born in Swanwick Hampshire but my home town is Poole in Dorset.

Appreciation for poetry began at school with the likes of Wordsworth and Milton. I haven't shown any of my works previously, because writing has been a personal and private way to relax and relieve tension.

I became a committed Christian at the age of twenty-eight and hopefully reflect that in my writing. I enjoy the company of my grandchildren and my only other interest is, now and always will be, Sir Cliff Richard in his varied career.

Poverty of a different kind
Steal away her days,
Thorn in the flesh underlined
In many diverse ways.

Afraid to be all alone
To walk along the street,
Choking fear, stumbling stone
Forcing her hasty retreat.

Afraid to live in this day
That will not set her free,
Thief be bound and go away
Return her sanity.

Friendship her insatiable need
Water in an arid land,
A friend in need is a friend indeed
Let the hearer understand!

Time alone can heal her pain
Of all that was before,
To feel and smile once again
Her love of life restore.

Reach out truth to help a friend
Set aside her fear,
With a beginning there must be an end
Let the hearer hear!

Jennifer Anita Colombo

209

Etherial Power

Notes

This poem, *Etherial Power*, is an expression of the nominous power that surrounds concepts of life. On the logical intellectual level we accept nomogeny, but on the irrational, illogical level we are inspired by and driven by thamatogeny.

We search for meaning to nature and life, but our natures are not set as with other creatures our unconscious gives us Gods or demons that drive us up or down. Ludwig Wittgenstein (1889-1951) once expressed it best, 'When all the technological questions have been answered to mankind's needs, mankind shall still have to face itself.' As impalpable as Wittgenstein can be, I believe he may have meant ourselves, solus ipse and at the end of the intellectual quest that mankind is on, the question why! Will still be on mankind's lips.

Briarean Brier is 41 years old, works and lives with his family and pets in Kent. He has two awards in information technology and has read widely in literature, philosophy, psychology and art and hopes to publish an anthology soon.

The power that drives
The green fused root
That pushes through tar
The slow blade shoot
Drives our will to life.

The power that drives
The dark cloud storm
That gives fresh life
To the dappled fawn
Drives our will to life

The power that drives
The bright dawn in place
That gives to nature
A chaotic grace
Drives our will to life

The power that drives
The celestial sky
And drives us on with
Why why why?
Drives our will to life.

Briarean Brier

Photographs

Notes

I am a housewife and mother living in West Yorkshire - a grand setting for an amateur photographer. My passion for photography was inherited from my father, who must have spent half his life behind a camera. His collection of photographs allows me to revisit my childhood. I, too, will leave my children with a visual record of their lives - moments in time that can never be repeated.

To my father, (who now wanders the Elysian fields snapping angels), I would like to say, 'Thanks for the memories.'

Elysian fields: Greek myth: the dwelling place of the blessed after death.

Favourite places,
Forgotten friends,
Familiar faces,
Fashion trends.

Newborn babies,
Dogs and cats,
Elderly ladies
In awful hats.

Weddings and birthdays,
Carnivals grand,
High days and holidays,
Children in sand.

Steeples on churches,
Castles with towers,
Begonias and birches,
Colourful flowers.

Hues and views,
Snaps from the past,
Memories you lose,
But photographs last.

Rossline O'Gara

The Meeting

Notes

My name is Ann. I'm 24 and I now live in Manchester where I am a teacher of English in an 11-18 school.

It is generally essential to be liked in order to get on in this world. The Meeting is about one way people seem to achieve this by flirtation and flattering someone's ego in order to get what they want; how many people use sex to succeed?

Trying to look innocuous
Yet full of purpose and pride
All those doubts and fears
Must be kept hidden inside.
Put on a show for the bosses
It seems we must perform
We females must smile and flutter
And try to give our massas the horn
He can plump himself up and strut
We can lower our eyelashes and smile
It's not overt, a silent game
Unspoken, just to please while
They give us the power we crave
But only as much as they think
When he's sat down with his loving wife,
He'll smile while sipping a drink.

A Northfield

Notes

Terry Matthews was educated at Marling School, Stroud and Leeds University where he read Psychology. Terry has spent 22 years in the Royal Navy.

Things of Love is dedicated to his mother.

Things of Love

Earth, sky, sea;
A bird, a flower, a tree.
Are these things signs from
One above?
A name, synonymous with love!

Terry Matthews

Read the Question Always

To what to be reconciled?
Some there are, who drive one wild;
There's yet no quarrel, mere irritation,
Nowadays, no devastation.
Lost jobs, lost love, lost self-esteem.
All one was able to redeem.
Much talk of reconciliation
Means only resignation.
Never the world's first ballerina for one season,
But Sadler's Wells is there to save one's reason.
Modest career success, not really tough;
Enough just has to be enough.

Joanna Mackay

Heaven Knows the Secrets

Through the power of your love
I have managed to sort out the most
intricate problems that had previously bewildered
and frustrated me for such a long time

and I'm sure that without your love
devotion and seriousness of matter I would still be
searching for a way out of this misery never
to be free like the birds and the trees

your warmth and encouragement
has set me free opening my eyes to bear
witness to the living reality thereby breaking all
the chains that surrounded me causing my
loss of free will and liberty

you're such a daring caring
person blessed with sincerity and a
sympathetic listener possessing a heart everlasting
with patience I'm sure was given to you above
with grace as pure as a dove

you helped me to see straight
through the misty fog that had previously
clouded my vision and perception but now I'm able
to see more clearly now the mist has gone

being with you taught me now to
trust my innermost feeling and to discover the hidden
inner strength that I possessed laying dormant deep
within awaiting instructions

but the most important thing of all
was in knowing you cared and by knowing
that made my world a dream come true by realising
that you kept on believing in me encouraging me
and pushing me to believe in myself

you helped me to recognise the
gift bestowed upon me from birth and
how best to utilise it effectively bringing out the best
in me and carving a place for myself
and loving family

Jonathan Hanley

Movin' On

Notes

I am 18 years of age and live in Bideford with Colin Baglow, my boyfriend, in a flat above Old Town Stores. We both work in the convenience store and plan to buy it. I still attend college until June when I take my final A level exams in Art and English literature. I have a sister called Gemma and my parents are Neil and Jackie Joy.

I have had five poems published entitled The Circle of Love in Awaken to a Dream, Bad Influence in Poetic Justice, The Struggle in Addictive Poetry, The Loving Feeling in Inspirations from the south west and 1990's in Back to the Future.

I have won Successful Writing by Teresa McCuaig from Poetry Today for Movin' On and the Editor's Choice award for The Circle of Love from the International Library of Poetry.

I like to write and draw so I practice illustrating short children's stories that I write. I have 4 rats that occupy my time and I collect memorabilia from the X-Files and Star Wars.

This particular poem was written when I sat my A level English mock exam, we were studying Carol Ann Duffy and had to write a poem in a similar style to her, I developed it as I moved in with Colin. A lot of my poetry has been written with connections to Colin and some of my best work was written during a time when we split up. I have only been writing for 2 years but most of my inspiration comes from being with Colin or listening to music, especially songs from the 1980s when I first started to listen to the charts.

Today I left my home, the place that I had grown in and called my own. You have a home, don't you? I thought of all the times that I had, had there, in my room, so big once.

This room is where it all happened. Discovery. The nights of high passion, clichés. That one drag that sent my body buzzing. The rain against the window. Bullshit, I shouted.

Now it is time to move on. Scary, isn't it? The times of this room are now objects in a dusty box labelled; *Past.* Up in the attic with the spiders. Memories long forgotten.

I remember that day. Don't lose your mind, I said to myself. It's a routine. Everyone has them, nothing special. As I slept it feels like home. Today.

Nicola Louise Joy

Faces and Memories

Notes

I am 22 years of age and have just finished a three year English and literary studies (with health studies) degree at Worcester College of Higher Education. Originally from Tamworth, Staffordshire, I have recently moved to Wales. Although I've been writing poetry since the age of 9, the first competition I have entered was this one.

This poem is dedicated to my Polish grandfather, Marian Zubrzycki. It has attempted to reflect just a few of his thoughts, as he remembers the second world war - as a prisoner in Auschwitz. Although it's been a long time since we've seen each other, the poem is dedicated to him, because I'm proud of my heritage and I'm proud of him.

Ebbing away, another,
never-ending
always coming, yet then going
Where?
Knowing, caring, unto loving
and then gone
as quick as lightning.
Never with a goodbye,
and never with a smile
and often leaving heartache.

Memories, happy and sad memories,
to dwell upon until the time is up.
Thinking, wishing and hoping,
perhaps dreaming,
but these dreams will never come true.
Every morning, often emptiness,
every evening, often tears.
And then time moves on
but never forgetting that face.

That face which brought mysteries
and dreams.
Bringing on happiness
and then tears.
The face which sheltered and protected
and then withdrew,
quicker than lightning.
The face which will never be seen again.
The face which once had a name,
now has no identity whatsoever,
only a memory.
And when the time is up for somebody else,
the memories and that face
disappear for ever.

Zara Zubrzycki

Notes

I have only recently revived my childhood passion of writing poetry. I am a 23 year old history graduate searching for a full time permanent job. For the last year I have been working for the Employment Service and my experiences there are my main inspiration for this poem.

My job has made it clear to me that there is a small minority of young people who belong to a dysfunctional sub-culture which has emerged as the result of British social decay. They have no concept of morality or respect and believe that it is their right to do whatever they please - no matter how socially unacceptable. They lie, cheat, taunt, abuse, insult and threaten until they get what they want from myself and my colleagues. They really believe that this society owes them everything.

Unless resolved very soon this sub-culture will grow. How it can be dealt with I have no idea. All I do know for sure is the attitude that I see in front of my every single day.

Attitude

Don't look - stare
Don't ask - demand
Don't speak - shout
Don't request - command
Don't listen - ignore
Don't smile - frown
Don't care - abuse
You young, vicious clown.

Claire Thomas

Baby H

Notes

When my daughter Heather
April Dawn was born, her
grandmother came to the
hospital and said 'Heather,
what a wonderful name, it
can never be abbreviated', *so*
from that day, she's been
known as *Baby H.*

Martyn Hudson has been
writing poetry for 12 years
and performing it for 2 years.
His successes include winning the Bristol Poetry Slam,
starting the Glastonbury Poetry Slam, founding the Poetry Whores on Tour, who
play Dutch dates and are appearing at Glastonbury festival 1997.

Martyn has had three poems
published in anthologies and
looks forward to one day being published in his own
right.

Emerging from, warm security
Into chaotic bright uncertainty
Entering a strange new world
My perfect little girl
A delicate shade of purple
Like the moors at dawn
Gradually changing colour
Becoming earth-bound Heather

Imagine cobalt blue sapphire jewels
Liquefied into sparkling pools
Then magnify endless, cloudless skies
Reflected in deep clear water
Combined and captured in two eyes
Glimpse the visionary gaze
Bestowed upon my daughter

Priceless gift from the Goddess
Our lives enriched and blessed
By this precious pixie star child
Her illuminating fairy smile
Refreshing as the white spring
Unlimited natural potential
Attuned with forces elemental

Just like a tiny flower growing
Or a raging river flowing
Her magical effervescent presence
Embraces each day with beauty
Fascination in discovery
unquenchable thirst for knowledge

Martyn Hudson

Burial Ground (Trompan, Skye)

Notes

It is only recently, since I moved into the countryside to live, that I have begun to write poetry.

First lines 'come' to me which must be written down quickly or the poem is lost. With luck the lines flow and an idea emerges (often to my surprise!)

The luscious bleakness of a small graveyard on the Isle of Skye prompted *Burial Ground.*

If ever you find that place, seek out the headstone erected by the Glasgow neighbours of a Skye woman who lived many years in that city.

Read the inscription. Raise your eyes to the headland.

Their empty eyes
see Dunvegan Head,
the aird below
with its black-ringed beaches.
No flowers bloom,
just thick green grass
and granite stones
where cold rain reaches
each weathered memory,
long gone, lost loves
whose lives are written
in one line speeches.
No tears can fall
from empty eyes.
Cold hearts are safe
from what life teaches.
But in that silence
hear their lonely moan
as the wind of time
fades and bleaches.

Alice Bell

The River Dee

Notes

I am 51 years of age, born and brought up in Wiltshire where I received my formal education. I moved to the south west nearly 30 years ago and for the past 25 years I have been a serving police officer in the local force. I have an honours degree (Plymouth University) BA in organisational studies which I took part-time over five years. I live on the outskirts of the city in my own home. Our grown up son is a business banking manager in the City.

My interests include keeping fit by cycling and walking. I enjoy gardening and I read extensively across a wide range of material. I also travel a good deal in Great Britain (short breaks). I started writing about nine months ago as a part-time interest.

This poem was inspired my the scenic beauty of the north west, in particular Snowdonia, to which I have applied my creative thinking and ability. I found as a result of many stays in the area, that with so many beautiful features and spectacular views I wanted to capture just one part in verse, through observation and feeling.

The mighty waters of the Dee,
Travel headlong towards the distant sea

Through deep pools and past wooded vales,
Tumbling swiftly with all your tales.

Through craggy valleys you flow with glory,
Over rocks and boulders you tell your story.

We watch in awe from distant bank,
But your majesty and might we have to thank.

Past tree-lined field you have far less pace,
Your waters move with the finest grace.

To those who watch, you give such pleasure,
To them you are a special treasure.

Flow on, flow on you mighty Dee,
In all your moods and changes,

Nature has decreed eternally
You journey from those mountain ranges.

G Knipe

A Vivid Dream

I saw myself in another shape
With wings soaring high,
And as I rode on thermals soft,
I never thought to question Why?
That I who was born in the shape of man,
Now soars under an alien sky
Whose mountains appear not on earthly map,
And only God knew where was I.
A leap of mind through space and time,
A form of bird and man,
But the strangeness, never crossed my mind,
For I remained as I am.
Man or bird it may sound absurd
But the shape it matters not,
It's the mind within;
The body is just a sham.

William Donovan

Writing Pen

Notes

I am 49 years of age, a retired service man and live in County Cork, Eire. I have nine children, sadly my wife died 7 January 1996.

I started writing about a year ago. I write about things of interest, my family and other things in general. I have had one other poem published in a book entitled Daybreak on the Land for which I received an Editor's Award.

To understand the meaning in what the writer is expressing as he puts pen to paper, try to be free in character.

My other interests are cooking, treasures of the earth, reading, fishing and art.

Writing to you of poetry done.
What splendid words were wrote upon.
Endless toiling words spoken with in jest.
But fruitful thoughts of joy and happiness.
I have told you this but never before.
You were the inspiration that brought forth thought.
That set my heart a-fire.
But it's just at the point of getting there.
Grants me but joy in achievement.
In the hope that I should go on.
With the firm understanding I know,
which is the forward way.
So with my pen in hand.
Here shall the point write,
with pen in motion.

Jeremiah Kenneally

Nature - a Forgotten Mother

Notes

This poem was written during a rare quiet moment in Sarajevo during the summer of 1995.

Unlike many of the other poems written at the time, it is not shrouded in the shadow of the war. Instead I see it as an expression of inner peace whilst the world (myself included) seemed to be going insane.

Do you remember the Old ways?
The ways of the rising,
And of the setting Sun.
When we did attend the Wind,
Paying heed to the Trees.

Does your heart recall,
Those exalted and halcyon days.
When we walked in the tall grass,
The World's first light still clean.
Hark! Your Soul speaks.

Observe our odyssey,
Blown with the sands of time.
Ancient hearts, entwined in Eternity,
Their lessons to be heard.
Do you remember the Old ways?

Simon Parkes

Needle Chill

Notes

I am 30 years of age, born 9 November 1966 in Bellshill, where I still live. My family consists of my mother Millicent, father Stephen and older sister Annie. I am a registered nurse (RGN and RMN) and I am working within the Glasgow Drug Problem service at present.

I have had 27 poems published over the past three years by Anchor Press, Poetry Now and Arrival Press.

My hobbies include reading, writing, drawing, music, most sports, movies, concerts and plays.

I began writing poetry at the age of 17 years as a means of catharsis and expressive release, inspired by life and living life to the full. I write poetry to express thoughts, feelings, issues, problems and other thoughtful issues motivate me and inspire me.

I have worked in the field of addictions for 10 years. This inspired me to write *Needle Chill*, this poem gives an insight into addiction problems.

Suffer the Chill,
the Needle Chill.
An injection of hope,
reality we try to kill.
Another escape,
another thrill.

Steal the freedom,
the comfort,
the hope,
another way by which to cope.
Cope with the troubles,
the anger and pain.
An easy way out,
we hope to gain.

An overwhelming urge,
that is hard to constrain,
another injection of hope,
right into a vein.
Clutching at straws,
in this deadly game.

Stephen McGeeney

Notes

I have seen how terrorism can instil fear and suffering into the lives of innocent people. I can never be persuaded that any act of terror can be justified by religion for that is a profound contradiction.

The best poetry for me comes only when I feel disillusioned or depressed, this is also the time when I find myself reading other people's work. I hope not to write many more poems in future!

Terrorists, Lunatics and Heretics

The building lay shattered, broken down
the air fetid, not a sound.
A crowd gathered, all passers-by
mother with child, started to cry.
Deafening sobs, against the silence of time.

Memories only of tragedies past
people's lives wrecked by the blast.
Crazed men with guns, shouting the odds
religious fanatics, all different gods.
Why they do it only they know.
Do they like how it feels, to stop a child grow.

Suicide bombers loyal to the cause
with mad men for leaders, a powerful force.
Following the faith, strong to the teaching
listening to figure heads, proud of their preaching.
Who is oppressed? Who are the free?
My god is best, but really is she!

Mark Patrick Hannigan

Notes

Married to Jim with two boys, James and Stephen, I am a State Enrolled Nurse working with the elderly.

This is my third poem to be published and I recently won the editor's choice award from the International Society of Poetry for my poem *Hope* written in memory of my late father. I have recently taken up short story writing.

I tried, in this poem, to create a feeling of life's fragility, questioning the meaning of death and how none of us can escape it. Although this poem is sad, not all of my poems follow the same lines.

Defeat

The stream of life goes ever on,
The moon is dimmed, the sun is gone,
Beats of radiant activity slows,
The meaning of reason too.
The gentle heartbeat of life strums on
embryonic in its fragility.
The weaving waves of the tangling tide
tying together ancient stones
and the anguish of my moans,
Strangles the yells of the gull.
And with the omnipotent black hollow of the sky,
tormented, captured in the night going by,
I submit to my defeat in keeping the night open.

M L Paine

The Apprentice

Notes

I am a Christian and I am employed as an accounts clerk for a local motor factors. I have been writing poetry for two years and have had several poems published.

The inspiration to write poetry comes through my faith. I believe for everyone who finds themselves in a situation where they feel 'the reins have snapped', God has an answer for them in his son Jesus and I feel that my poetry reflects this.

It is reaching out to a hurting world.

Imagine you try riding upon a horse's back
When all of a sudden the horse bolts
And you find the reins have snapped

Only if you were a skilled rider
Would you be able to render control
Like when we make a mess of life
Only Jesus can mend the soul

It's when we find we struggle on
And we think it's expertise
When in fact we should recognise
God's love
And accept we're just trainees

Belinda J Howells

Alleycat Jack

An alley cat whose name was Jack
Thought he would try another tack
Instead of foraging in the bins
For fishes heads and salmon tins
He hung around outside the shops
Seeing only joints and fat pork chops
For several days he had no dinner
And Jack was getting much, much thinner
He wandered round the town each night
But dustbin lids were all on tight
No chance of any food from there
All he could do was sniff and stare
He slipped off quietly to the park
And prowled around in the dark
He wished he had a fish to eat
That would be a welcome treat
Then up ahead he heard a splash
And alley cat Jack, in a flash
Was there beside the boating lake
In time to see the fading wake
Made by a fish quite near the shore
So skinny Jack dipped his paw
Into the water and he waited
Like fisherman with hook well baited
He lay there in a semi-doze
'Till suddenly his body froze
He saw a fish begin to rise
Poor Jack could not believe his eyes
Tensing muscles and staying cool
He flipped the fish out of the pool
With relish Jack began to eat
Then lay there smiling, quite replete

Maureen Bastable

Memories

Memories - of you:
When I close my eyes I see you on the crumpled bed of a London Airport
Hotel
With a fag in one hand and a beer in the other and a self-satisfied smile on
your face.
You still have the taste of me on your tongue, your lips, your mouth:
That tongue, those lips, that mouth - spilling kisses and caresses, cries and
lies.

I shouldn't have loved you - but I did.
I shouldn't still love you - but I do.

I often wonder: do you still think of me as I do you?

L Thompson

The Cat Is

Notes

I am Stephen Panting aged 36. I live in Banbury with my parents. I am on trial in a part-time job.

I like sport, writing and walking.

I like interesting people; 19 sportsmen have acknowledged my work; Neville Southall, Peter Shilton, Lee Dixon, Maidstone United, Andy King, Joe Royle, Andy Hinchcliffe, Terry Venables, Peter Reid, Ian Botham, Eddie Hemmings and Neil Smith are some who have written letters back, sent autographs, and colour photographs autographed.

I wrote a story to Spice Girl Mel C, receiving a colour picture which was autographed and another photo signed by all 5 Spice Girls.

I had part of my Neville Southall story published.

The cat has whiskers to measure space
The cat the independent animal.
They leap to get up high.
The animal that has balance
Milk, kitty cat, fish amongst their food
The time the cats can sense.
There is always the friendly cat, the nervous cat
At night cats' fighting stop the silence as we sleep
Purr a happy contented cat
The cat may leap to your lap.
Chase the wool around the room
The Persian, Siamese, the long-haired cat
Many breeds of cat
Cats at shows, cats that roam the streets
Cats a comfort for many
The cat has a roll on its back
The cat will paw you for affection
Meow goes the cat, it wants to talk
Always on alert for dogs.
The smell that senses food.
The cat with the long-haired fur.
The cat has a sleep in its own world
Some cats have a collar for name and address
They have a roam and roll around
The cat may be happy or give you a scratch
Hey! Watch the milk on your doorstep
The birds that flap around
The mouse that squeak around
Hey! Where's my salmon gone? The cat's around

Stephen Panting

Notes

I was born on 16 July 1967 in Edinburgh and am the proud 'mother' of three cats!

I have been writing since childhood and apart from poetry I also write short stories and plays.

I am an actress currently working for a Ghost Tour Company in Edinburgh as a guide, entertaining tourists with stories of Edinburgh's history.

I write purely for pleasure and prefer to write in standard and simple dialogue. I try to encapsulate moods and feelings that the majority of readers can relate to.

I am also involved in writing for a new magazine on the Internet, at Café Cyberia in Edinburgh.

Mr Mitchell

The young girl sat quietly facing the wall,
comfortable in her own nakedness.

Her long hair tangled down her spine
and her lean arms never left her lap.

Quietly she sighed
but she never took her eyes off the wall.

She had been motionless for nearly three hours now,
thinking bland thoughts, or planning her life.

She would sit until she was told to move,
for she was in love with her art teacher.

Sarah Wilson

The Spinning Wheel of Spring

Notes

The farmer had left the gate open leading to three fields surrounded by undulating woodland. It was January and I walked in the fields. The gate was open because of the BSE crisis. No cattle. I was sad also but felt the strength of the earth and the inevitability of the seasons.

I am sixty-seven, have been a teacher, but since retirement have been a carer. I have been writing since 1973. I have published a book of poems called The Rosemary Bush.

The hoared fangs of winter
Bite the dwindling soul,
Baring the bones of love.

Ice laces the sea edge,
The reed swords guard the shivering lake,
Which, ice-carpeted, clutches to itself
The wraiths of summer.
Pine trees, white-candled, pagoda-styled,
Loom, mist-curdled.
Brown, skeletal leaves of holly lie,
Prickles piercing the recumbent snow,
Love crouches beneath the flail
Of winter.

The still roots of trees, moss-ridden,
Succour-stretched into the earth,
Mole deeper to escape the delving frost;
But dormant and alive they wait
The spinning wheel of spring.

Rosalind Taylor

Notes

I am an eighteen year old student at the University of Glasgow where English Literature is a major component of my course.

I began writing poetry two years ago at school, Originally I submitted poems for examinations but afterwards I began approaching publishing houses. To date I have had around seven poems published.

I have received an Editor's Choice Award and a nomination for Poet of the Year 1997 from the International Society of Poets. I have also reached the final of competitions with other organisations such as the Poetry Guild.

The inspiration for 'The Dove' came during the broadcast of harrowing pictures of young Somalian children. This poem was my way of hearing their message.

The Dove

She flies above so white and pure,
Gliding through the heavy grey, smoky skies . . .
Of Ireland, Bosnia, Somalia, Rwanda.
Ascending, descending, her white feathers fluttering in the breeze,
She dodges the scuds from below.
In her beak she bears an olive branch,
The one from our dreams.

She flies within our minds becoming our hope, our dream . . .
Of peace.
Hovering overhead, as people's lives fall,
Believing in the message she personifies.
Wishing they are all listening she hangs in the sky
Wings full span, white and beautiful,
In her beak she bears an olive branch,
The one from our dreams.

So many people suffering for sins committed by others,
Caught up in a fight, fatally failing.
The dove falls from the sky, her white body splattered with red.
She is dead -
Torn apart as were many promises and compromises.
There can be no winners in this war of evil,
When peace and hope are ignored.

The olive branch slowly glides down toward the ground,
Paying homage as it falls to the dove and her message.
Its journey ends beside the dove, but the branch is not withered.
Who will pick it up . . .
And resurrect the dream of the dove?

Lorraine Wilson

Notes

Dale Christian Ranson was born in Melbourne, Australia 31 March 1975, he is one of two sons.

Dale is currently a world traveller but is returning to be a history student in Melbourne University. A man of many worldly interests with no real conviction to any particular one as yet. In respect a man of nature who spends most of his time in the bush and who adores nomadic lifestyles.

He always enjoyed reading and discovered poetry in a time of isolation. Thoughts and dreams often provided better company than superficial friends.

'The poem is filled with comparisons to my own affairs and is better left to interpretation.'

The Dam of Love's Flood

The heart's dispassionate course is riven,
with the flood of lust's last embrace.
Words are inadequate, inept to describe,
the confusion and turmoil, of subconscious mind.

Words are embroiled,
in the mystery that's their own.
Although I understand,
I can barely comprehend.

The Athenian games, with which you plot your moves,
on the tri-dimensional bao-board,
serve only to twist the conscious,
in your subterranean labyrinth.

Why is my brain so starved of oxygen,
just enough to prevent death,
but dull the nerves,
stem the senses.

Placed in a tighten struggle of wants and realities.
Selfishness prevents from recognising,
the form that has been so evident,
so long.

Feelings apparent,
in their own recognition.
Dashed and draped,
bloody against the wall.

Words written, understandable,
unpermiated by slurs and pronunciation of speech.
Like poles of a magnet, drawn to their own,
unhindered by logic, and restrictions of law.

Sacrificial beast. too heavy to lift on the altar.
Innermost thoughts, never meant to be read.
My face a facade, that envelops the mind.
Stoic in approach, to most of life's hurdles.

I am a plasticine, I have weathered the cold.
Once solid and immovable, your warmth making me pliable.
Yet selfishness, and lack of conviction,
may yet, still stand in the way.

Chris Ranson

Behind Closed Doors

Notes

Hello, my name is Yvonne Maiden, I am 24 years of age and my hobbies are aerobics and of course writing.

I have only been writing for a year and a half.

Behind Closed Doors is one of my favourite poems and I hope you enjoy reading it as much as I enjoy writing it.

As I shut the door behind me,
I'm out of harms way,
But with all these feelings bottled up inside me,
What do I say,
As I sit here with my inner-self,
I'll pick up my teddy bear,
I'll hold him close,
For he is always there,
No one can see me now,
They do not know what I feel,
Or why I hide away,
And not conquer my fear,
I sit here all alone not knowing what to do,
For locked away deep inside me,
I know I must face the truth,
Behind closed doors no one can see,
That behind there,
There is someone lost inside of me,
No one can see my tears of sorrow,
Nor my pain of heartache,
All they can see,
Is someone who is out of harms way,
One day I will conquer my fear,
And not run away,
For whatever life throws at me,
I will not hide away,
But until that day comes,
I will always be that someone who is out of harms way.

Yvonne Maiden

236

Notes

I have always written hu-
morous poetry, but wrote my
first 'serious' poem recently
called *A Purrfect Life*, published in the anthology The
Cat Got the Cream.

At 28, and agoraphobic for
the past two years, I've found
writing poetry both therapeutic and rewarding.

I compare myself to the butterfly in *Breaking Free*, as I
too look fine on the outside,
but I'm not living inside,
'preserved' behind closed
doors.

*I wish to dedicate this poem to
my mother, Margaret, as with
her love and support I know
one day, I will be able to
compose the sequel - I am
Free.*

Breaking Free

The cold, speckled pebble skims rhythmically along the
surface of the murky lake,
Tiny ripples erupt through the water, creating a
pattern of expanding rings.
The lone figure lets out a wistful sigh, as she
contemplates how much more she can take,
No longer does she have faith in the
Adage: see what tomorrow brings.

A rare species of butterfly may look beautiful,
Preserved behind a clear, glass frame,
But only by being alive in the freedom of the world,
Can it ever thrive and grow.
For too long than she cares to remember, her life
has been painfully mundane,
To expand and become emotionally fulfilled,
She must be like a butterfly, she must be let go.

As she looks down into the murky lake,
She studies her sorrowful reflection,
She knows she must bury the ghosts of her past,
For they blind her and she cannot see.
She's been living at a crossroads most of her life,
And longs for a new direction,
Invisible chains sap her strength and make her weak,
And she desperately wants to break free.

As she tosses another pebble into the lake,
She wonders where it will land,
Like the pebble she doesn't know where she's going,
But she hopes she's on the right track.
She decides to rid herself of all her restrictions,
And grips her future firmly with both hands,
Then she walks away from the murky lake with the world at her feet,
And not once does she ever look back.

Jacqueline Cheryl McLean

Notes

I was born 7 January 1972 in Glenroyd, Blackpool. I am married to Serafina and have one child.

My hobbies are poetry and life.

People and circumstances that have influenced me to write are poets such as James Douglas Morrison (The Doors), William Blake and Oscar Wilde. Also having an illness called Crohns Disease. 'Pain is but time and time shall surely pass'.

Friends

I have got such good friends
    that I can call my own.
Enter their place
    I enter a communal home.

A brother of my age,
    a sister I never had.
We chose each other as friends,
    for this I am truly glad.

I've never known us to argue,
    as we never struggle to talk.
Throughout our lives,
    together we shall walk.

W B Dowman

To Spencer . . .

Fate is not on our side
The distance between us is far too wide
I know some day we will be together
Hopefully it will last forever
It will happen in later life
Someday I may even be your wife

It's good to know how real this seems
It's just a shame that it will only happen in my dreams.

Hayley Morgan (14)

Darker Days!

Angry words
Shouting voices
Echo through the night.
Angry words
Muttered curses
Hatred burning bright.
There shall be no laughter now
The darker days are here,
The love has gone
The bad rules on
Reigning with the fear.
Angry words
Muttering voices
Shouting through the night
Angry words
Tears falling
As my parents fight.

Emma J Franklin

Warmth From Within

Notes

Although I was not inspired to write this poem through personal experience, I feel that Warmth from Within reflects my concern for those without love in their lives, those who have been abandoned and others in similar situations.

I have been writing poetry since I was 11 years old and this is my second poem published.

I am a full-time student in my hometown Liverpool and I am studying in both A level English language and English literature at college.

I look at these walls and I shiver with fright.
I look at the window but I see no light.
I look for help, but nobody cares,
for the one's who once love me say I'm
no longer theirs.

Oblivious to emotion and unconscious to love,
is the language they use to define my
falsehood.

They abandoned my cries, my screams
and my pleas
They refuse any love like destructive
disease.
They cannot see that I am frightened
and that deep down I have learnt.
Please loved ones forgive me for
this hole that I have burnt.

Instant forgiveness - I no longer
expect.
Recent discovery of my true self is
all I have left.

Claire Elizabeth Gregson (17)

I'm Asking Why?

Notes

I've been writing poems since 1985, but it's only been since October 1996 that I have entered any competitions. So far I am to have three published, including I'm Asking Why?

This poem comes from the anger I feel from the constant murdering of wild animals for their skins, or even sadder, fun.

I dedicate this poem to all the wild animals and their fight for survival.

Why was a life just taken,
If it was not for meat.
Why did you kill the animal,
If you did not want to eat.
Why do I feel so guilty,
For a crime I did not commit.
Why am I ashamed of the human race,
Ashamed to be part of it.
Every minute a life's being taken,
Nobody to mourn the dead.
No revenge for they don't understand,
Until they've been shot full of lead.
We need to ask for answers,
To the many questions why.
We need to stop them killing,
Before too many have to die.

Amanda Woodcock

Adieu to a Philanderer

Some day when you are tired of chasing rainbows,
When selfish games of pleasure start to pall,
And still you have not found what you are seeking,
What every soul desires most of all.
Then as you sit, alone and empty-hearted,
Reflecting on your 'victories' of yore,
Perhaps your wandering eyes will chance to linger
On some word that I wrote long years before,
And memories, long dead, may come to surface,
And wisdom dawn, and clearly you may see,
And sadly say, 'There was, among the many,
Just one who, truly, did love me.'

Barbara Rowley

Notes

I started writing poetry and lyrics about four years ago. I had my first poem published in March of 1996 and From *This Day to Forever* is the eleventh poem I've had published since then. I'm a member of the International Song Writer Association and the Irish Musicwriters and Songwriters Association. I won a certificate of excellence in a lyric contest run by the International Songwriters Association last year. I'm currently in collaboration with two other songwriters, one based here in Ireland and one in Liverpool.

I wrote From This Day to Forever as a wedding present for my cousin Geraldine and her husband Christopher when they got married on the 29 December 1995, and it's dedicated to both of them.

From This Day to Forever

This day to you, my friend
This day to you, my lover
Of my heart, my soul, a mirror
I swear my love forever
A promise pledged eternal
In faith a kiss will seal
My life, my love, to you always
No greater care you'll feel
From this day to forever.

Before all souls here gathered
Of histories old becoming new
Bear witness each as my heart declares
Its passion, loyal and true
An eternal flame well guarded
To darken no shadow shall dare
For beyond the grasp of tomorrow stands
Our love in the good Lord's care
From this day to forever.

From this day to forever
As heaven has rules shall be
From this day to forever
You're all I'll ever need
The comfort of your touch
The peace within your arms
You're my harbour in all storms
My safety from all that harms
From this day to forever.

Tony Sullivan

Notes

Hi how you doing, my name's Stephen Gibbons, I'm twenty-six and come from the town Greenock in Scotland. I've been back in Greenock on a permanent basis for the last year and a half, before this period I spent some time in London, and then worked or wandered, mostly worked through a chunk of Europe.

My effort conveys the feeling of forced normality on my return home, I plan to travel again in the future.

My other published work include *Thank God for Windows* in the Glasgow and Strathclyde Anthology, *An Honest Love* in A Message of Faith, *Home Coming* in Quiet Moments and other pieces going to print at the moment.

Fact

Not born for this life we lead
Follow the crowd with despising heed
The gaze still upon wonders of this world
That dreaded gift of memory plays again and again
Uncontented with mundane acts forced upon my person
Lucky to have they cry! Convincing themselves once more
Acting out my part well insides churning
The road I will one day tread runs straight and true
Through canyons and scrub tasting the dust
Filled winds watching that courageous
Sunset filled with red and blue
I'll be there one day make no mistake
For if the day comes for me to take
My leave and that road I did not tread
A wasted life I've abused

Stephen Gibbons

Horizons

How wondrous you look
As you reach up,
To kiss the morning sky
Powdery blue, fluffy white clouds
How I long to be covered
With your golden shrouds
Floating free to ride
The winds of destiny
Surging through the laps of time
See how I rise and fall
As I gaze upon
This wondrous land, so pure and clean
Where men's minds do roam free

D J Smith

Work

Notes

I am a 53 year old spinster. I had to give up work, or more precisely, work gave me up, when it was found that I had osteoarthritis in my spine.

For the first time in my life I am having to live in poverty.

Writing and reading are my main hobbies, as I cannot afford any other hobbies. I have been writing on and off for most of my life. Just about anything can set me off.

I find I can usually see the odd side of any situation, and then write about it.

I wrote my poem, Work, after having a very uncomfortable time with the DSS, and the evil Tory government. I believe they really hate sick and disabled people. One wonders who they will pick on when they have killed us all off. Jews perhaps, or the blacks.

Work, what does that word mean?
What is dictionary definition,
Expenditure of energy, enjoyment,
DSS understanding, god only knows.

Work, exertion of mind or body or both,
Work equals remuneration, money, does it?
Work equals entitlement to what?
Money, no, a happy life, not necessarily.

A gardener a manual worker works hard,
Gets very small remuneration, perhaps none,
Man in office sleeping his day away,
Receives loads of money, lots of prestige.

Is he really necessary perhaps not,
Person making steel heavy lifting hard graft,
Person in wet and cold picking vegetables,
These souls receive very little of anything.

Woman skivvying for even less two pounds an hour,
Woman at home skivvying for even less no prestige at all,
Writer poet, artist, painter, is this work,
Walking, driving to shops, is this work?

Old Cornish saying, he who does not schemy,
He has to louster, Cornish saying right,
Look about, they that stand, shout and schemy,.
Tory thieves have got it down to one fine art.

E B Hawken

Notes

Born a Londoner in Balham in 1919, I have been employed as a church of England clergyman since 1943, most of that time in the suburbs of that town but towards the end of my ministry as a Vicar in a Northamptonshire country parish and later, as a retirement task, at a small but lively Devonshire daughter church.

My literary experience has been confined almost entirely to the composing of several thousand sermons and, as editor of numberless Parish magazines, I was nearly always granted by myself a niche for some small effusion. Owning an appalling memory, my opinion of poetry has been very negative for most of my life, that is, until I took an Open University course on Romantic poetry about two years ago. This gave me some insight into what poets are trying to do and some of the techniques they use and so, while my memory has only got worse, my appreciation of the written has somewhat improved. I shall therefore look forward with some excitement to the arrival of Beyond the Horizon and to reading the work of contemporaries.

The poem Totally Negative was triggered off by the fascination I experience, mixed with a frisson of fear, in reading the popular works of scientists and biologists such as the excellent rhyming couplet of Stephen Hawking and Richard Dawkins. My hope springs from the fact that the universe seems designed to force questions and continually to demand answers, ie a dialogue is occurring.

My present hobbies are gardening plus an allotment, playing outdoor bowls, painting with water colours, collecting postage stamps, especially those with maritime pictures or connections, playing the flute badly and, at present, struggling with an Open University course on Religious Diversity in Great Britain from 1945.

Totally Negative

Just suppose that Hawking's right
And all existence turns on rushing galaxies;
Wheels whirling, winding worlds
To a final mindless extinction;
Expanding irreversibly, expending energy
Towards an everlasting nothingness,
Meaningless even to itself, a self
It has not got.
Clock-like the unwinding continues
Constantly unobserved and oblivious
Until, quite unintentionally, a tear
Appears, ripping a cry of protest
In the stone cold heart of the matter
And, chance-like, creates a kind of watch,
Ticking pathetically, to offer
A hand of hope and a point to meaning;
I mean, in a momentous molecule of DNA,
Which for a fleeting moment makes
Mud plants and bloody animals and man,
Merely to look with horror at hell's reality,
For there is no one to say 'Thank you' to;
Just Jacob's strangled yell at the hard headstone,
'How awesome is this place!' but no God
To make it sensible
In the heart of our soul.

Peter Rowe

248

I am 29 years old and live with my husband Chris and my son Nathan in the small fishing village of Port Isaac in North Cornwall.

This is my eighth poem to appear in an anthology since I started writing 18 months ago although I had previously written poetry at school.

Living within a tight-knit fishing community, and with Chris being a fisherman, the weather has a particular significance on all our lives. It was whilst waiting for the boat that Chris was on, to come in, that I wrote this poem.

Untitled

It came with the day
Creeping into the light,
Timid at first
Like a well beaten dog.
But as the minutes ticked by
It gathered clouds for its strength
Raised its head and then howled
And the storm began.

Amanda Aldridge

Moon January 20 1997

Notes

I have been writing poetry for many years but am known better as a painter. I won the Woodmans' Press poetry prize in 1993 for *The Chartreuse Spring*.

I was so sad
That I wanted you to dissolve me
Or make me merrily mad forgetful
                    oblivious
I was watching you outside the bedroom window
As you loomed and scooped great sky-fulls
                    of Prussian blue
And poured them over your perfect spine
Then you slowly swam over our house
Scrutinising broken tiles
                    tut-tutting at cracked windows
Seeping through cracks
                    illuminating my distraught
                    face
So that you exposed me to a lady
Watching my window
                    from the other side of the street
And I swore at you
                    and went to bed.

Marina Yedigaroff

December Journey Westward

Notes

David lives in rural Oxfordshire and works as a garden
centre planteria manager,
after a previous long, professional career in social work.

His main interests are nature,
particularly flora, and medie-
val, social, religious and local
history. He has only started
writing poetry in the last
year, 'in the feel of the moment' most of which reflect
these interests as well as the
inspiration from Shakespeare
and Spencer's love poems, the
nature poems of John Clare,
George McBeth's less cerebral
ones and Betjamans majestic,
nostalgic ones.

To date he has two other poems published *Dunster Castle*
and *A Lover's Plea* in anthologies by Anchor Press.

This poem was written during the last half hour of a
train journey through the
wetlands of Somerset as an
instant atmospheric see, feel
spiel and response.

In the grey mist and quiet-dripped dankness
Of a December, drizzled, dark dogged, dismal day
Greenness, in the winter washed and watered meadows
And in the isolated sky looking perpendicular rush
As also more often in the form of the wild berried holly
Fiercely fire dancing in romance within an embrace of wild rose
Still pervades; softly conquering the repeated intersects
Of brown dark ribbed skeletal arch of naked bush and tree
A proud victory, albeit one insidious, over that just deciduous,
Well mirrored so in the silvered grain of rain-filled dykes and ditches
That in their muddied bankside holes held hungry voles, drowned moles
Whilst framing pastures that drained to water slapped, lapped boles
Of oaks and ash, willows and the black foreboding alders.
Such was the vista from the window of the westbound railway train
As it digested its track across a narrow corridor of Somerset
Until the sudden, straightened aqueduct, a brick signal box
A brutal concrete motorway spur and a line of rusting allotment sheds
Announced, with the same discordance of the train tannoy
Arrival in the terra non firma of Westonzoy and it's caput for the hoi
polloi.

David Viall

Pain

The author, now 33, started writing in her teens after a school-mate shared her own poetry with her: 'That night, I didn't go to bed until I had put to paper the torrent of emotions I had kept bottled up inside for so long. A secret door had been unlocked which never closed again.'

She has been writing poetry ever since, some of which was published in student magazines. She has also written songs and performed before a large audience.

Her poetry explores a wide range of emotions, from love to hate, pain to joy, in their complexity and depth.

Pain tells the story of silent suffering, the kind which nobody wants to see or know about because it makes you feel uncomfortable.

I saw a look in your eyes
That told me of your pain.
I saw despair and a cry for help.
I saw agony and torment.
I saw your fear
Of losing life and sanity.

And I was touched,
And I was moved,
Your tears I cried,
Your anger I hurled at the world,
Your pain I felt.

I felt real poignant sorrow,
Regret and disappointment,
Because your eyes hit my heart
And I understood.

Lydia Berton

Notes

I am 31 years of age, single and work as a process technician. My hobbies and interests are poetry, calligraphy and psychology.

I started writing about two years ago; after departing from my girlfriend.

My inspirations are beauty and form, the future, the past, nature, psychology and women.

The poem, inspired by Britain's drug culture, is a symbol of what the future may hold for the thousands of youngsters who are taking drugs, and who think it will not affect them in the future. Especially from a social and psychological point of view.

This poem is dedicated to the youth of the nineties.

$D + L = I$

As my unconscious lay amongst the roving poppies;
opiates of strife.
Aberrant misguidance of wrongful man,
Doting on life.
A condition eased temporarily,
By the coming of a wife.
Or a neurosis ended permanently,
By the sharp-side of a knife.

Ken Peacock

While You Were Away

(Kraków July 1995)

Notes

I am 26 years old and live in Gillingham in Kent.

I started writing poetry in 1991 and have received favourable reviews from all my family and close personal friends!

I am a very keen climber and traveller having been travelling for about five years now - financing my trips with stints at climbing and camping shops and trying to sell photographs and writings from my travels.

My original poetic influence was Laurie Lee (I like the way he wanted to live). Now I write very much in more modern style of free verse.

The poem was written to a soon to be girlfriend in Poland, and describes the activity in the Rynek (market square) in Kraków.

I hope to publish my own collection in the near future.

The idiot's pride of the square's purple soldiers.
Have sounded retreat to the trumpeter in the sky.
And men's healthy music - rhymes tunelessly down,
Counting the shadows 'round the washed yellow hole.
And the high empty evening, stretches the lengths of the lonely.
Whilst colourful gatherers stand, and stare at the crown.
And a million black clouds -
Circle and scream at the setting sun.
Whistling the end of the song.

But the window's slammed silently.
The note is shut in history.
The camera is bagged sourly,
Having stolen no one.

The wide sky chills him warmly.
The globe blowing gently.
The stones shine in the shade,
Stinging his eyes.

So he says.

And the swarm will dance high forever and ever.
And the swarm will gaze at the fairy-tale tower.
The poet will grow more blind with every dawn that will rise.
Whilst the painter's pencil will darken and blunt.
The past will fade flatly -
And wink at the world knowingly.
And the windows of wet houses turn away.
Still all the while, all the Gods, in all of the churches.
Will keep all their lovers to themselves.
And thank each other loudly;

> For this city;
> this atmosphere;
> this evening;
> this smile;
> this tear.

Damon Coulter

Salute to Australia

Didjeri don't
Didjeridu
Into Australia
A quest for the new,

Tropical forests
Barrier reefs
Coroberee dancing
Native man's chiefs,

Sky scraped cities
And barren red lands
Beaches of glory
With silver white sands,

This country so fair
A gift land from Heaven
Crystal clear oceans
Beautiful women,

Oasis of dreamscapes
Mountains of blue
Mystical fortunes
God gave them to you.

Vance A Carson

Love Like a Bird

My love for you is like
A feather in the breeze
Always quivering
Like birds on leaves on trees
But always trying to reach the
Next height.

C P Grant

A Visit

Notes

Lines written after the loss of
a brother, Peter Sumner, (29)
in the UTA Air Disaster
(UTA772) over Niger, Africa,
19 September 1989.

Geoffrey Sumner, (46).

It was a grey day in Paris the day we came
The day of All the Saints
A Public Holiday.

The builders' bricks and sand lay moist, forgotten.
In the Paris rain.

We stood, forlorn damp figures
On the steps of the Institut Médico-Légal.

'Is this where they brought them?' She asked.

I nodded.

She started to cry and moved away.

'You should take a photograph,' she said.

I stood well back and took in the tree, the sign,
The round Parisian lamp.

There will come a time when we can look at them again.

G T Sumner

Time

Notes

I was born 27 February 1970 in Blackpool, where I still live.

Time is the first poem I've written and was inspired by my granddad, George. A brave man whether fighting war, loss or crippling old age.

Dedicated to Audrey, my friend, lover and soul mate.

If time was in essence, and not in decline
The length of a circle, the taste of fine wine
To do things so different, to keep them the same?
To change paths of wisdom, to tread them again?
In twilight years, and movement of stone
The greying of hair, the creaking of bone
The body is dead, the mind so alive
But all is not lost, for memories revive.

Of many a year, I sit and remember
The haze of July, the dawn of September
Of snowy capped mountains, the birds in the sky
My envious thoughts, of days now gone by
The birth of a baby, to grow to a man
To visit as often, as often as can
The photo's as faded, as the life I now lead
But all still hold moments, that's all that I need.

Paul Holliday

Our Jack

Notes

My name is Ria Moore, I am 15 years old and a year 11 student at Little Hulton Community School.

Our Jack is the second poem I have had published. I wrote my first poem, *Waiting*, when I was 14. After waiting for what seemed like a lifetime for the birth of my cousin Jack, I decided to mark the occasion by writing a poem about him.

I would like to thank my Auntie Michele and Uncle Colin for having our Jack, and a special thank you to my Uncle, Steve Fennell for entering my poem in the competition.

Jack David Medhurst, this is his name,
His cute little face could bring him fortune and fame.
He's yummy and scrummy and ever so cute,
He's smooth, pink and chubby in his birthday suit.

His mummy and daddy are ever so proud
Ever so caring, but papa's quite loud.
His brother and sister are loving him too,
Everyone loves our sweet Jacky Jew.

He's now getting big and ever so sweet,
It won't be long before he's up on his feet.
He giggles and laughs and squeaks like a mouse,
And since he's been born, there's a joy in the house.

Ria Moore (15)

The Lady in the Public Bar

Notes

I was born in Dublin, Eire, and emigrated to England in my teens. I finally settled in Birmingham to work and raise my family of five daughters and two sons.

I've lifelong enjoyed reading poetry but only seriously considered writing and submitting my own poetic efforts for publication as recently as the summer of 1996 - I am fortunately rewarded with several of my poems into print thus far. Poetic inspirational moments often find me atop of a barstool at my local pub - the accompanying poem is composed of some of the lighter of them.

Like an angel from afar
The lady in the public bar
Drinks her gin and smokes her fag
With the swiftest sip and the longest drag
Then lets her face relax awhile
In the station of its best profile.
In a low-cut, black, seductive dress
That wraps her curves in sweet caress
She sits alone. Oh, could it be
Perchance she wants some company?
I drink to that and drain my cup -
And another to get my courage up.
She looks my way and in her gaze
I freeze, I heat, I burn, I blaze
In the smouldering coals that smoke and singe
Along the line of her auburn fringe;
She speaks to me - spellbound, I hear
From Heaven's door upon my ear
The dulcet tones of angels . . . But wait!
From where did he originate?
Appearing like a shining knight
With flaming sword he loans a light
To her cigarette. Oh, it's plain to see
The lady's found warm company
In his burning overture -
Now all I see is him and her.

The pub-bell tolls and in deep gloom,
As everyone vacates the room,
I watch them trip into the night;
He high, her 'low-cut' far too tight
And straining at the seams; he proud
And tall, she small and thinking far too loud.
(As they passed; as she tripped by
I caught her calculating eye -
It was the eye of a hungry pike
That knows its meal and waits to strike.)
Poor him! No lady that by far -
You'd find her like in any bar!
Goodnight! I'll find my own way home
By the lamp of the alcoholic moon.

Austin Murtagh

Notes

The Mill was inspired by a visit with friends to Salts Mill, Saltaire, West Yorkshire. As we wandered through the David Hockney gallery and the furniture and clothes departments, we were accompanied by a vociferous impromptu guide, who claimed he used to work at the mill. He expressed his distress at the transformation of a working mill into a fashionable tourist attraction.

Though he irritated us at the time, his anger and passion at the decline of Britain's industrial base certainly left an impression with me.

Mark E Connors was born in 1970. He lives and works in Horsforth, Leeds. He has been writing poetry since the age of 16. He is currently working on a new collection of poetry which he intends to publish in the near future.

The Mill is for Faz and Diane.

The Mill

He worked here in this mill -
Before the carpets came,
Before in-vogue fashions,
Gallery and Café.
He drank coffee from a flask;
There were no exotic spring waters.

Kojak from Poland worked
By one of Hockney's dogs:
A sketch of his Boodgie.
A rude, impromptu guide
Is ranting back the clock;
When tourists pose, he's quick to deride.

He frequently accosts
The art house café staff.
He pays his pound for tea
And resents each mouthful.
He joyfully explains
The demise of our industrial base.

The salesmen don't approach;
They've witnessed his long rants
On humid afternoons,
They've seen that burning roach
Between those nicotenes.
They would love to fit him out in new clothes.

He patrols each section
With the required scorn,
While diligent workers
Weave their own traditions.
Rejuvenated floorboards
Now creak under the pressure of new shoes.

They sand-blasted the grime.
This bright, angelic mill
Was never fully exorcised.
He browses in the Gift Shop
With angry, tearful eyes,
Accompanied by an old familiar hymn.

Mark E Connors

Notes

I am a seventeen year old English student. I have lived in Cornwall all my life and began writing poetry seriously at the age of thirteen.

I always write my poetry for me - not with an audience in mind. It is a form of expression and I use it as a release when I cannot talk to those directly concerned or when circumstances overwhelm me.

This particular poem was written after a temporary split with my boyfriend, who then encouraged me to send it.

Hollow

I feel like Chernobyl
Walled up, still unsafe
You shouldn't come near me
In case the walls break

The reason above
Is the reason why
I sit by myself
Feeling lonely and cry

Louise Burslem

Notes

I am twenty years of age and an only child. I live near the picturesque village of Bruree in County Limerick, Ireland. My hobbies include reading, especially anything by Stephen King, listening to rock music and anything to do with motorbikes.

I have been writing poetry off and on for about seven years. I was inspired to write *Humility* after a friend said she wished she lived the life I do. The 'he' in the poem refers to an ex-boyfriend.

Humility

He despised my intelligence, I hated his ignorance
The day we said goodbye I threw a party
She said she wished that she were me
I smiled, I laughed and thought of her tolerance
If she were me she would be dead
All facts must be stated with clarity

'Miss Anorexia' is his nickname for me
So what if I am thin I am also healthy
My mission is to prove everybody wrong
My sanity is not questionable so let me be
I am the queen of self consciousness
And I am paranoid too

They think they know everything but they do not
How then can they possible judge me?
Human behaviour is so strange it is almost frightening
All my bad memories are being left to rot
Nothing pleases me more than the decay of evil
O friend of mine do you still want to be me?

His laugh makes me want to cringe and hide
My ears have become immune to his comments
The he of now is not the he of before
I needed him like I need a thorn in the side
She is miles away thinking about her beau
The person she so much wants to be is here . . . alone

I came across a picture taken of me years ago
Thankfully I have changed for the better
My future looks extremely precarious
There are many things that I do not want to know
Through no fault of mine I am prone to depression
No I can assure you, you do not want to be me

Ann O'Rourke

Gettysburg

Notes

Anyone who visits Gettysburg, scene of the famous battle which was the turning point of the American Civil War, will be impressed by the way in which the town and its environs are dominated by monuments commemorating every stage of the battle.

As a reflection of this, the poem is self-consciously 'monumental', elegiac in mood.

At the end of the three days fighting the casualties were 23,000 for the Union army and 27, 000 for the Confederate army.

Frozen in stone the General stands,
more than man-high, binoculars in hand,
on the very rock where he first discerned
the need to hold this hill.
Other battlefields, elsewhere, are quiet now.
Nature and Time have done their work.
Seeds fall in the blood-sodden earth,
the mud dries and greens again.

But here we have said 'No.'
Men, each so dear-achieved, died
by the thousand here, in half an hour.
We will remember them.
The grass and the trees may grow,
but Nature shall not work her further oblivion.
Time here, here, at least, shall have a stop.
No more houses, farms, flux of life.
Let the ruins of those that were remain.
Henceforth let us build only monuments.

And it is surely right that there should be,
on this earth, freighted so with suffering,
some places consecrate to memory.
For untold years these fields were merely fields,
till those three days in 1863
when such a violence concentrated here
as to sear the very earth, imprint the air.
Elsewhere, in half-forgotten places, there are tales
that ghostly armies ride on certain nights.
But here, perhaps, all ghosts are laid to rest,
exorcised by monuments.
The earth is healed; the air
but merely rent momentarily.
Nature does not remember. Only we,
and that imperfectly, can stem the tide
of her forgetfulness. This place,
a rock in a relentless current,
must stand for all that we too have forgotten.
Such is our glory and our tragedy.

Margaret Mihara

Light Breaks Throu'

Light breaking through the boundaries of the outer hemisphere
Just to hear the sound of cheer
Ere's happening, never knowing, knowing nothing and everything

Dust breaking through but never knowing what to do
The crows crowing, boatmen keep rowing, rowing the Nile, the idle canal

The Ship and Owl, the fate of the everlasting child
Ren the big fat mother hen, the son of Mr Ken
Ney, hey let's get out yeh!

Lights too bright, just to cause a fright
To end all nights and give men his rights
To ensure there are no more fights.

Hate nights, love fights all in a day's night
Tracing the bright and everlasting moonlight fright.
So let us reach the highest of all heights
Wuthering light now ends in a everlasting blistering blight.

Rhinebeck

You Can't Change Fate

Our lives are but a written book
In a library on high
And we can't change a word of it
No matter how we try
The opening page is at our birth
And each page will foretell
Of joys and pleasures in our youth
Of how we might do well
Each day is planned, some will bring sorrow
As we journey through each page
Waste not a moment of each morrow
Too soon will come old age
Then memories of each yesteryear
Come flooding back to mind
Did you do the things you planned,
Were you good and kind?
Did you give your heart to one
And was your love returned?
For love returned can only be
What one has truly earned
Respect and honour, a faithful heart
Did you give them to your mate?
For every word and thought and deed
Is writ in the book of fate.
No use wishing for what might have been
Could I have done things better
For all is writ within my book
And I can't change a letter.

Iona Watt

Warm Things

Warm things I've loved both long and much,
Sunlight on sand and a warm rock's touch.

The sweet warm smell of new mown hay,
Long sunlit shadows at close of day.

A dog's smooth coat and fur's soft touch,
Red poppies glowing, these I love much.

But best of all when evening falls
And warm lamps glow on shadowed walls.

Soft curtains drawn and firelight gleams,
Your hand in mine to share our dreams.

Dorothea Boscow

In Between

Notes

I am a 19 year old qualified Nursery Nurse working and living in Redruth, Cornwall, with my dad Ken, mum Sue, brothers Stephen, Marcel and Stacey and my sister Donna.

My hobbies and interests include music, dancing, , drawing, playing keyboard and sports.

I started writing poetry at the age of 12 or 13 years and it was influenced by liking a major pop band. School inspired me to write a poem about a wolf. I have been writing for over six years. Everyday life experiences and traumas inspire me to write. I have another poem being published in an anthology and on tape, entitled Fearing for his Life. I also wrote an article in a local magazine about Bullying.

I wrote this poem to express my anger and feelings on how I feel about being overweight. Stating that I would like to be in between so that no one will hassle me again.

It is dedicated to every overweight person in the world.

Why be fat
Why be thin
Why can't I just be in between
Hassles from here
Hassles from there
I get hassles from everywhere
All they do is scream and shout
And then they wonder why I walk out
Then they shout be thin be fat
Which makes me feel like a total prat
How do I know what to be
When all they do is chat at me
Why be thin
Why be fat
How do I know I've only been fat
At times I feel like being thin
But that only means I want to fit in
It makes me angry just to see
The way people go on at me
Other people look and stare but should
I change it's only a glare
Should I worry
Or should I not
There's only sixteen miles on the clock
I don't know what I want to be
I wish people would stop shouting at me
I would like to be in between
And then people might stop digging at me
Do I take notice of what people say
Be fat
Be thin
I'll decide one day

Emma Rowe

Muse

Notes

I just wanted to understand and create.

Inspiration is the darkwell of creativity.

I started writing and reading poetry two years ago.

Muse: is not finding the well.

I would like to dedicate the poem to my late father Mr John Cantwell.

She has abandoned me
left me alone
a lock without a key
a statue a stone

Seamless sea sky
white upon blue
a seagull's sigh
do birds coo?

Yet here I am
a jaded misery
a pregnant dam
a clouded mystery.

John Cantwell

My Love is Constant

Notes

I wrote this six months ago and I am very please that you like it, it has given me pleasure.

I have written articles on all sorts of things, which most people say make good reading.

My circumstances are poor just now, as I am not well. I have very bad arthritis as I am 76 years old.

Though we are separated by distance and time I look forward to the day when I shall look upon your smiling face once more.

The secure memories and the power they bring makes me feel warm on the coldest nights when I am alone sharing my dreams with the constellations.

My thoughts return to the pure ecstasy of the lovely feel of you entwined in my arms and the secret success we made of living our lives together.

Thinking of these days and nights made in heaven brings tears of joy and distance is irrelevant.

May God be your guardian until the day dawns when I can count the seconds on my fingers for our everlasting reunion.

Until then the separation is a pain that sears my heart.

M Chidgey

Chameleon Youth

Notes

I am a housewife and mother
of six. I first started writing
about 20 years ago and then
stopped because no one
seemed interested in publishing my work and also be-
cause I was so busy with my
large family.

Five years ago a local woman
did a tape of songs she composed herself. It set me
thinking about my writing
again and having more time
on my hands for it.

I remember it so well, it was
a day in March, I sat down
with my pen and paper and
composed a poem called
Spring, which I sent to a local
magazine. It was published
straight away and I've never
looked back. I've had my
work published in several
anthologies and in local
magazines and I've won a
few small prizes also the International Society of Poetry
in Kent have included a poem
of mine on a tape they have
made for their personal collection. A book of my poems
called Penned into Submission also on sale printed out
by myself.

My hobbies are reading, gardening, watching television
and having a good old natter
with friends.

He stands at the bus stop
Indifferent to those around him
Arrogant almost, face dotted with pimples
Evoking (unknown to him) sympathy
From his unobserved watcher (me)
(The sympathy coming through remembered moments
Spent agonising over same in
Some far off almost forgotten time)
Hair cut in a modern style
Greasy now, needing a wash
One ear sporting cheap catchy earring
He adjusts the bag
(Not properly closed and
Slightly frayed at the corners)
On his shoulder with
Lean smooth hands
(Their perfection marred by
Their obvious grubbiness and
Two bruised-black nails)
Some books threaten to escape
As if overcome by
A sudden claustrophobia
The regulation army coat
Frayed jeans and scuffed runners
(Blending with his companions)
Giving him the unkempt look
Of someone neglected
He says something to his friend, smiles
And the lively intelligence in his eyes
Transmits a picture of
The real person concealed
Under all the trappings.

Annie Doherty

Notes

I was born on the 6 April 1941 and was brought up in a village called Hendley which is on the outskirts of Huddersfield in the county of Yorkshire; I am now residing once more in the village of my childhood.

I wrote my first poem shortly after failing the 11 plus! I have had a book of poetry published

I also write short stories; am a humorist; satirist, write limericks, do sculpture and am a would be inventor. I am a life long member of the YHA and in my spare time I'm a paranoid schizophrenic!

Blot on the Landscape

The roar of the ocean
Caressed their ears
A cushion of sand
Intimate in its silence
Bodies leaving their loose imprints
Soon to be washed away
The rising tide
Cares nothing for man

Joyce Turner

The Realisation of Lost Love

Notes

The poem was conceived at
dusk, on a piece of waste
ground by a river. Weather
was gloomy, heavy drizzle
and gusty wind - the kind of
ingredients that matched my
mood, and made me feel as
though the heart and soul of
creation sympathised with
me.

I wrote this poem for a lady
who proved to be a 'Russian
Doll'.

And all the Gods who know my pain
Shall tell their angels 'Shed a tear'
And their tears shall blot out the stars
And my soul will live in darkness.

And all the Gods will sigh
And despair at such a tragedy
And all the stars will fade and die
If I'm losing you.

Theodore Seasons

Contemplating a Peacock

Notes

My son's wedding reception was in Syon Park where I saw this beautiful bird.

Later, I was sent some wedding photos, one of them of myself gazing at the bird, captioned *Contemplating a Peacock*. Hence the title of the poem which expressed my thoughts.

Bright, brilliant bird, all iridescent glow,
Stately and self-contained as on your 'progress' go.
Head held with regal pride, and neck a lustrous blue.
Enthralled we gaze - our homage pay to you.

Your plumage spread into a glorious fan,
A hundred eyes aglow within its span.
Rich blues and greens - your native Indian's pride
Reflected in that elegant, slow stride.

A visitor from such exotic strand.
How do you fare in this cold, alien land?

Margaret M Osoba

Notes

At twelve I won first prize in a poetry competition, but it was thirty-three years later, when my two children were grown, and I had to give up my job through ill-health that I began to write again.

With my husband's encouragement I entered a few competitions and approached a local publisher too.

That was eighteen months ago, and so far I have had thirteen poems published and reached the finals of most of the competitions I have entered.

I write in a simple form about everyday happenings, serious issues and the funny side of life.

Millennium

The millennium draws nearer
But where does it begin?
The far off islands battle out
The race to cash them in.
The TV companies clamber
To film the dawning age,
Commercialism rules the roost
And fights for empty page.

Exotic islands kick and scream
While scientists measure start,
Afraid they'll lose their new dawn dosh,
It's pushing them apart,
But who can blame them? For this chance
They've never had before,
So with both hands and business-like
They barter out the score.

Religious Leaders call their flocks
To gather and to pray,
Let's hope that it will do some good
For world peace on that day.
How great if understanding dawns
And makes our world unite,
And brother hand with brother stands
In peace and not in fight.

Our universe is special
And if globally we bridge,
There is hope to solve the problems
And span the open ridge.
Unrealistic to expect
That peace would reign world-wide,
But what mark for millennium
If everybody tried.

Irene Carter

My Love for You

You walked by me one day
and made my heart cry out in pain
I knew that if I couldn't have you
I'd rot away insane.

You looked me in the eye
as you walked on by
your eyes an emerald green
you don't look all that mean.

Yet my friends didn't like you
they tried to change my mind
but I couldn't explain to them
the way you made me feel inside

The pain was unmistakable
when I couldn't hold you
I tried and tried but you just slipped from my side
I couldn't stand to let you go
but now I know I'm all alone.

They say I'll find someone new
but they didn't know
the love I had for you
I hope one day you'll remember me so
and the love we had might just grow

Lorna Cobban

Notes

I am a 65 year old retired painter and decorator living in Melton Mowbray, Leicestershire.

My hobbies include indoor bowls and snooker.

I started writing for the sheer pleasure of creating something from nothing.

The story behind this poem is pure imagination on my part. A short story version of this poem called The Reluctant Soldier was recently published by Caring and Sharing, so a double has been achieved.

I had a lot of faith in this particular poem, as I consider it one of the best pieces I have produced. It is therefore very satisfying to know that it will occupy a place in a Poetry Today publication.

Not a Shot was Fired

Was this my moment of truth?
Would I survive to see the dawn?
In my cold mantle of uncertainty
I shivered in frantic anticipation.
It was my first engagement,
the initiation of a new recruit.
The order was 'kill or be killed,
taking prisoners is a liability.'
With loaded gun and fixed bayonet,
I followed the flag of glory.
Demanded that the dense jungle,
reveal the elusive hidden enemy.
'Hit the deck! Enemy patrol.'
The words infiltrated my soul.
In the embrace of Mother Earth,
I silently prayed for my salvation.
Moonlight glinted on deadly metal,
the gun barrel moved towards me.
I felt the bullet's penetration,
and its lethal message of death.
I even wiped away imaginary blood,
from a non existent wound.
Tasted the acrid burning sweat,
pouring from my petrified brow.
Fear ruled my tormented mind,
the fatal shot was never fired.
Yet I still carry the scars,
of the battle I never fought.

Dennis Stevenson

Time Enough?

Notes

I was born in Oxfordshire in 1975 (I'm 22) and still live there now (although I've moved out of the family home). I started writing poetry at school on long bus journeys about eleven years ago. I've collected quite a bit now. I've never won anything for my poetry, but then, outside of my friends and family, this is the first time anyone has seen it. I wrote *'Time Enough?'* last year in response to a Time Management Course I attended.

Much time is spent
On management
Of how we spend our day
But writing lists
And planning things
Just waste that time away
Kindly tell me, if you would
How I can get things done
When all my time is spent on just
Prioritising them
You ask me if I've finished this
And if I haven't - why?
The answer's very simple
I'm planning it, aren't I?

Angi Arnold

A Question of Meat

Notes

A Question of Meat is one of my earliest works since I began writing in 1995.

The poem was inspired when a friend asked if I would prefer to be burned at the stake or boiled in the bag and I wondered how I would eat someone if that did happen.

I have lived in Edinburgh for 8 years since moving from Shetland, when I was 22, to study Drama. I use my acting skills to enhance performances of my work.

I have written several children's plays including a one man show, 'Geordie the Viking', performed on the Edinburgh Fringe.

If you had to eat someone,
Where would you start?
You could start with the toenails,
But joking apart;
Would you cut off their head,
To boil in a pan,
Or maybe a leg,
Or should I say Ham?

I think I would start,
With a shoulder or calf,
Or maybe a bottom,
Not the whole, just a half;
Maybe a bicep would cook just like Bison,
But what if that bicep had come from Mike Tyson?
Would that make it sinewy, tough and all stringy?
How hard would you chew if you ate Tyson's thingy?

In China some thingies are held in esteem,
They make a man potent,
You know what I mean.
Not thingies from men or from sheep or from goats,
But from Tigers, all souped up help men get their oats.

But back to the question,
Just where would you start?
I think I would start off by eating the heart,
'Cause that's where the soul is,
Or so people say,
Though how can we prove it?
There's no easy way.

So maybe the answer to this situation,
Is don't think too hard,
And avoid the temptation,
To tell someone else what you thought in the end,
They might lock you up,
Say you'd gone round the bend,
But then you'd have plenty of time on your hands,
To plan how you'd eat humankind as it stands.

Robert Williamson

A Young Conservative Speaks

When I grow up, I'm going to be
Boss of a filthy great company
That was once a public utility
But is now a private monopoly.

Telephones, electricity,
Water or gas would quite suit me,
Rail or the nuclear industry:
The returns are juicy, don't you see?

I'll introduce advanced IT
And cut services, for economy.
The axe will be part of my strategy
For anyone older than forty three.

With share options and perks, my salary
Should exceed a million, annually,
Thereby rewarding appropriately
A chap of my true blue pedigree.

I'll live in a castle, luxuriously,
With a drawbridge and moat, for privacy.
From the top of my tower I'll shout, 'Fiddle-de-dee,
You filthy poor - you can't catch me!'

Norman Bissett

Untitled

Notes

Having at different times been a miner, farm labourer, soldier, teacher, foster father, chef, gardener and life model, I now do a bit of odd jobbing, write poems, paint pictures and play bridge.

This poem is one of the sixty I have not destroyed in disgust. It was written when I was trying to see into the mind of a suicide.

Black velvet water felt among the rushes,
Kissed at parting
Then crept beneath the bridge.
Make me inevitable as the river
Who has no conflict with her sons
And keeps her every lover.
She moves with grace
And leaves her beloved with tears
Falling from his fingers

Beautiful you are, oh black woman,
Coal is your breast.
I pillow softly and rest.
Float me in your grasp
To suit your silent sought for purpose.

Quick now, hold me fast and take me,
Morning tears night's mantle
The workers in the fields see where I lie.

Bruce Hoyle

April

Notes

I am nineteen and studying for an English degree at university. Poetry and creative writing has always been an enjoyment of mine and this will be the fourth poem I have had published.

The poem was inspired by the break-up of a relationship.

April brought you and happiness,
and with it too, all the best
times I've ever had my dear,
the good, the bad, throughout my year.

May brought presents and a ring,
subsequent happiness meant everything.
Temporary misfortune held in its place,
life ran as normal at moderate pace.

June became slow, happiness ran dry,
I just became a fixture in your mind's eye.
The cogs still turned, along with everything,
I was immune to what July would bring.

July was quiet, weekends were long,
nights were restless, something was wrong.
The TV was turned off, the telephone didn't ring,
I was immune to what July would bring.

Chantele Bigmore

Iris Plants

Thrusting out of fissures push tiny plants,
The spaced leaves are like fingers on a hand,
No, too thin and delicate for fingers
For there is no substance in these flattened
Shapes. They are the hollowed-finger forms of
Empty, elegant gloves, smooth-suede gloves
Empty now but once receptacles for
Long, cool fingers with sharp-pointed nails,
Nineteen twenty's hands holding leaf-thin
China cups. Birds hop and peck at speckles,
Sunlight suffuses surfaces, tits swoop
Their wings also fantails lightened by the
Sun. Soft-grey feathers spread into fan shapes
Repeat the design of the Iris plants.

Valerie Conway

Glorious Day

A jug of yellow daffodils stands on the kitchen windowsill catching the
morning sun,
shouting it out through their trumpets that spring is really here.
Although I already knew for the birds sung it to me as I woke today,
lying bleary eyed in a rumpled bed, waiting for my limbs to take lead from
my head
in which my mind has already limbered up and is ready for today's event,
tensing at the starting block, eager to be off.

The air feels still and faintly heavy, as if weighted with the promise of some
longed for heat,
and the smell of coffee from the kitchen finally gets me to my feet.

A jug of yellow daffodils drinking up the sun.

Washing hanging on a line stirs faintly in the breeze that whispers past,
brushing tendrils of hair against my face, tickling the leaves still scattered
on the grass from their winter leap.
And life seems so much better now if it is to be lived under such a sky as
this,
as blue as the wisps of cloud are white, as the grass is green and those
daffodils are yellow,
in their jug on the kitchen windowsill,
singing out the sun.

Suzy Tyndall

A Sad Departure

So sad last night was my departure,
No parting kiss did brush my cheek,
Nor soft caressing hand my fingers meet,
No smile did grace those lips of rapture
Nor e'en a subtle tear creep down her cheek,
With leaden steps I walked the silent street,
For I may never tread again life's narrow way,
As eternal sleep this night might me embrace.
'Tis sad to ponder that no farewell did she wave,
And should again I see the light of day,
Will not she hastily her steps retrace,
To kiss, and smile, and once again to wave.

Basil Van Sertima

Notes

I am about to retire as a sci-
entist in medical research. I
have written poems intermittently since I was seven,
usually to try to capture the
essence of a moment or a
feeling, but this poem is the
first submitted for publication.

It grew from a conversation I
had with a stranger while
flying to Toronto. He and his
son had just spent a holiday
in France on a study-tour of
World War 1 battle fields.
'The war to end all wars' yet
we are still fighting.

I wrote the first draft when
they went to sleep.

Headlines

I crave kaleidoscopes that I can shake
And see the patterns whirl in sparkling spate
To form a living, breathing crowd of folk,
Whose wit and music, loves and homes all rate
More than a mention in a headline stark,
When hunger, war or fear have torn to shreds
The warp and woof, and careless spread
Trampled lost certainties which Nightmare treads.
Can it be incorrect to joy in variance?
To lift the heart at one another's song?
To marvel at the myriad countless ways
That men have rolled the ancient world along?
There is enough of wonder in the stars,
Enough of beauty in the solemn hills,
The seasons, and amongst the world of men
An endless dance of interweaving skills -
Enough
To leave a space for each and every one
To live and work and worship as his kind.
For 'different' is as fine a thing to be
Innately, as a dull conformity.
Come, catch the changing laughter on the wing,
As children play together in their Spring
Too young to designate fair/dark, tall/short, wide/thin
The limits they can feel at home within.

Frances Searle

New Chalet

Come, join me in my chalet by the sea,
Where landrails crek and larks trill in the sky.
Where wind blown wheat rustles in mystery
And time stands still wherein the poppies lie.

Come walk with me in cornfields ripe with grain
Below blue skies a-mist with summer haze,
And ponder far off vistas kissed by rain
Refreshing to the soul and to the gaze.

Come sit with me in gardens gay with flowers
Where roses reach full blown maturity,
And with me while away the golden hours
In blissful peace and perfect harmony.

And as we roam along the sandy shore
The gentle waves white-crested at our feet
I know you will return to savour more -
I know that once again we're bound to meet.

Muriel B King

The Horror of the Seas

Wailing mournful cries carried on the wind that no one hears,
Nobody caring to share our tears,
Biting, cutting, stinging nets destroying me.
Half conscious now, death lies waiting, pulling me down,
Insides hanging out, drifting out to sea,
Longing for my death; release me now . . . from this torment all around.
Reverse the role; those pirates of the sea
Harpoon themselves tied in their nets, then jump into the swirling deep,
Slowly drowning, bleeding, this horrific death
Too weak to cry for help beneath this sea,
This sea that once, 'Belonged to me!'

Liz Dicken

Dangerous Summer

Notes

I am 44 years old and have two children, Kelly aged 18 years (very artistic) and Jodi, aged 13 years (loves writing poetry). I am divorced.

Dangerous Summer is a poem about my first love, whom I met in Gibraltar in 1970. It was a very passionate affair but I was too young to cope with it, We split up in 1972. I haven't seen him since, but, I am *still* in love with him! So I am thrilled this poem was chosen for publication, thank you.

We kept right on as the sun fell
Into the sea
And the cloudless sky
Blazed a flame red orange
That quickly faded
Into an incredible green.

The stars and moon were suddenly with us.
Our love came along and
We were engulfed in a
Pale spectral light.

The sea lifted in great waves
As the water we had displaced
Flooded in behind us.
We walked along a thin white line
Across a moonlit sea.
We were in deep water now.

Cilla Ashburner

SPQR

The eternal city, Rome the divine,
Ancient, modern, baroque or just sublime
Gladdens the eye and feeds the hungry soul
With its grandeur, beauty and arching grace.

What remains of the Empire's marbled halls
Down the barbarian centuries calls
Us to conjure up those famous days
To see Augustus, Cicero and all.

The palaces and statues, side by side,
With the fountains and churches are the pride
Of the Rome of Popes and Cardinals
Of Bernini and Michaelangelo.

Rome lives joyously in the modern age:
Here in the glories of this urban cage
Politics and money, fashion and food
Drive the people, amidst the swirling traffic.

But, Georgie, while in Rome what have you done?
Have you climbed all seven hills for fun?
Perhaps you lazed by the Spanish Steps
Or bought handbags, silk scarves and chic new shoes.

But if, despite the joys, something still jars
Think what it is: the noise? The crowds? The cars?
Perhaps you'd do well to remember that,
As the Milanese, laughingly, recall
'Soni porci questi Romani.'

Richard Hopton

The Pool of Ice

Notes

My childhood years were spent in rural Suffolk but I now live in Coventry, working as a primary school teacher. I have been writing poetry for about two years and was pleased to be invited recently to read some of my work at a local librarian's conference.

My ideas for writing come from many directions, and I find the writing process both exhilarating and relaxing. The inspiration for this particular poem was a country walk in winter.

I would like, one day, to produce my own anthology of poems for children.

All night long
In the silent silver moonlight
Winter's strong sinewy fingers had worked
To create this masterpiece.
The small pool
Covered in layer upon layer of ice,
Patterns of exquisite beauty,
Curved contours of crystallised coldness,
An opaque covering
Unspoilt
Frozen in time.

With a crack like gunfire
The ice shattered,
Like the ending of a dream.
Shards of ice, razor-edged,
Disintegrated and dispersed,
Disfiguring the cold smoothness.
Ripples of icy water surfaced, then retreated
To the remains of their protective shell.

The ugly, jagged hole made by my boot
Stared accusingly at me,
A Cyclops eye in this now distorted image,
A gaping wound in frozen flesh,
An aching pain which I knew could never heal.

Jane Hill

Notes

I live in south-east London with my husband, a dog and a cat.

I have always loved writing but lacked time to pursue the dream of being published due to a busy career of mothering four children, a very happy fifteen years sandwiched between two busy periods of teaching culminating in retirement.

I turned to writing poetry after one of my sons was tragically killed, *Lost Dreams* was inspired by the plight of so many young people and memories of Centrepoint.

Lost Dreams

The walls were cracking,
Paper peeling and ceiling sagging.
The house was lonely,
Lacked company, humanity
How could it be otherwise
When it wore its shabbiest garb
And shunned its neighbours in the square?
And then the squatters came,
Homeless people, looking for a roof, a shelter from the rain.
They filled the empty house
And into the cracking walls
Brought life and love and laughter
And their dreams.
And the house turned joyfully
To meet its neighbours once again -
Until the demolition squad arrived.
Soon the house and its neighbours were gone
And in the square was a useless, meaningless heap of rubble,
Filling the workmen's eyes with dust
And the eyes of the squatters with tears.
Now there is a chrome and steel-plated office block,
Full of glass and light,
But no lettings,
No life, no love, no laughter
And no dreams.

E Ward

Babylon a Burnin'

Notes

'This poem is about you.'

Brothers and sisters are you ready
I speak only truth the prophecy has begun
Let light shine out of the darkness
Keep your faith follow the righteous

The fire has started can you see the flames
That burn the wicked that judge and blame
They not know like I the power and the glory
Love and truth are the only story

Babylon a burnin', yes it is burnin' down
Everything is just an illusion, take a look around
You better be careful, better watch every step
For whatever you decide you may regret

Chris Wills

Memories of India

Notes

A retired school teacher I am a vegan for humanitarian reasons. My hobbies are gliding, gardening and foreign travel.

Noisy horns in busy street
People begging at my feet.
Ladies in beautiful saris riding pillion with such grace.
Rickshaws, cows and bikes and taxis, all at such a pace!
Pavements where the people sleep
Ragged bedclothes in a heap.
Grand hotels are for the wealthy
Shanty towns are not so healthy.
Lovely flowers in the park
Scented gardens when it's dark.
Sandy beaches by the sea.
Monkeys swinging from a tree.
Temples where your feet tread cool.
Palm trees crowded round a pool.
Camels working in the fields -
Lots of fruit the country yields.
Flooded rice fields, tea and salt flats
Cotton, Carob trees and, - cowpats!
Elephants walking in a line.
Smiling waiters when you dine.
Spicy food and graceful dancing,
Indian music is entrancing.
Soon the heavy rains will start.
Time for us now to depart.

Joan Bryan

Notes

I was born in Birkenhead, Wirral, Merseyside.

I have attended LSOA Workshops for poetry and writing, One Eyed City Poets, Poetic Licence and Mentholyptus Eaters.

My hobbies are writing, painting and gardening.

I have been writing poetry for two years and performed poetry at Bluecoat chambers, in groups at clubs and pubs and have been interviewed three times on local radio. I have also recorded for the internet Liverpool. I have had work published in magazines and newspapers and have recited my work on Arrowe Park Hospital radio.

I have written about twelve hundred poems in two years, I had a couple of children's stories published in magazines. I write ghost stories and long funny monologues, plays and sketches.

I really enjoy my writing, it gives me great satisfaction when people write to me and tell me they enjoyed my poetry.

You Were Really Mine

Even the rain can weep real tears
Even the wind can moan
Even the moon has lost his smile
Now I am here all alone
Even the house is silent and still since you went away
How I only wish my life was back
In my dreams of yesterday
Never to see your dear sweet smile never to hold you tight
To listen to your sweet laughter
Since you quietly left in the night

Never to share my troubles with you
Never to hold your dear hand
Never to kiss your dear sweet face
The best face in all of the land
Never to tell you I love you never to show how I care
For you were mine for all the time
And my darling I was just yours to share.
Oh how can I go on without you and how can I cope through the years
For we were so happy my darling and you were my king on your throne
As the bitter tears flow you are happy I know
But how will I cope all alone

Oh what's the good of half a love, when the other half has gone
And what is the good of just half a heart
How on earth will I still carry on
I shall miss you my darling for the rest of my life
Till the stars they all cease to shine
But one thing I was so proud of my sweetheart
That you were really mine.

Eleanor Brandes-Dunn

Notes

Darren Bailey is an Anglican parish priest working in Yorkshire, he is married to Stephanie, and has two young sons, William and Joseph. He was born and raised in Shropshire, and wrote this particular poem while training for the priesthood at Lincoln Theological College.

Mortality Is

I felt like a saviour,
But nobody offered
To build me a cross.
I suppose I could build my own,
Suffering is suffering,
I thought,
Though some
Is worse than others.

My uncle died,
I felt nothing for him
So it was OK.
They said:
'He died in his sleep,
it was a good way to go' -
I wondered if he thought so.
Maybe they were right,
But I was glad
It wasn't me.
Sleep is sleep
I thought,
Though some
Is worse than others.

Darren Bailey

Life Service

Notes

I am 27 years old and work as a Civil Servant in a government agency that is supposed to benefit people.

I have never written 'poetry' before but wrote this in five minutes after being given yet more red tape that makes my job much harder.

I am just an average bloke that loves his beer, his football and especially his girlfriend.

I struggle each day to live my life with paper all around just bringing me down.
There's no longer the room to do things my way, give a piece of me and enjoy my day.

Can't they see the tape they're giving, its colour is red; Entwining my arms, squeezing my life and just doing my head.

My reason for joining now makes me leave, a carefree soul to right the world, now struggles to breathe. Those I despise I've nearly become, pushing round paper and repeating the rules, from pushing in numbers my fingers are numb.

Build me up to break this cycle. I need the strength to start again. For those people I'm here to help I'm just numb to their pain.

Mark Cayzer

Notes

I don't like to say much about my work or myself, I just let readers find different levels and meanings in my work.

Wild Roses

Wild roses
I found some on a plate
how rare these plants
took the dog for a walk
to the middle of the island
wrong time of the year
for roses more likely
in one of my poetry books
the ones sold in florists' shops
hybrids of someone's
imagination
not natural
wonder if I'd seen a dog-rose
would it have barked at me?

Barry Edgar Pilcher

A Son's Praise

Notes

I am 15 years of age and attend Bradfield College. My hobbies are writing and tennis.

I started writing poetry about two years ago. Themes such as birthdays, Christmas and other special occasions inspire me to write.

Inspiration for this poem was a trip to Greece on a boat (which my mother was not set to enjoy).

This poem is dedicated to my mother.

What can I say to you but thanks
You've been a great mother all the year through
And it's time I gave some praise to you.
Firstly well done on your tennis match
I'm now afraid to give you a game
In case I come out very ashamed.
Next well done for going to Greece
I know you would have rather gone to Spain or Nice:
You gritted your teeth and made no fuss
Even though the form of transport was a boat and not a bus.
What I'm trying to say in this poem of mine
Is that I love you Mum and that's what counts.
I wouldn't swap you for anything,
Not even money in huge amounts
So this Mother's Day I will think only of you
And how you've been the best mother all the year through.

Edward Peel (15)

Patient

Notes

I am an 18 year old student studying A level English literature and political history at Sheffield College.

I have one other poem to be published in the autumn of 1997. I've entered just two poetry competitions and have had two poems accepted.

Patient was written from a very personal point of view, after visiting my doctor and being prescribed anti-depressant drugs.

I'd like to dedicate this poem to the one person who helped me off the drugs. She knows who she is. 'If I could be - who you wanted, -all the time . . .

A quarter to three
And still no summons.
Where is she?
She prolongs my problems.
I saw her punctually last time,
Now her absence distresses me.

I wait impatiently.
Scanning the room for a cure.
Newly-borns screaming,
Maternal instincts hit zero.
Please arrive soon
Or these babes will cry me to death.

My identification ignites her throat.
Names turn us into statistics.
Cautiously, I follow.,
As not to catch the babes' eyes.
Seated, she digs out my file, my life.
And opens her dull mouth -
As if to speak.

'How are you this week?'
She knows how I feel,
But she asks as though she could be wrong.
The first time it was 'Why do you cut yourself?'
As her lips moulded back together,
I knew she was incapable of understanding.
I decide to play along with her depressing interest.

Nervously, I try to be polite.
Her knowledge is strangely limited for a 'croaker.'
But seriously, I expect no sympathy.
'Make another appointment,' I'm warned.
I guess that I must need more mind-numbing pills.
Feed the world the drugs and leave me alone.

I close the door between our lives and leave.
The waiting room, where I (suspiciously) sat forever, is now bare.
The babes gone, disappeared back into the womb
Where it's safe and the nothingness turns to ignorance.
I appoint myself to courageously come back.
Without a further thought
I walk out on bail, into the freezing, January questions.

Alan Davison

Waiting

Notes

Arthur Phillips was born 1913. Apprenticed and awarded the C and G Full Technological Certificate in 1939. Examiner for Full Technological Certificate, awarded OBE in 1973.

Author of Computer Peripherals and Typesetting HMSO, 1968 and Handbook of Computer aided Composition - Marcel Dekker, New York, 1980. Lectured at LSP, London College, Reading Technical College. Joined HMSO in 1935, war service as commissioned radar officer. Deputy Head of Typographical Design under Harry Carter. Worked on Mathematical Composition, published by Monotype.

Has been writing since he was 17, and writes because he needs to express himself. He has five daughters by his first marriage and two sons by his second marriage.

Explanation of 'Waiting':
Line five 'Telegraph' refers to the 'Crossword'
Verse one up to line eight 'Waiting' in the city of London
Last five lines of verse one and two - Twyford Station
Verse three 'City of London'
Verse four 'Waiting' for the steam train from Budleigh Salterton (Railway Line now closed)
Verse five 'Waiting' by the fountains in Hyde Park.

Waiting where the busy throng
amorphously confuses
departure time and terminus
this station undefined
I'll add a word to Telegraph
my presence waits reply
to my appeal
please come and leave me not alone.
Waiting; the cold rain's beat
upon my face
a nettled hand of stinging sleet
chilling my body warmth
which I would share.

Below the bridge the trains retreat
washing the banks with yellow light
who homeward go to greet their loves
Ah come to me.

Waiting: the twirling traffic's tortuous path
denying refuge here;
Commerce in walls reaches the sky
like you beyond my grasp
Yet come, that we may touch
in silence, still the traffic of my heart
come, leave me not alone

Waiting on the slow branch line
St Mary Ottery, Tipton St John
Ora pro nobis
we know what love can give
yet do not dare to take,
Ah come to me.

Waiting in green embroidered dress
from Panama
He sees me as a Grecian maid
in Panathenaeic festival process
the votive offering I bring
is all my love, and that for him
The fountains sparkle in the evening air
yet chill wind blows across the park
Ah, come to warm my heart
and leave me not alone.

Arthur H Phillips

Ode to a Woollyback

Notes

I'm 27 and single and live in London. I am interested in performance poetry and am planning on going to the Poetry Café in London.

I enjoy escaping to the countryside going for long walks and climbing trees, meeting people, music and writing song lyrics.

I've been writing poetry for a few years, producing more work over the last few months, the more intense my emotions the more I will write.

This poem is about Andy who I loved deeply and whom no longer wished to see me. Writing down my feelings as a poem helped my friends to understand and for me to remember.

Perhaps you will call when the moon is full
and the dog beyond the fence begins to howl
Until then I'll continue to live life wearing a dressing gown
You share a name with my first true love, at the age of seven
and so it would seem I've come full circle.
Night after night my face is awash with streaming salt
as I wait to continue my adventures in the Empire of Sleep
I wish you could come with me but I can no longer see your face
and I'm too weak to fight against time and space
Eventually I'll emerge through layers of sleep, as heavy as lead
Opening last night's eyes which have become puffed up balls of gloom
feeling the fingers of my dream wrapped around my brain
inviting me back to an easier life, inside my head.

Michelle Allwood

The Green Night

Notes

I was born in 1950 and have lived in Holland and India. I have travelled around Europe, Morocco and Turkey and am now living with my partner and five year old son Gabriel.

The wind is growling tonight like a black dog,
his bated fangs flashing like the stars
in the night sky.

Bending round corners,
wrapped in misty shadow,
the wind heaves across sleeping lawns.

In the deep of night
the multitudinous blades of grass
increase in sharpness, silently,
while the soil slumbers, each blade
becoming a knife capable of slicing
through pink finger flesh.

People shudder as they travel
the routes of their dreams.
The green revolution bangs against their
bedroom doors, fresh mud between the
toes of her feet.

D L Finlayson

Notes

I am 29 years of age and live with my partner Andrea, who is expecting our first child in late May early June 1997, and Dexy the Doberman. I work with adults who have severe physical/psychological disabilities. I am currently studying courses related to social science with the Open University.

I have been writing poetry for approximately 15 years (off and on). I am inspired by my emotions and 'feel' for a topic. I have been attempting to write stories for approximately two years and I'm still working on a Science fiction/horror (ish) story but commitments to home study restrict my writing for pleasure. My ambition is to one day have a story turned into a book.

Essentially, *Millennium* is a personal observation about wanting and needing. This means that although millions and millions in cash is being spent on huge projects *wanted* as a means of marking the millennium - (such as rugby stadiums or theatres) - we must not forget, nor ignore the fact that those millions could be spent for the benefit of humankind and generated into projects concerning education, NHS resources, medical research, crime prevention, homelessness and poverty - (the things we *need*).

Millennium

Millennium approaching
and still no change,
gun law, knife law
ignore ignore.

Millennium dawning, still no change.
Still poverty and depravation and the homeless and hungry
across the nation,
a dire situation!

Millennium calling.
Millions and millions spent
on aesthetic splendour, cloaking the reality
of a secret governmental agenda.

Millennium.
Dreams and schemes? Fantastical, it all seems.
Impressive too - at least - to the global eye.
But what the eye can't see, the eye won't know
nor be concerned . . . just as long as there's a show.

And now there's a saviour
from the lowest waged labour
to rescue the one parent mum
from her life of struggle and despair,
at last her life could go somewhere.
Indeed, life could be a lottery - without struggle, worry or care,
play twice weekly - it's tempting - but unfair

If there's money to spend, then spend it with earthly wise.
Let us prevent global wars, cancers and crimes
the scourge of our earth,
the scourge of our time,
the source of our anger
the source of our decline

As the millennium draws near
sadly, selfish - destruction and global revolution
I fear.
Millennium millennium
Oh Dear!

L Hale

Notes

Zenda Cooper lives in the heart of the Norfolk Broads with her partner and their 18 month old daughter, Kimberley. Born in 1969, Zenda has been writing for pleasure since childhood and has had a number of poems published in various books.

Zenda is a busy working mother, employed by a manufacturing company as their company accountant. Most evenings are spent writing. Zenda's second love is cars and she is the owner of a 1959 Ford Popular which she shows during the summer.

Silent Replies

The unspoken words I want to say
Are written clearly in my eyes.
I search your face for unanswered questions,
I wait anxiously for your silent replies.
My thoughts drift into memories,
Far away to some distant land.
Back to the days of smiles and laughter
Where love and joy ran hand in hand.
You say we must go our separate ways,
But you won't even tell me why.
Please don't lock my closing doors
And leave me here alone to die.
Tell me where our love went wrong,
Give me reason to your rhyme.
Can't we retrace our steps
And take a walk through time.

I want to say I love you
But you deter all my devotions.
You blew the sea into a storm
And sank my dream boat in the ocean.
No matter how you hurt me
You know that forever I'll care.
I'll bandage up my weeping heart.
For you I will always be there.
Our communication is in decadence,
You say this is the end.
You've left confusion to unravel
And a broken heart to mend.
The unsaid words are wasted
On ears that have gone deaf.
I'm lonely in my nightmare
Now I only have memories left.

Zenda Cooper

Notes

I became interested in writing poems in 1995 aged 15. I have had one poem, entitled *The Family*, accepted for publication already by The International Library of Poetry, in their anthology A Lasting Calm. I write as a way of expression, to let out thoughts, feelings and dreams.

Taste of my Love

Take half a pound of understanding
and heat it in a pot,
when it's cooked add some warmth
but don't make it too hot.

Add two spoonfuls of happiness
and a pinch of humour,
pour in a large glass of romance,
'cos my love ain't just a rumour.

Sprinkle a touch of braveness
and a teaspoon of equality
and half a pint of sharing
and a handful of honesty.

Get a piece of sensitivity
and drain out the fears
and a shoulder to cry on,
to place all your tears.

Find the purest of love
and the sweetest of caring,
showers of gifts,
but only a twist of boldness and daring.

Don't forget heaps of smiles
and tons of charms
and hundreds of roses
to fill your arms.

Add sweetness and protection
and lots of hugs and kisses
and spoonfuls of affection
and all of your wishes.
Make sure you stir it enough
then have a taste of my love.

Let it set and let it cool,
mix it fully and grab a spoon,
tuck in gently to a man so true
and all these things I'll give to you.

Dean J Wing (17)

Silence

Silence means consent, you see
Established by the law
But Sir Thomas More discovered
That may not always be so.

Silence is golden, so they say
Yes, I know it's so -
Reaching home some dreadful hour
Silence, then, is bliss.

Silence can be full of meaning
Pregnant, some would say
Charged emotions, yet unuttered
Speak when yet unsaid.

Silence comes in music
To give each one a break
Taking in what's gone before
Leads us to the rest.

Silence means so many things
And here are just a few
Next time you find that you are quiet -
What does it mean to you?

Sarah J Reid

Radio Broadcast

Notes

I am 44 years old, married with no children, live in Nottingham and work as a social worker.

I write poetry and music which I sometimes perform but have not been published before.

I write when emotionally 'hit' by an experience, either personal or second hand. Injustice and absurdity usually get me going. On this occasion the radio broadcast made me cry and re-affirm how intensely devastating and cruel we are. Technology is developmentally ahead of our thinking and can amplify our cruelty.

I would like to write more and collaborate with others, perhaps incorporating music.

Tortured by dreams
Kept awake by the light
A million scattered voices
Burn into the night

I was not there
But I can remember
By listening to the dreams
And words of other people

The stories of a million
Burning eyes
The black rain
And boiling rivers

The last desperate measure
To extinguish the flame
A hopeless attempt
To avoid destiny

The blind
Leading the blind
Trying to find a few shreds
Of what life used to be

I will not forget those voices
Those sounds on the airwaves
Those children speaking to me
I thought
Only children can speak this clearly

So
I am left in the night
In hope
That I am not woken up
By the blind flash of light

John Herod

My Angel

Notes

I am 29 years old and live in Gosport, Hampshire with my naval husband, and four children. I have had another poem printed in a similar book, but have only recently begun to submit poems, although I have been writing them for years.

My inspiration comes mainly from my life experiences, I feel the written word is my only true form of expression.

I thought I saw an angel today
Thought I felt him touch my face
I saw him smile at me in a special way
Felt him slip his hand around my waist
And when I turned to hold his hand
To let him guide me forth
I spied a beautiful paradise land
Leading away up to the north
And so as we began to travel
Along that wondrous path
I saw many familiar things
Places, faces from the past
And even with theses strange things happening
He made me feel at ease
And at last I knew for definite
All my fears could rest in peace.

Maryanne Gibbs

Accidentally

Love is a bird with all the feathers picked off,
Shattered battered ashen-now hearts,
Scattered around the temples
Of idolised selves.

I came in between the two,
Separating him-her, she-he,
Departing that 'It,'
Shattered battered,
Scattered -
Two warm hearts.

Anne Vair Shanklin

Inclination White

Notes

Adrian Shaw is 51 years of age and an ex- 'Midnight's Child', who was born in Madras, India and British-Canadian, he lives in Tottenham, London where he studies art at Central St Martin's College and lectures chemistry part-time to support his creative work - photography and painting (besides writing).

His poems, published over twenty-five years here and in North America have been broadcast. His awards include a GLAB Creative Writership in Schools, shortlisting in an 'Artrage' magazine competition and an Arvon Foundation Bursary.

Past themes reflect his concern with the 'odd and disturbing' and 'politics'.

Inclination White - dedicated to Georgina Lock, his partner, fellow-writer-and-traveller - celebrates their love.

This love . . .
like sickness in my heart
sweet with pain and longing
with its vacant spot for you, my Love,
its cardiacal beat . . .
my Heart . . .
springs forth within each second
tents to encapsulate and keep you here
for ever . . .
This parting space we'll fill
when we are one, together . . .
Never fear or worry -
I am your certain home
if you are needful of a shelter . . .

Adrian Shaw

The Individualist's Charter

Notes

Thanks to Stevie Smith

Warring world - feuding world - crazy world spinning
Everyone's fighting - nobody's winning
Children cry out - widows are weeping
Soldiers lie dead - politicians lie sleeping.

Grasping world - gasping world - must make a living
Everyone's taking - nobody's giving
Pamper the rich - the rest aren't worth saving
Poor folk are drowning - politicians are waving.

Clutching world - thrutching world - pushing and shoving
Everyone's lusting - nobody's loving
Perverts abound - nudging and winking
People not sharing - politicians not thinking.

Itching world - bitching world - gouging and biting
Ignore the peace talks - carry on fighting
Maiming and killing - sniping and stalking
Victims still dying - politicians still talking.

Warring world - feuding world - crazy world spinning
Everyone's fighting - nobody's winning
Children cry out - widows are weeping
Soldiers lie dead - politicians lie.

Graham Unsworth

Niche Market

Notes

Born in 1968 the youngest of
five girls I currently live in
Hendy, working as a secretary for accountants in Car-
marthen.

I entered *Niche Market* into
the Poetry Today competition
hoping to be one of '250
runners-up' to acquire a copy
of Successful Writing. As this
is my first serious attempt at
writing I am very pleased
that my poem has been se-
lected for Beyond the Horizon.

Rushing through town, I
averted my gaze and quick-
ened my step in order to
avoid a market researcher.
Hurrying past, I thought
what a thankless job it was.
However, on my return I was
surprised to see 'a lady of advanced years' conversing
enthusiastically with the researcher.

'Excuse me, hmm, excuse me!'
'Would you be so kind'
I hear myself ask

'To answer a few questions, perhaps?'
'You're in a bit of a hurry'
'Yes, but it won't take too long'
'Just a few more to be answered'
Oh no, please don't run off!

To succeed, I will have to be tough
Demand their attention and time
So what, if she is in a hurry?
It's her time I'm using, not mine

I think of the holiday I dream of
Paid for by the money I earn
Demanding time and attention
From those who have no time to hear

Then along comes a lady of advanced years
Who looks at me straight in the eye
'Aren't you going to ask me your questions, dear'
She says with a long, drawn out sigh

'These days no one can be bothered'
'To stop and talk for a while'
'So I thought if I answered your queries'
'It may help the time to pass by'

So I look her straight in the eye
'Of course you can answer my questions'
'Well, at least you could give it a try'
'I don't mean to sound so disdainful'
'But wait and you'll clearly see why'

'These questions are for a young lady'
'To tell us what method she prefers'
'Contraception, you see is the subject'
'And which option is currently hers'

'Oh dear'
She says, disappointed
But then I just know what to do

'How old will you be today then?'
'Between eighteen and say twenty two?'
'Oh yes, that sounds about right, dear'
'Now, how shall I bias my view?'

Claire Rees

A New World

Everybody listen and let me be your teacher
  you are my disciples I will be your preacher,
Go out to the world and tell everyone
  All war must cease a new peace has come,
Leaders of the nations you sit and gather round
  making each one promises and no solutions found,
It's time to stop your talking, take heed of what I say
  Yesterday is history and a new world starts today,
For a light will shine out of the skies

  and take the evil right out of our eyes,

  and the rich man that walks down the street
    will help the poor man onto his feet,

  and the hungry that lives on the lands
    will be fed by once greedy hands,

  and war will be a thing of the past
    for peace will be here at last,

  and our children will be the ones who
    will know for they will preach all that we sow,

  and we will all give thanks to the light
    for we all have gained a new sight,

  and everyone will be beaming with love
    by this light that shines from above,

  and the world will be fruitful and young
    in this new era that has begun.

Ernie Larkin

Notes

This poem is a part of a cycle collectively know as 'The Voyage of Baron Skylark.' It is a mantra to be partly sung like a football song.

The poem tells of hope beyond the approaching event horizon, the next millennium. I am Welsh, twice self-published and enjoy diverse performance based arts.

Everyone is Everything Again

No more History,
now it's Herstory.
The rising waves are growing,
decreasing and then flowing.
Leading spiral boundless,
toward the final wholeness.
No more History,
now it's Herstory.

Life and times merging
are clasping hands tomorrow.
Throw yourself towards
the all encompassing over-mind.

Hypereal visions blinding
earth mindful connecting.
Vibrating gardens curling
the rising time waves swirling.

Everyone is everything
an absolute this will bring.
A oneness here now once again
to ease the weight of grief and pain.

No more History,
now it's Herstory.
This final wholeness glowing,
the old order gone or going.
The boundless spirals leading,
to where the god greens bleeding.
No more History,
now it's Herstory.

Chris Jones

Notes

I am a 27 year old New Zealander, and have been living in London for the last eighteen months. I have a keen interest in the outdoors, and began writing newsletter articles for a local outdoor club several years ago.

Coming from another country has made small differences in culture and climate particularly noticeable, and I have been struck by the contrast of seasons in Britain. The feeling that winter is the end of a cycle is much stronger here, and I wanted to capture the dark wait for the new cycle to begin.

December

Scolded by the black wind
Crouched low in the shadows
Of a long twilight sun

The heather on the heath
Knows winter's icy reign
Has only just begun

Soft snow falls on the land
In gusty shifting drifts
That are watched by no one

Awaiting season's change
To wash away the dead
And flush life through the young

Paul Rowe

Yellow Dog

Notes

Whilst travelling though India I witnessed many dogs in appalling conditions. Dogs so sick it was a miracle they were still standing.

One yellow dog in particular broke my heart and I would like to dedicate this poem to him and the countless others that endure the bitter struggle to survive.

The dust
Swirled around his tender paws,
The heat
Beat upon his back,
Crackling skin, hot,
Red with livid sores,
Showed through where hair did lack,
His mangy head,
His mournful eyes,
Turned here and there for food,
And all around
Man passed him by,
For few of them were good.

Oh yellow dog
You seldom find,
Some kindness in your path,
How tortured
Is your canine mind,
And yet you have no wrath,
Against the hand
That feeds you not,
Nor offers you a home,
Destined to travel
Yellow dog,
Through life's cruel lane
You roam.

Gemma Edwards Gill

The Dead are No Longer Lonely

If you walk with me
you're on the long path
between dimensions

Look for me in graveyards
as the sun sets, and its
last rays punch through
the thickly leaved trees

As the shadows grow long
I walk your earth,
searching for the lost souls
and hear their anguished
cries in the twilight

So think of me as you die
and I will help you
unlike the ferryman
there's no payment
for I too was once lost
now I am the sender of souls

Steven Gray

The Age of Contentment?

Notes

Elizabeth White is a retired practice nurse living in South Norfolk for the past thirty years. She is a widow and has one daughter.

A lifelong love of poetry, she has entered one or two local nursing theme competitions for 'fun'.

Other interests include music, singing, walking the countryside and book browsing. Church and the community.

This poem was written shortly after her mother-in-law died at the age of 96. (She was a wonderful character who regaled us with stories of her early life as one of 11 children. I have drawn from those).

See the old lady asleep in her chair
The smile on her face shows that she's free from care
In her dreams are the memories more precious than gold
A lifetime of living - she's 90 years old.

Her memories go back to the days of Queen Vic
Of friends from her schooldays, the Headmaster's stick
Which he used with such vigour if only you dared . . .
(During reading of scriptures) to utter one word.

Her school-friends she left at the age of fifteen
To search for a job, and there were umpteen . . .
To choose from, and all were hard work
But it was a living and too good to shirk.

In service you started at six on the dot
Cleared the ashes, laid fires, made tea in the pot . . .
To take to the Master and Mistress at seven
Their lives she was sure, was her idea of heaven.

A little relaxing at the end of the day
When mending was done, but alas for no pay
But tales there were many, told by the coal fire
And a warm cup of cocoa when time to retire . . .

To the small attic bedroom, just under the eaves
A candle for comfort and light for a read
Of a paper-back romance and dreams in the leaves
Of her own special hero, for her hand he will plead.

A husband and children are in the next scene
Life's pattern unfolding, a family serene
In their two up and downer, but oh! What such bliss
To heal life's tribulations with a hug or a kiss.

But children grow up - it seems at such pace
That the business of living seems almost a race
To cram so much action and pleasure in life
Interwoven with sadness, successes and strife.

But the old lady dreaming alone in her chair
Just remembers the *good times* so happy to share
Now nearing the end of her own earthly days
She is older and wiser in so many ways.
So God bless the old lady, she's far from alone . . .
With her memories of life, love, living and *home*

Elizabeth White

The Wedding

Notes

Pat Cartwright is a secondary school teacher specialising in English but has taught all ages. She has an interest in students with learning difficulties and currently, with her husband John, is writing a series with reluctant readers in mind. She has written articles about her early schooldays in war-time West Riding of Yorkshire.

Poetry is a special love. *Reunion* and *Labour of Love* have appeared in Poetry Now anthologies; *Thoughts of Love* appeared in a Heritage anthology.

Her parents had sadly both died when *The Wedding* took place, making the occasion somehow seem more poignant.

The Church was hallowed, warm, inviting . . .
The flowers vernal, their scent inciting . . .
The Choir sang, their voices soaring
Like larks with every note out-pouring.
Melodious voices finally cease,
To leave tranquillity, calm and peace.
The chalice gleams, the wine is passed;
Rings are exchanged, they are one at last!

'You were invited but you did not come!'
My eyes welled up, my heart felt numb.
To see their well-loved grandson wed
And to give their blessing on his life ahead
Was all I wished - how could they stay
Away from this place on their Wedding Day?

With head bowed on hand I prayed that he
Would walk in happiness and find the key
To lasting joy and light and love,
And guidance from the One above.

I stemmed my tears and raised my glance
Absorbing the atmosphere as in a trance.
The organ played, the candles spluttered,
The Father blessed them and thanks they uttered.
The procession formed to leave the Church
And I gazed at the candle; my heart gave a lurch.
It flickered, it lowered, then burnt with bright flame
That glowed and intensified; it had only one aim -
For there, in the circle of light which it cast
Stood my parents, both nodding and smiling - at last.
'We came as you asked,' they both assured me.
'We couldn't miss this, so we just came to see.
We have to go back now. We love you. Take care.'

And the candle lowered - and no one was there.

Pat Cartwright

1 Nil to Malcolm?

Notes

Wayne Reid was 16 years old when *1 Nil to Malcolm?* was written. At this time he had just left school, he was unemployed and rather depressed, so he wrote poetry on depressing subjects—mainly racism. In the time he was unemployed (3-4 months) he wrote 100 or more poems.

Now aged 17 years old, Wayne works at Irwin Mitchell Solicitors and his life has more direction, unfortunately no new poems have been written but his past poems are enjoyed still by colleagues, family and friends.

This poem is dedicated to Shauna-Marie.

I get my philosophies from Malcolm. I respect him deeply,
Even though I'm not a Muslim, I read his words and they feed me.
I don't copy, no I appreciate,
Relate,
Debate,
Then demonstrate.
By writing poetry for others to feed,
I try to fulfil their needs,
By showing the lives others lead.
Some of the opinions, most are from people around me,
Just because I make them rhyme doesn't mean they don't astound me.
I try to write both sides of a story, against and for,
Some people like them, some don't, but I still write more.
I'll continue to, until I'm on my death-bed,
And I'll always try to appreciate what has been said.
Whether it's from the KKK or a white man,
I can never understand.
But I can be open minded,
Never blinded.
By the media, the devils,
Or the countless rebels.
I have my opinion, you have yours,
Either way, we both know the score.

Wayne Reid

Notes

I am a fifty year old married man, with three children and three beautiful grandchildren. My wife and I have been wed for the last thirty-two years, she inspires me in everything I do.

I worked as a professional musician, but now work as a professional stand up comedian, also an actor/writer. I recently finished and passed a BTEC National Certificate in performing arts.

I have had several stories and several poems published over the last couple of years, and have been writing poetry since 1995.

I am very fortunate to live in a beautiful part of the country, Yarm in Cleveland. I am also very fortunate in having a wonderful family, and enjoying everything I do in life.

Gentleness

Can you see the flower
at your shoulder
How soft it feels it's alive
you know.
Put it into this small basket
before it weeps itself away
please don't harm it
in anyway.
Drop it slowly, drop it straight
drop it gentle, before it's too late.

Let me do it for you please
let me do it before I leave
that's it - it's done it's done
it's done.
Nice and smooth
what a good job - done for everyone
well I must be off
I'll take myself away - to go
it's been nice helping you, for sure
see you soon . . . I hope.

Peter de Dee

Adversity

Notes

A victim of multiple sclerosis for thirty-seven years the poem Adversity, is just one reflection on his life. Age fifty-nine Tom Quinn was educated at Tonypandy Grammar School he is well travelled and spent a great deal of time being deeply involved with disability in general. He has written as a journalist for many years with the local paper The Rhondda Leader, and has secured his own poetry spot under the pseudonym (Wheel Walker).

In his travels he has met many disabled people who bear the cross adversity, with courage and dignity, and the poem reflects this philosophy.

Adversity is the silent seeker
no warnings does it give,
it comes to one, it comes to all,
in a life we all must live.

There is cruelty in its passage,
there is pain and suffering too,
but one must strive to seek an answer,
one must find a pathway through.

It is difficult to fight an enemy
sheltering in the caverns of your mind,
a friend is the key who slips the lock,
and whose hands are there to guide.

To the one above who knows it all,
we must utter the silent prayer,
and perhaps the answer He might give,
is so often waiting there.

Tom Quinn

Some Oaks

Notes

I was born in Galmpton, near Brixham, Devon. I had one French grandmother, and one Devonian grandmother.

I have been writing poetry, prose, humour and fiction since the age of six. I draw my inspiration from everyday life, past and present.

There were three oak trees in a field near to where I was born: they are still there today, giving life.

I dedicate my work to my children, Rosie and Harry and my wife Sue.

As I gazed upon some oaks, someone uttered,
'Those oaks you see ahead, they do nothing.
Just standing, may as well be dead.
That is not the life for me, an oak tree.'

Oh, how clouded his gaze must be, if he cannot see
The myriad lives being lived within just one oak tree.

Here there are three, planets revolving, solving
A housing crisis in the animal kingdom.
Lending your life to the human race, your trace
Of oxygen released, borrowed and returned.

All are thankful to you, if only they knew,
The years you have stood here, firm.
Watching many years of humanity, their insanity
Clouding your atmosphere and the planets you are.

Your barks are scarred by individual lusts,
Declaring love falsely and without consent.
But your out-stretched arms welcome all, even call
With mystic Druid language drawn from below.

The parasites enter your scars, and would fell you
Like the woodsman's axe; protection comes from friends.
Dwellers of your wind bent boughs feed and seed
Your offspring to make a new planetary system.

Some only see a table and chairs, a flight of stairs,
A door and its sturdy frame: a shame.
Insects, a squirrel, boys climbing. The flight of birds
In this once worshipped race of giants.

The final refuge. The last soldiers of time,
And space. Hurricanes snap your limbs, your trunk
Stands firm. We humans can't afford mans' hurricanes,
Our limbs, our trunks disappear like burned embers.

Someone disappeared gazing at some oaks,
He had no chair to support his limbs.

Ian Harvey

Roses

Notes

Dedicated to my father, Alexander Pow, who died of cancer 20 April 1996.

His bravery shone through his pain and it was this that lead me to start writing poetry again after years.

The very first poem I wrote was a Christmas present for my father. Also something he could take with him, it was entitled *You Maybe Weren't Perfect* followed by *Missing You* then *My Little One* and of course now *Roses*, all published in different anthologies.

I hope my father is watching over me and I hope he is proud of me, like I was proud of him.

Shimmering shades of red,
Leaves deep green.
One soft pink
So precious as seen

One by one
Laid upon
Like a wreath
Your heart beneath.

A simple act
We carried out,
Like a pact
There was no doubt.

A final Goodbye
to part of us.
Trying not to cry
or make a fuss.

Covered up
Purple cloth,
Gold trim
Then your hymn.

The story of your life
We had put aside
The dancing
We couldn't hide.

Then disappeared
Amazing Grace
Now only memories
And your face.

Lesley-Anne Pow

See, Hear and Feel

Water cascading down a mountain,
Bury your head in a foaming fountain,
The sound of children, out at play,
The smell of new cut grass and hay,
Look at a cloudless, moonlit sky,
A gentle tiredness making you sigh,
A drink of clear water to quench your thirst,
To run the race though you weren't first,
To feel and hold a baby's hand,
To stand with your feet in hot, wet sand,
Sink your teeth in newly baked bread,
Or an apple or pear, try those instead,
Smell a rose covered in dew,
Run naked through a forest try it, please do,
Remember when you passed your driving test,
When someone said 'Babe, you're the best,'
There's many more, you know what I mean,
Most of us all, have been and seen,
That's great, you say, what's the fee?
No charge, my friend, all this is free.

Brian Reece

Notes

I've been writing poetry
about three years now, and
I've gone through a lot of
subjects, that are inspired by
just about anything, stuff I
read, see, things around me.
Some poems are put together
with my art work I do.

This poem is done in the
same way and probably ties
in with my Irish background,
but in Dublin,

Circle of Belfast

As you travel through
The streets of Belfast

You seek the freedom
From the killings
That haunt our past
Which makes your mind
Turn in the space
That it has

Which leaves you alone
To fight the misery
That entails the fear
You so much hate
And so they plan their
Next murder

Which follows on
From the last one

Which is bred in
The next generation
Of the IRA race

P J O'Toole

Poole Bay

Notes

John Cartwright, a retired educationalist, has an interest in local history, theatre and writing.

Other work published includes most notably Sonnet to Self-effacing Love (Heritage), A Paean of Poesy (Poetry Now) and a series Growing up with Grandma (on Cannock Chase) for Staffordshire County Magazine. His biography of his mother Time is But the Stream is recently published by Regency Press, London.

An historical novel The King's Pirate, telling of Poole, Dorset and Faversham man Harry Paye and the King Henry IV is just completed. Poole Bay written on Southbourne cliff, was inspired by research into Adventurer Paye.

I stand on a cliff top near my home,
And let my mind's eye freely roam.
There are Roman galleys in the bay,
They're Paye the Pirate's cogs another day.
Was it Drake's drum sounding from afar,
When the Dons misliked the way we are?
Roundhead and Royalist battle it out,
Smugglers flee as the Revenue shout.
The visions fade and a new scene rises,
U-boats lurk and they'll take no prizes.
I shudder and cling to the present day,
When Ferries and Pleasure-craft cross the bay.
From Purbeck to Wight, Bournemouth, Christchurch, Poole,
Lie peaceful, I know, for I'm nobody's fool.

John Cartwright

The Ancient Crone

Notes

The author is sixty-two, retired, and living in Sussex.
His previous publications include a short story in the local press, and another, together with a poem, in a national magazine. He is currently proofing a first attempt
at a short thriller, he is sup-
ported by a patient and understanding wife.

He draws upon experiences
as a child for much of his
inspiration, and in fact *The
Ancient Crone* is a piece of
imagery from a well remembered, repetitive and vivid
nightmare from early childhood, that often left him
thrashing among knotted and
twisted sheets. That particular
ghost is now well and truly
laid.

The ancient crone is all alone,
For reasons that are clearly shown.
Grubby raincoat, handed down,
Rumpled stockings, dirty brown:
Safety pins and ragged belt,
Pot shaped hat and Fox's pelt.
Button shoes, both down at heel,
Lipstick that's begun to peel,
Claw like hands, veins blue and thick,
Shuffling steps with walking stick.
Grimy nails too long and cracked
On fingers by rheumatics racked,
Warted nose that's hooked and huge
Twixt sunken cheeks with two days rouge.
Toothless mouth, lopsided grin,
Above a hairy pointed chin,
Bright beady eyes are never still,
Reflect a cunning evil will.
This ancient crone is only seen
Just once a year - on Hallowe'en!
Yet in my nightmares still I fear
This dreadful creature will appear.
Simpering, sniggering apparition,
What is the meaning of this vision?

Edward Butler

City Rush!

Notes

Originally from Great Britain I was born and lived there most of my life. I have an English father and a German mother. At present I am beginning an apprenticeship in Hotel Management in Germany, Hamburg.

I am interested in theatre, acting and I enjoy painting.

It is certain circumstances or situations which tend to inspire me to write poetry. Sometimes the words just flow.

They stand and wait
Look and stare
each in his own world
not daring to look up
into the eyes of another
the fear's of man
becoming evident.

All in it together
But all afraid of the other
It is strange how man doth function
we are a race
All quite different
And yet the same.

In this cold world
there are just numbers
sad empty looks . . .
But there!
There was a spark in someone's eye.
A bit of human touch
A peace of personality

A pair of eyes did meet
A flicker of a moment . . .
. . . then again all is enveloped in it
A cool fear all around us
We look not
We speak not
And we feel not.

Where does it all lead to?
Standing, sitting . . .
And waiting . . .
Waiting for what?
Who are they? I ask myself
What are they doing?
And where are they going?

It is a sterile world,
the city life . . .
for me, the country,
it is right.
Where I am happy and content
It is fulfilling to be
a part of nature . . . free!

Heidi Deans

330

One Less Than Us

Notes

I'm a 29 year old Geordie who's into: hedonism, self-pity, weight training, football, music, tall women, Cary Grant, Lloyd Cole, Charles Buchowski, Scott Fitzgerald, Stevie Watson, Selina Scott and being a large buffoon.

My poetry relies heavily on the clichéd tortured artist syndrome. The poem featured, being a perfect example of this. I'd broken up with the woman I'd been living with and this was my obligatory 'Oh woe is me' response.

I was informed of my inclusion in this collection on the anniversary of my dad's death, so I'd like to dedicate it to him.

a dance of crazed insanity
one less than us leaves only me
to dance alone with no fair maid
alone I sway, alone I fade
into the blackest black background
I disappear without the sound
of loving address
no tender caress
so here I am
alone and damned

Julian Lee

There are Other Dead Fish

I must remind myself to breathe.
To take the polluted air,
into my shrivelled lungs.
To draw it in and choke it out,
the fuel that moves my brittle cage.

I must remind myself to move.
Force my bones and muscles
to take even a few steps.
In any direction.

I must remind myself to eat.
To chew and to swallow
the mutated garbage,
the processed poison,
and put fat onto my yellowed limbs.

I must remind myself not to feel.
To numb my being,
to laugh at pain.
To smile a sick smile,
when you fall down.

I must remind myself to move on.
I must remind myself there are other
dead fish in the fluid sewage.

Zoë Jackson

Room at Night

Notes

Christian McConnell was born on 11 August 1978. The youngest of four children, he attended Alsager Comprehensive School, where he gained 9 GCSEs. He started an A level course, but gave it up when his family moved to Congleton to run a family business, The Three Arrows Hotel. He is now working and studying part-time. In his spare time he enjoys reading, writing and walking.

This poem was written soon after his move to a new town and life style. The feeling of isolation and futility reflect his sense of disorientation, a young man at the cross-roads of his life.

Four walls, a window and a door,
the cruel reality of being poor.
Money comes and soon goes,
I'm left again in this room alone.
Settled in to enjoy the night,
of watching people who have got it right.
I did, I once, I could again,
become ambitious and play the game.
I would rather lose myself,
and write my thoughts to calm the night.
A chilling thought then split that night,
how Christian McConnell could get it right.
As soon as the good thoughts flew,
I remembered I was still in this room.
There is no way for someone to escape,
the rain and deadly pitch black night.
I'm a lost soul in a room somewhere,
with no possibilities of getting there.

Christian McConnell

Notes

I am 22 years of age and live in Gainsborough, Lincolnshire. My parents are Donald and Jennifer; my brothers David and Andrew and my sister Julie. I am employed as an agricultural parts person.

I had my first poem published by the International Society of Poets, and have five other published, or pending publication. I received the Triumph House Editor's 2nd Choice for my poem entitled Passage (twenty quid!)

My interests include reading, writing, listening to music, driving and walking. I have several pen-friends, established through mutual interest in Sci-Fi/Cult television shows.

It took me some time to bring myself to submit work to poetry anthologies however, I recommend it to those contemplating it, what have you got to lose?

Creation

The daylight succumbs to the darkness of night
The birds, to their roosts, deploy their last flight
The moon, in its wisdom, replaces the sun
To supply, on reflection, small light where there's none

Distant bodies, far off planets, speckle the dark sky
With twinkling starlight from years long gone by
Somewhere streaks a comet with long, fiery tail
Unseen from this distance as it burns its own trail

We know very little of what is to know
We find little snippets and onward we go
There is so much out there that we, in our days
Will never discover to show and amaze

Our history lies out there, beyond furthest sight
The key to existence in faraway light
The day we discover the absolute proof
Signals the world's end through knowing the truth

Since man first appeared he's wondered just how
He came to exist as he still does now
There are two main theories that keep us in line
The first evolution, the second divine

In both we are led to believe the unknown
What someone has written in book or on stone
Both contradict, yet both could be wrong
Some unthought of truth could still come along

We can be restricted by what we are taught
For we, as mere children, are fed others thoughts
In hope we'll believe the first that we hear
And not voice opinions to confuse and to fear

Whatever did happen to create what we are
It should make no difference, we have got this far
With truth as unknown we have our beliefs
So life gives fulfilment, then leaves us in peace

Simon Blacknell

Britain

Land of future promise, land of grief and pain
Will it never rise to see world greatness once again
Little gem of contrasts, with emotions running high
Deep dark pits and soaring hills, reaching to the sky
Where man fights man in Industry, as well as on the fields
Just like in other foreign lands; what will the future yield

When I think of all the beauty that abounds in our fair land
The lovely leafy corners, the green fields hand in hand
The fresh air hilly vistas, that one can reach with ease
To get away from polluted air; which doth the nostrils tease
The quiet lanes and calm thatched roof that is still in village found
What aspirations in the mind, the quiet air may abound

Man needs time to think, it must not all be rush
Where one is pushed and harried, with no time to hear the thrush
Sweet song of bird can still delight the unaccustomed ear
Reluctant heart can still abound at each new promised year

But we must all pull together to reach the promised land
Instead of shaking angry fists, we must learn to shake the hand
In friendship, trust, and courage, unite to pull together
Through sunshine, sleet or snow, whatever be the weather
Corner reach to corner, country reach to find
That joining hands together, can elevate the mind

Although the different Cultures must ever have their say
The common bond must keep us close, together, day by day
May we ever freely roam in this green and sceptred land
Set like a jewel in the sea, with tree and rock and sand
Let the heart be free; not like the rock; but reach out like the tree
Hand in hand upon the strand; Britain can yet again great be.

Walter Botterill

The Field Trip

We paced purposefully along the open promenade at Hythe,
The schoolteacher and I,
Looking for evidence of tourism -
A hopeful hotelier daubing bright paint,
An overlapping lady titivating her tea shop,
And deck-chairs.

'A field trip must be carefully prepared,'
The schoolteacher explained,
'Reconnoitres, roneod sheets, aims, projects, graphs, charts, maps . . .
And I pondered all this as with synchronised steps we covered
the imposing front.

And with each step a sadness overcame me
As I became one of the day field trippers,
Watching the roneod sheets served like writs,
Their reluctant recipients openly dismayed
As their delusions of liberation evaporated.

They won't race delightedly across the solid sand,
Nor dabble around the water's edge with favourite friends.
The secrets of shallow pools will elude them
And the sharp taste of the mighty sea will pass them by.
It's just a field trip.

Elizabeth Ann Barnard

Notes

I am a 28 year old Public Service worker from Swindon. I started writing poetry at junior school. At the age of 10 I won 2nd prize in a competition run in conjunction with National Tree Week. My poem was about *The Plain Tree*, those that lined one of the streets that I walked down every day to get to school.

I have always enjoyed writing both short stories and poetry, rhyming humorous poems being my favourite.

My inspirations are real life experience/situations I find myself in, feelings, dreams and what makes me laugh.

My hobbies and interests are competitions, walking, dancing, music, my 2 cats, (Cagney and Lacey!) and travelling.

Now I have had a poem published I will probably write more as I'm now feeling inspired by this success! I usually only share my work with friends and family but hopefully I will be able to expand on that.

Angel of Darkness

When the Angel of Darkness descends
I am hopeful.
But alas he has come and he knows.
I am not ready, I am beating, I will fight.
But he suffocates me with his power
And I cannot see but only one thing - destiny.
And when he clouds over me I am frightened.
I struggle.
But he knows he has come at the right time.
When he takes me I go, afraid to stay for fear
of what will be left.
But when I'm there I see myself - I look serene and peaceful.
Now I know why and now I am ready.
When the Angel of Darkness descends
I am hopeful.

Theresa Williams

Buried Alive

Notes

I am a student living in Dublin, Ireland. I started writing about two years ago. My favourite poet is Sylvia Plath.

This poem is about bad memories that seem to be gone but can return to haunt you, even if you think you have dealt with them.

This poem is dedicated to Jenny Harrow.

I won't go back and you can't make me,
Those are the things I can't see,
Sometimes I wish it was over,
And then remember,
It is.

I won't go back and let it take me,
Those are the things I could be,
Sometimes I forget,
And then remember,
Them.

I can only burn myself,
Destroy from within,
By those who destroyed without,
It is buried and hidden always,
Not dead.

Dervla O'Keeffe

Falling

Notes

I am a 17 year old 'A' level student who only started writing poetry a few months ago. This is one of my first few poems and the first I have had published (being the first one I have submitted).

My first and greatest influence was a girl, and my love for her was my first inspiration.

This poem is dedicated to her - the light I couldn't quite reach.

Where am I?
Asked the man to anyone who could hear him
Are you sure you don't know, replied a voice from the darkness
I don't remember this place, said the man
What can you remember? The voice inquired.
There was a light. A bright light.
A light so bright I could see nothing else.
And the light was warm, warm and comforting.
It sounds nice.
It was the most wonderful thing I have ever felt.
Why did you leave then?
I didn't want to.
I tried to get closer to the source of this divine radiance,
But whenever I came within reach I was thrown back.
Time and again I neared this object of perfection,
This thing of pure joy,
But always it was beyond my grasp.
What did you do? The voice prompted.
I knew my chance was fading,
So I gathered all my strength for one final try.
Yes?
I lunged forward,
Closer and closer, until I was blinded by the brightness
And enveloped in a feeling of pure pleasure,
Greater than anything ever before.
I reached out my arms,
And was about to embrace the light when . . .

. . . it was gone.
The light had gone.

I was surrounded by darkness.
And I was falling, falling through the blackness.
I fell for hours, weeks, years, who knows how long?
And I was cold.
Cold; blind; confused;
Alone.
And here you are now.
Yes. Where is this place?
Are you sure you don't know? Asked a voice from
        the darkness.

Daniel Rust

Passage Through the Bluebell Glen

Notes

Poetry has always been a source of enjoyment to me, both reading and writing it. I also enjoy reading about the history of Scotland and the Great Wars of this century. This poem is about the 1745 Jacobite rebellion in Scotland, a sad part of Scottish history.

I live in Glasgow with my partner and am presently unemployed. I came from a large family and have always been encouraged to write.

I enjoy the outdoors, walking, fishing and gardening. I also enjoy travelling both in Scotland and abroad. This has been a source of inspiration during the many hours spent writing poems and lyrics for songs.

Twenty five hundred marching men
Ploughing through the Bluebell Glen
Twenty five hundred dreams of do or die
Thoughts of glory
Held together by a broadsword chain
Passing through the Bluebell Glen
Left behind a mother and many a hungry wean
Off tae fight for freedom tae keep a family name.

We're off tae see the red coat who slandered
Ma Heilin hame.
We're a' men no a' the same
But heilin men we ur by name
Passin through the Bluebell Glen
Born part o' these mountains that born this
Glen part o' the runnin water that feed this glen
Plan tae kindle a family in this heilin glen

If it takes a lot of killin' then let it be
The redcoat came before into my house
But never used the door
In this Bluebell Glen
Took my mother for three days or more
Took away her heart
And no more weans could she bear
In the Bluebell Glen

Now a man wae a blacksmith's forge for a heart
We're off tae see the redcoat and I will
Duly do my part.

Stephen McGowan

Notes

Living in Dorset, from Bri-antspuddles countryside, to Weymouths seaside town. The seaside and countryside are my main inspirations.

My life consists of taking our surroundings, adding all the senses and my personal touch. I follow the Wiccan Path which evolves around nature and spiritual love.

I have had published *'All the Trees Wave Their Boughs'* published in 'Voices in the Wind', by The International Society of Poets'. I have also received a certificate of commendation for love poet of the century from the poetry club in Wales.

One More Night

Cascades of velvet
touched the moonlit night,
shadows danced
against the silvery beams,
distant stars glittered
in the background,
rippling waves
moved slowly over the sand,
over the darkened seas
rode a dolphin
moving over the water
gliding over the waves
droplets shone out on his back,
seagulls take flight
as the tide flows out
leaving prey vulnerable
to the keen eyes
and sharp beaks,
gently the breeze
caresses all in hand,
forgotten seaweed travels lightly
rolling over and over
dizzily to the next stop
to meet with torn paper-cups
and rubbish left to decay
mixed with flat pebbles
cold and wet and glistening
under the night glory
the air full with sea
the smell of salt
lingered in the air
silent as can be
the night slipped
into the west
ready for a brand new day.

Daniella Reed

First Taste

Notes

I began writing about how living affects me during a complete breakdown of everything in my life and never stop.

As an adopted adult, my concern is for those who experience an enforced 'emotional crippling' throughout life through denial of knowledge of their roots.

The social worker who worked to find my father, unsuccessfully, utilised my negative experiences as an adopted baby to improve the overall attitude of the right of the child's access to knowledge of its truth from the start. We need to know, good or bad!

I have raised three precious children mostly as a single parent.

Thus, it begins with no choice.
Thrust into life with no voice.
No control in her world.
Here and there to be hurled.
Abandoned to alien power.
First taste of life is sour.

Mother's breast absent, withdrawn.
Maternal heart brims with scorn.
Papa with mama has fought.
Confusing message is taught.
New infant alone with her tears.
First taste of life is fear.

Slashing babe's soul with a sword.
Comes the adult pain of discord.
Cold arms of a stranger.
Emotional danger.
No comforting motherly tone.
First taste of life . . . 'alone.'

Chartered, stormed life then begins.
Sad child bears the parent's sins.
Future patterns in place.
The 'fight' etched in her face.
Licking wounds from the knife.
Seek the 'honey' of life.

Trisha Williams

Notes

I live with my girlfriend Louise in Glasgow where I work
as a staff nurse, working with
adults with physical and
learning disabilities.

My hobbies include football;
travelling; entertaining children; keeping fit
(reasonably); socialising and
having fun.

This is my first poem I've attempted to get published. I've
been writing for around five
years. My inspiration usually
comes spontaneously when
my emotions are stirred by
something I feel strongly
about, for example romance;
the unknown; comedy; anger
and world-wide issues.

A Day in the Life was inspired
whilst working in a
ward/house, with adults with
special needs. In a ward like
this physical disabilities are
sometimes all that people see
and acknowledge where
through ignorance and non-
education people do not see
the human being. I've tried to
write the poem from what I'd
imagine that sort of life to be
like and the inner strength
that would be required to
cope with this.

A Day in the Life

I hear the all too familiar voices
Coming ever nearer down the hall
Another long; lonely day is dawning
I don't want to be part of it all

They awake me from my fantasies
And my dreams quickly drift away
It's suddenly back to reality
What can I do or say.

You see nobody understands me
Handle me like a child does a toy
And conversation is made around me
As if I'm just a little boy.

And suddenly I'm lying naked
It's as if they've even stripped my soul
I feel so vulnerable and so cold
As I begin my everyday role

Blunt metal burns my tender skin
Blood and water mixes in with soap
In this twisted body I feel so trapped
No dignity; no hope.

Two hours have past since I left my other world
But it seems like two long weeks
Because time doesn't pass in a crowded room
Where nobody ever speaks

The day it passes like time standing still
Not many come and go
As I sit alone with my own thoughts
Which no one will ever know

Then darkness descends like a vulture
And I feel its prey is me
Reminding me of my day gone by
Laughing that from this life I'm still not free

And as they put me to my bed
Some say goodnight; some just walk away
I say thanks to them all; forgive their faults
And hope they'll be rewarded when it's their day

It's quiet now as I lie here
Through the curtains I see the flickering moon
Maybe that's my perfect world
If it is; I hope I go there soon.

Stephen Caine

Reflections

I am disillusioned by the human race
I look around and see disgrace
Man's humanity to man
Is so evident today.

Genocide, torture, starvation and fear
The human legacy from year to year
Is this the purpose of the human race

Often I am consumed with shame
To be a part of universal blame
Is this the purpose of the human race

There must be a way - a way for the future
While mankind continues to destroy
Hell-bent on profit and loss

Hundreds know the profit
Millions know the loss

The holocaust should be history
The holocaust is here and now

Anne McLennan

Mistaken Identity

Notes

Avrille McCann was born in
Sheffield is married and has
four adult children. She has
written in verse since the age
of thirteen and regularly uses
poetry in her work as a
teacher for the Multi-
cultured Service in Middles-
borough. The 1985 Open
University Course 'Art and
the Environment provided an
incentive to put the collection
into book form to which she
has added ever since. A dozen
of these have now been
published by Arrival Press.
After the first one Avrille realised that most women
change their name on mar-
riage and thus could not be
recognised by old friends. For
this reason she decided to add
her maiden name 'Oxley' to
make her nom-de-plume.

Inspiration for this poem, as
with many others came during a walk along the local
greenbelt.

I thought it was May,
But when I got closer
I realised it was you,
Looking so debonair
In your spring finery,
The black suit
With the frilly furbelows
And those sharp nails!
My dear, how could I
Have been mistaken
Especially in April?
I should recognise
A Blackthorn anywhere.

Avrille Oxley McCann

345

Notes

I am a forty-two year old plater/welder currently unemployed. I live in a village called Parkgate which is on the outskirts of Rotherham. I have never written any poetry before but decided to have a go after reading the advert in the Guardian, in November.

My interests are reading, walking, listening to music and watching Sheffield Wednesday and obviously poetry, in particular Shelley, Brecht and Auden.

I like to write on issues that inspire my social conscience.

I would like to dedicate this poem to my father who died on 16 July 1996 and never made it to see the publication, and to my mother, who did.

Spain

Sixty years ago this week
Things in Spain looked rather bleak
The Republican government were in place
Which the army sought to replace

Led by Franco and the Fascist militia
Attempting to create a political fissure
Big business, the church and landowners too
United together to support the coup

Franco desired a rigid Catholic state
A despotic regime would be the country's fate
The workers were left to go it alone
As their leaders lacked any backbone

The workers formed militias arming themselves
Liberating weapons from the armoury shelves
Now the Republican government didn't want to offend
Their allies in Paris and the London friend

They needn't have worried because in the end
The popular front proved their best friend
The Spaniards and the international brigade
Heroically fought as their leader reneged

Workers united from all over the world
As the Socialist banner was unfurled
Spain was swept by a wave of rebellion
To stop the coup and this Machiavellian

Within a few days the Franco revolt
Was nipped in the bud and brought to a halt
Two thirds of the country under workers control
To seize the rest was the ultimate goal

They fought heroically against this rabble
Betrayal ripped the heart out of the struggle
The Republican government lacked any solution
They preferred Franco to a revolution

The people of Spain were sold out
Preparing the way for a Fascist rout
The lessons were plain as they are today
The workers; leaders will always betray

Stephen Watson

Salman Rushdie

Notes

I am a father, a teacher, a brother, a husband, a son, a grown-down. I enjoy playing with words and song and have several children's stories in the pipe-line. Any ideas to get these in print? Drop me a line citizens of the world.

Writing to the writer
Who's been turned into a fighter
For the right to survive
And keep his family alive
What are his sins?
They say he mocks
Blasphemes,
This man in blue jeans
Deserves to die
'Cos he tells a lie
I ask you why?
Surely God is great
He has the keys to the gate
He does not need us
As his bouncers and killers
He is father and mother
Sister and brother
Who was and who is
Allah the Almighty
The merciful

How dare we presume
To drag him from the tomb
And kill others in the womb
We have no right to destroy
And use others as a toy.
We want to act in his place
As if not part of the human race
Have we never done wrong
What happens when the gong
Goes for us?
Will we rush
And hide
Because inside
Is a shell
As empty as hell?

Gerry Martin

Candle

It sits there on my fireplace,
Burning ever so bright,
There are no switches on,
The candle's my only light.
I sit there in my own silence,
Forget about all the pain I've caused,
The hate and the violence.
The wax crackles, trickles then falls,
Like the tears rolling softly down my face,
Nobody wants me,
I feel so out of place.
The candle is out,
The wax has all gone,
Flick the switch, the light is back on.

Katryna Jane Fundell

Notes

I am Carrie and I'm 17 years old. I come from Manchester and live in Mereside, Blackpool.

I've been writing poetry for four years and this is my first piece published. This poem was written when I was 15. I thought I was in love and ended up heartbroken. Now I love and treasure every minute I spend with my partner John and our gorgeous son Jake who is one year old.

My heart inspires me to write; my parents always encouraged me to write what I'm feeling.

Dedicated to Vicki Holmes for being there through my pregnancy, birth and always mending my brokenheart.

Passport to Suicide

Every time you hurt me
Hate built up inside
But on the day you left me
You 'fused' my suicide

I read you like a book
But I must have missed a line
Because I always thought that you
Forever would be mine

You took me to the fun park
Without a ticket for a ride
Now you'll have to pay the price
Guilt gnawing you inside

And don't think you can run
Or you can ever hide
But live forever knowing
You caused this suicide.

C Beresford

Dawn

Notes

I am a 71 year old widow living in Surrey with my grandson and my cats.

I enjoy writing, gardening, painting and am a very keen environmentalist.

I have been 'scribbling' since a child but have only recently submitted any for publication. I have now notched up my sixth acceptance in eighteen months!

This poem was inspired by the beautiful skies I see from my bedroom window.

Dawn lifts aside the purple veils of night
And moves across the sky in roseate glow,
Caressed by sun her radiance shines through
To bathe in light the sleeping world below.
And all around her as she goes, floats out
Her raiment of cloud soft gossamer spun,
In an enchantment of changing colours,
Lit thru' with gold by an adoring sun
Her jewels, sparkling dewdrops, nature's pearls,
Shimmering like myriad beads of glass,
She scatters round her as she walks - and they
Fall soft to rest on velvety green grass.
Whilst now a lyrical outburst of sound
Pours forth to fill the air from sky to earth,
As birds sing out for joy at sight of her
Their thanks for giving this new day its birth.
Through fading rosiness she smiles, then bids
Farewell to waking world and slips away,
All's done for now, wrapped in soft cloud she sleeps
Till sun's warm kiss wakes her to start the day.

Daphne Lodge

Wicklow

As the dampness of the morning dew
Envelopes the tender blades of grass
The bleak and listless countryside
Emerges with the rising mist.
The skeleton trees stripped of their foliage,
Stretch their slender corpses to the sky.
A diluted blue sky, scarred crimson by the sun.
Life is postponed during a morbid season
As nature prepares for the rebirth.

Sarah Corcoran

Notes

I am 16 years old and have two brothers, Barry and Seán. I live in Wicklow Town, which is the inspiration for this poem. Wicklow Town is popularly known as the 'Garden of Ireland'.

Another of my poems entitled Snow was published in a book called Jewels of the Imagination, published by the International Library of Poetry in America. Also for that particular competition I am in the semi-final to win £1,000.

My hobbies are reading, writing and I regularly play badminton.

I have not been writing for too long, maybe 2 years. I write everyday things in a special way.

Notes

I am forty something I have two daughters. Nicola aged 30 and Tiffany aged 12, and a granddaughter, Lauren aged 2. I am a single parent.

Tiffany is dyslexic, very allergic and has been badly bullied. These very situations were my original inspiration, as well as poverty and anger.

I have been writing poetry for about a year, I have had one other poem published entitled Anger.

I love writing, it gives me a sense of achievement. I have collated my own anthology which I hope will soon be published.

I dedicate this poem, 2 am, to my late parents Ted and Betty Aubrey.

2 am

Alone with my thoughts,
A chance to reflect,
Mistakes I've made
Deep-seated regrets.

Judith Aubrey

An Ode to Me

Notes

To me, writing poetry is not about sitting down and thinking about what to write and what to rhyme; it's about writing exactly how you feel. Seeing your thoughts on paper can solve problems and relieve negative feeling, proving to be an inspiration to others as yourself. That is what I hope this poem does; inspire others to do what they want.

Dedicated to my family who mean everything to me, even though I am hard work at times, and to Heather who I love beyond the boundaries of life itself.

Greatly inspired, so my life is a pain
A romantic by nature, not a scholar in vain
Reality dreamer, away from the norm
You see I am me, I don't want to conform

Go on, take a knock, you won't be the first
Aggrieved though I am, everyone sees the worst
Respond I will not, the pleasure's not mine
Young I may be, I won't fall in line

God gave me my hands, I modelled my brain
Arsenals I created, so my heart can't be slain
Respect I won't get, sounds follow me round
Yielding the hurt, trying to hurt the profound

Governing bodies will rule, bringing the laws
Artificial intelligence will cover their flaws
Relating to this, I am nothing but small
Yet throughout my days, I will always walk tall

Gary Dougherty

Untitled

Notes

By the time this book is published I will have graduated from Exeter University with a BSc in Mathematics, had my 21st birthday, and will be travelling, mainly in Australasia and South East Asia, before deciding on my choice of career.

I have written poetry sporadically for about 5 years, but this is my first piece to be published.

I have left my poem untitled so that the readers are free to interpret it in their own way. It is not dedicated to anyone in particular, but it does stem from different experiences in my life.

I'm closing my eyes and my fingers are pressing,
The lids down tight to the balls,
Trying to block out real life for a moment,
And letting the random images rule;
But all I can see is darkness invaded,
By bright white forms of nothing familiar,
And instead of relieving the pain for that moment,
By stopping the flow of constant thoughts,
The feel of my heart sinking and swelling,
Over-rides the control of sense and reason,
And my tears seep out, wetting the tips of my fingers.

The cause of my sadness is hard to define,
No one thing to acknowledge, then make better,
But love is, as ever, an ongoing theme.
I cry for my friends, for their pain, for their emptiness,
Knowing, re-living, their shock that I've felt,
When thinking I was strong and completely in control,
I realised I was falling apart.

My eyes are now hurting, so maybe it's helped,
By replacing one pain with another.
But I had looked inside, hoping to see,
An answer emerging from the darkness,
But no such revelation is shown to me,
So I loosen my fingers' harsh pressure a little,
And let the blood resume its flow.
Now the images I see have a certain beauty,
As the darkness smoothly fills my view,
And as a sense of peace takes over my mind,
I realise it hurts less now, to think of you.

Caroline Pomeroy

Old Friend

Notes

I am a 32 year old mother of two (soon to be three) and I have enjoyed reading and writing poetry for many years, but until now have never submitted work for publication.

This particular poem was inspired by my first dog Tammy who was a loyal and much loved friend throughout my teenage years.

It's said that wisdom comes with age
And old I am that's true
But as long as my body clings to life
I'll always be there for you.
Summer strolls and winter walks
The best of friends you and I,
Though other interests took my place
As the years sped swiftly by.
You told me all your secrets
Knowing I would never tell.
I protected you from danger,
Kissed you better when you fell.
I watched you grow from a little girl
I remember the fun we had.
Now burnt by the fire of adult love
I grieve to see you so sad.
I'll go and get my greatest treasure
Buried by our special tree,
Perhaps my gift will make you smile
It gave hours of pleasure to me.
So don't be sad, dry your eyes
You know you're not alone.
Here, have it, go on take it,
Have an old dog's favourite bone.

Tina Aspell

Lost at Sea

Notes

I am 24 years old and come from Vancouver, Canada. My parents are from England and, after completing an English Literature degree, I decided to visit relations and tour the country. Here I am two years later, working for the Civil Service!

I've written an abundance of poems since my early teens, but it has only been during the past year that I've pursued publishing my work in the local paper and amateur anthologies - and I've been very successful.

Travelling has inspired me to write, due to all my new experiences. This poem was written a few months ago at a time of reflection. I realised I could not live abroad forever: my family and friends are too important. So in June, I am returning to reality (home) instead of drifting in limbo.

This poem is dedicated to my homeland!

One day I heard the dull, faint drone
Of a fog-horn moan . . .
Then realised where I am,
And discovered it was a sham,
I no longer live near the shore,
Of the Pacific, like once before,
Yet I have felt so uninhibited and free,
Who's not to see the irony?

I used to be a ship lost at sea,
Floating about aimlessly,
Sometimes the waves seemed too high and rough,
But since then I've learned how to be tough,
England was my light, my beacon of hope,
Showing me I was strong and could cope,
My cluttered emotions dissolved like the mist,
As life became cluttered with tryst after tryst.

But soon I will return to my native soil,
Where my heart now remains forever loyal,
For I've been on a voyage of body and soul,
Learning life's answers, discovering my role,
Viewing my past from a new angle,
No longer suffocating in an emotional tangle,
No longer drifting with happiness suppressed,
Hoping to never again feel depressed.

But these days I awake and think I'm back home,
Then reality sinks in and I feel so alone,
Alas, this country is becoming less alluring,
My needs and my future here are blurring,
Like at sea when the mist rolls in,
Surrounding, encircling,
Then - Bless! - The fog-horn blows,
And the lighthouse winks, showing where to go -

A sailor's comfort and security,
As my homeland now is to me.

Alison Courage

Chamber of Horrors

'Order,' 'Order,' shouted Speaker Bet
and Prime Minister's Questions Time hadn't even started yet
The dreaded Beast of Bolsover, unleashed his vent and fury
at the members opposite
Oh to be a Tory
Conservative back-benchers responded to the bait
New Labour!
Impostors, frauds and utter fakes
backed by the Cabinet sat on the front bench
they couldn't be accused of sitting on the fence
Accusing the Opposition of stealing their clothes
constantly changing policies even ditching the red rose
As the Chamber descended into attacks and accusations
was this a good example to set before the nation
With Members struggling to catch the Speaker's eye
did we really elect these people
Oh why, oh why, oh why.

Mark Pitter

Notes

I am 22 years of age and live in South East London. My family consists of my mother Andrea, father Leslie, brother Michael and sister Marie.

The person who inspired *It is Only in My Mind* will remain nameless. What I would like to say is that it is amazing the effect someone can have on you without that person even realising it.

It is Only in My Mind

It is only in my mind that I see a present
It is all wrapped, ready, and nice to see
It is only in my mind
This is a present for me.

It is only in my mind there is a knock on my door
Opened I see my present is now delivered
It is only in my mind
This scene is considered.

Impatience hijacks my brain, I must see inside
'Hold back,' that's the phrase for this day
It is only in my mind
I believe this phrase will pay.

It is only in my mind that I unwrap my gift with care
I feel your love envelop me with each tug of the bow
It is only in my mind
Yes I can feel your love for me grow.

Beauty and charm are yours to command
These things are there for all to see
But it is only in my mind
You were born just for me.

Jason Gunter

Notes

I am 26 years old, single, female and exiled Mancunian
living in Southport. I am a
junior school teacher in a
middle-sized primary school
in Skelmersdale (famous as
the setting or Blood Brothers).

This is my first published
work. However, I have been
writing poetry since primary
school and have attempted to
write lyrics but found I was
better at poetry.

I love music and am learning
the guitar in the hope I can
get past 'Row, row, row your
boat.'

My best poetry comes at the
worst times of my life, this is
a poem of hope and the title
is fairly appropriate to the
fortunes of my football team,
Manchester City.

Rise and Fall

I've seen this all before
Life holds little surprises
I need some time away
Somewhere different to stay.
I was in a different land,
Then I held your hand,
Sunrise.
Look at the state I'm in
Mass of contradictions
Confused and dying from within
People look to you
But will never be visited
You're the latest thing I know
Sunrise.
Sunrise lights a new day of emotional debt
As you light up my existence
But withdraw affection in an instance
It all comes to an end too soon
Sunset.

Lynn Fletcher

Delusions of a Schizophrenic Body

Notes

I wrote the poem *Delusions of a Schizophrenic Body* after coming across a seminar-programme 'Talking Bodies'. I was intrigued by an address by Guy Faulkner, 'Exercise as Therapy: Implications for the schizophrenic body'. The seminar had nothing to do with me but I latched on to the idea of a schizophrenic body, ie a body suffering from delusions and hallucinations; a body which has lost contact with reality. I think this happens to some extent to most of us as we grow older and have to get used to losing our figures and muscle tone.

The stream I used to jump has widened,
The tree I used to climb has lost its holds
The road I used to run is longer,
The hill is steeper and the surface harder.

What's the matter with the world?

I need some exercise to soothe my mind.
Where did I put my running shorts?
Ah, there they are
   under the racket
      and the roller-skates
        and the hockey-stick
         and the ballet shoes
      at the bottom
    of the cupboard
   under the stairs

How faded they are
   and how did
      they manage to
        shrink while
          just lying there?

Marianne Whiting

War, Tell me Why?

Notes

On the 15 August 1993, I picked up a pen and began to write. That was when I realised my talent and my purpose, which is to bring the enjoyment held within poetry to everyone.

I've written a lot of poems in varying styles, some I hate, some I love, but hey are all my work which I am proud of.

As a result of poetry competitions this is my second poem to be published, the other being *The Show* which is in an anthology called Light of the World by the International Library of Poetry.

Who invented life?
Was it Adam or his wife
Whose was the dream that thought it alright to create
A nation that one day would turn against each other
Even their own race
Everyone has a right to peace
To live in a house and lead a trouble free life
At the end of the day, no matter what race
We all have to live together, rubbing shoulders with each other
On this place we call earth
So tell my why we waste our time on war?
Why do we kill the loved ones of someone else?
To try to prove that we're better than them
Tell me the point of wasting valued lives?
OK, so the world's not a perfect place
But is death the answer?
Will it solve anything to kill with a gun?
War has already claimed many a loved life
And we seem to think this alright
To kill, an innocent life
We all love our country, but is that a reason to risk
Being killed to prove a point?
What does it matter who's better than who
We're all people, individuals who have a brain
To think for ourselves
Basically, we are what we are, why try to change that?

R Oldroyd

Sometimes Night Comes Soon

Who was she?
Alone and in spinning space,
Fighting through a path of life. It came to a sudden end,
A gaping hole sucked her down,
Spiralling she gave birth to confusion.
What had gone?
In some place she had been different,
Flying along a windy sky,
Altogether the blue faded.
Plummeting down some whitened ways,
Swooping, she spied prey as likeness.
Why so new?
Once, away she went, always,
Anywhere and at any time.
Nothing took her breath
But freedom no longer cared,
Her wings hung on the shelf.
Why so sad?
Losing a battle of wills,
A mirror image was leaking
Into some other world.
Greedy fingers robbed herself,
Someone else became.
Why so same?
Now alike every other clone,
Nodding, dog's lying down.
Inside a joint,
A casement of bone, of hers
Calling out her name,
Forgotten, so sweetly forgotten.
It's easier
Why so old?
Youth had merely passed her by;
Some naiveté remained,
In the wrong place.
She wanted it stopped,
The pendulum swung on, regardless,
She tried to regard nothing,
She failed.

S Gibson

Like the Serpent in the Tree

You watch as our heaven turns slowly to a hell,
You sneer as we cry out for mercy,
Serpent in the tree your reign of terror brings us to our knees,
You watch as we fall,
Smile as we walk in fear,
We lived in paradise but now the green and multi-coloured flowers
Are disappearing and from their ashes emerge concrete skyscrapers
And multi-storey car parks.
You're the serpent with the sickly smile watching from the tree,
You threw down the apple from which the hungry took a bite,
You weave and twist around our hearts,
You slither and squeeze turning love into hate,
We can't afford to die,
We can't afford to live.
We can't resist your hypnotic gaze,
We'd like to make changes but all we do is sit and wait silently
For someone else to make the first move,
You triumphantly sit as you bring the brave and fearless to their knees,
You sit and lie to us with your forked tongue like the serpent
Who bewitched Adam and Even long ago,
You're the serpent in the tree gleefully waiting for our downfall.

S Hooper

The Quest

Notes

My inspiration: memories of nights dancing around my handbag in 1980's nightclubs. It was difficult to locate friends amongst the throng of dancers, loud music and 'atmospheric' smoke! Nostrils were accosted by dozens of different perfumes and feet attacked by women's handbag handles.

The poem is, of course, a play on words, but I'm sure many thirty-somethings will understand the sentiment of this poem. The man, 'hunting' for a woman and maybe facing rejection in front of his mates; the woman feeling apprehensive or excited, dependant on how welcome the particular man's approach is!

Quietly, stealthily, he stalks his prey.
He pads across the wooden slats,
Eyes cast on the ultimate quest.
He loses sight - he panics -
It's over - once more in the line of vision.
The noise engulfs him, it's deafening,
The lights appear, they turn - they flash.
Smoke pours out upon him from all sides.
He must not lose the scent.
He weaves between the objects in his way.
Pushing, tripping, moving around them,
He arrives at last.
'Excuse me love, fancy a dance?'

Teresa McGoldrick

Every Step of Life is a New Battle

Every step of life is a new battle.
I will succeed.

Life is like this poem.
Endless in its content.
Never ending, never stopping,
Never knowing what will be written.
    Every step of life is a new battle
What has this world given to me.
Will I leave with only a trail of tears to show for it.
As one by one they leave my side.
Trust turns to deceit.
Love turns to hate.
Friends become enemies.
These are the hardest steps to climb.
    Every step of life is a new battle
But life puts you to the test.
Conquer and the world is yours.
Lose and pay the penalty.
Will I let life slip through my hands,
Like grains of sand.
Look, feel, capture.
I won't let it go, I will not let it slip away.
    Every step of life is a new battle
Will I ever sleep in the same place more than once.
Will I ever rest, will my feet walk,
Forever,
Along this path.
    Every step of life is a new battle
My feet stop, yet I still keep moving.
I run but get nowhere.
Imprisoned in my own life, I cry for you,
But will you cry for me?
    Every step of life is a new battle
Will I sink in my own tears.
Will I drown in my own fears.
When will death come for me.
    Every step of life is a new battle
Death is just another step of life.
As I climb the new steps,
I see a light, new beginning a new life, a fresh start.

Juwel Aktarruzzaman

Winter Colour

Notes

The arbutus or strawberry tree is unusual in having this year's clusters of white flowers on the tree simultaneously with the berries from last year's flowers, against shining evergreen leaves.

This is my first poem, but now I hope to write some more. My great loves are literature, music and natural history, particularly trees and flowers.

After having three children I qualified as a piano teacher. Later I took an honours degree in German at Birkbeck College, London University, part-time. I am now retired from teaching German, but organise concerts for charity in Chichester, where I live with my husband.

I shall be very thrilled to see myself in print.

Look! The arbutus bears berries in October, bright
Yellow, orange, then red, with heather bell flowers white.

The hawthorn and rowan, their berries ripe red
Call in November to songbirds to be fed.

Winter jasmine, in December sure to be seen,
Weaves green stems and yellow stars, an embroidered screen.

In January the pale snowdrop's thrusting spear
Attacks hard ground, frost and snow, without fear.

Early iris and crocus in February unfold
Arrayed in ceremonial purple and gold.

March bursts in with blossom, bud and catkin, as flowers
And soft pussy willow open to sun and showers.

When tossed by tempests and greeted by great gales
March gives way to April, so spring never fails.

Kathleen Harris

Wave

Notes

I was born in June, 1956 and live in Seaham, County Durham, with my wife Carol and our three children. I am employed at the local port of Seaham Harbour.

Working with the sea inspired me to write *Wave*, which is the first piece I have written since leaving college in 1975. While at college I enjoyed reading Ted Hughes and Norman Nicholson as their writing really fires the imagination. I now intend to write more as I have again discovered a love for poetry.

I lie in wait for wind's mighty hand
To push, to lift me from my sleep
To journey on, to kiss the land
My voyage from the deep.

It comes, I stir, I slowly rise
Strength builds I'll soon be free
My shoulders grow in size
My shackles gone coursing o'er the sea.

My power builds, my body grows
Into a giant, running strong
Running where. Who knows?
Running, pushing along

I'll soon be there to lay at rest
My foaming white arms reaching out
Run on, run on and do not rest
Roaring! Hear my body shout.

I see my end a bed of gold
I'm pleased for I did not want the stone
I must push out. I must be bold
My journey almost done.

Reaching, stretching for the land
I'm crashing, tumbling down now
Toward my grave of sand
To die if I'm allowed.

I crash gouging, probing fingers deep
At last I've reached my end
Strength gone, now I must sleep
Ocean, leave me to die old friend.

Terence B Kennedy

The River

Notes

This is my first and probably my last poem, I have never been interested in poetry, so this 'poem' was a complete shock to both my wife and myself.

I have attempted writing short stories, and one longer children's story but have had nothing published yet. The inspiration for the poem was the river Tone, near where I live, and take my dog walking.

Bold and careless, free and wild,
Tumbling, splashing like a child,
Sometimes abandoned, always moving.

Bubbling and tumbling, flashing and reckless,
Sparkling, reflecting, never feckless,
Sometimes falling, always rippling.

Puddle and ponds, flowing over weirs,
Turbid in channels, showing no fears,
Meandering through places no one will see.

Hiding in shadows, searching 'round corners,
Brushing through flora, ignoring the fauna,
Bumbling through branches, broken and dying.

Flying over rocks, wallowing in mud,
Trickling through shallows, floundering in flood,
Passionately turbulent, riotous, rebellious.

Dogs and ducks, willows weeping,
Flies and gnats, small fish leaping,
Rodents living in holes in the banks.

Children swimming, people in boats,
Ducklings fussing 'round fisherman's floats,
Lolly sticks floating as if in a race.

Current is pulling, starting to eddy,
Starting to strengthen, slow, cool and steady,
Destiny drawing it on to its delta.

Maturing and growing . . . then one with the sea.

G A Spicer

Untitled

Notes

I am a retired school secretary and NHS clerical officer married to a retired journalist with two sons and three grandchildren. We are Liverpudlians exiled in Middleton near Manchester for 37 years.

I am an enthusiastic crown green bowler and gardener.

I have had poems published in Poetry Zodiac 1971 and in Metric Muscle 1993.

My enjoyment of writing verse came from helping my nine year old son with English homework in 1969. Since then I have been moved to write hundreds of times and keep them in diary form.

This verse was written as a project about a famous person without mentioning the name, in this instance Bill Shankly.

This man was famous in his life,
Remembered now with pride,
Thousands talk about him still,
As they stand side by side.
He always was outspoken,
Said just what he thought.
But never an unkind man.
His wisdom often sought.

He played the game for many years,
That must have been a sight,
And then he was made manager,
With colours red and white.
The game it did consume his life.
He really loved that side,
And when the Queen rewarded him,
Our hearts near-burst with pride.

This man will live in history,
At least in our fair city.
We won't see his like again,
It's true, and more's the pity.
'King Billy' we all called him,
Mourned by Nessie, his sweet spouse,
Though he spoke with broad Scots accent.
There's no doubt he died a scouse.

Pat Eves

Notes

One of my husband's life
long dreams was to have the
ability to write short stories
and poetry. In the two years
that he spent writing, each
poem was thought about
deeply and every story was
researched thoroughly before
he started. He knew that his
grammar wasn't perfect and
that is why we take so much
pleasure in reading and remembering this poem. Chris's
greatest wish was to see his
work in print, this is one goal
that he himself wasn't able to
see.

*The family dedicate this ges-
ture to him.*

If I Could Only Write

If only I could write,
I would tell the world of this planet we live in,
of the bright sun, with the angelic moon opposite,
the sky, with all its temperance,
sometimes with a serene smile, or a tempest of anger,
the bright stars, that tell of other planets,
we dream,
I could tell.

If only I could write,
About the hills, and the mountains,
that stand up tall, or ramble in the distance,
the rivers that flow, some more gently,
whilst others are explicable torrents, raging rain, or gentle mists,
it's all the same to them,
I could tell.

If only I could write,
to show the lovely trees, and plants, that keep us alive,
the grass, that is essential to our beautiful animals,
the wild deer, the horse, sheep, and other species,
we people do depend on them, that we take them for granted,
is it not a shame,
that we sometimes abuse them,
I could tell.

If only I could write,
that life, plus love, is precious to us all,
our families, of children that grow up so quickly,
then all too soon, we see them with their families,
the laughing, the crying, all over again,
with a smile, we look on, remembering,
I could tell.

If only I could write,
so that angry people, could understand,
that hatred in this world, have so few moments,
our lives, are just a spec in the universe,
once gone, gone forever,
the dreams, the hopes, the lives,
oh yes, I could tell,
If only I could write

Christopher G James

Winter's End

Notes

Semi-retired 'Seisneg' now living in a rural West Wales community, my career has been as widely based as it has been unfocussed; except for a core period as a photographer and technical journalist. Incomplete war-time education limited my awareness of poetry's broader aspects.

I write spasmodically - on some inner prompting - mostly humorous verse and short stories, feeling gauche and immature where emotional demand is involved.

My current interests range over science and the paranormal, philosophy and comparative religion.

This is my first published poem.

Faint whiffs of slurry on the breeze;
Magpies noisy in the trees.
Docks and nettle clog the ditch
And now the tractor's sheared its hitch.

The feed man's late again, today.
'Don't blame me,' is all he'll say.
'Fog/frost/snow, computer errors -
We dropped your load at Woodham Ferrers.'

Rain-filled pot-holes in the lane
Have lagged the car with mud again.
While round the house's frigid stones
The gale gives voice with shrieks and moans.

So while we shiver 'neath the sheets
The stock stay snug on corn and beets.
And Bob, the dog, lives up to form
By rolling in what's soft and warm.

There's hawthorn out, and catkins blow;
A crocus peeks above the snow.
Though rooks build high and skylarks sing,
You'd never ever guess it's spring!

Mutch Merryweather

Animals

Elephants thumping through the forest thump thump,
Antelopes charging at one another in a stampede,
Birds swooping and diving down to the ground,
Fishes swerving side to side,
Dolphins diving in and out the water,
Dogs chasing the cats in other people's gardens,
Bears having a fight,
Lions roaring at one another,
Polar bears in the icy cold water looking after their babies,
And seals doing tricks in a show.

Lucy Miles (8)

Catastrophic Pillage

In jungle green alive with eyes,
strange sounds all through the night,
your habitat, so shrill with cries,
that chill my spine with fright.

Tiger, Tiger! Break of day,
fleeing from those prowling men
with their nets of captive prey,
to cage you in some distant pen.

Which country's zoo, a life you'll spend
or, circus travelling round,
what plight will be your silent end,
remote from freedom found.

Alas! Now caged you sit and stare,
I wonder what you think,
of all those humans yonder there,
who've condemned you to this 'clink'.

Tiger, tiger, night and day,
I know that you are fed,
the sweetest dreams I always pray,
you'll retain on your straw bed.

J S C Webb

St Mary's on the Hill

Notes

Tony Green, a retired architect from Hull, started writing poetry at the age of 65 and is now 76. He has had work published in Scotland in Borders Poetry Anthology and Glasgow and Strathclyde Unabridged. He has a collection of 100 poems entitled *Poems of a Pensioner* (unpublished).

Tony believes all verse should be intelligible to everyone and have rhythm, rhyme and reason.

St Mary Magdalene's
Still stands upon the hill
Built in Eighteen-sixty
For people at the mill.

His name was Butterfield
The architect I mean,
Great buildings he'd created
On the fashionable scene.

He made large wedding churches
For chaste Victorian dames
In better parts of London
I can't think of their names.

His work got in the art books
Along with Gilbert Scott,
But pictures of St Mary's
Most certainly did not!

As gaunt St Magdalene's
Still squats upon its hill
In little beknown glory,
Folks don't now work at mill.

Tony Green

My World

Notes

I am now retired, aged 69, and live in Hampshire, and I have a husband, two daughters and three grandchildren.

I have been writing poems for as long as I can remember, about everything and everyone that I care about, but until my sister sent one of my poems to a publisher I had never thought of submitting them before. That first poem, *Memories of Childhood* was published in January 1997, and gave me the incentive to submit *My World*.

I love reading and painting in water colours, and have an abiding interest in people and the world around me. This particular poem was inspired by a seemingly never ending period of continuing dreadful news in the press and on television I really felt ashamed to be human! Hence *My World*.

There is so much pain and hatred in this world of ours today,
'Our lives are just existence' so many people say,
'Ugliness and evil are the things that seem to rule,
If you think otherwise, then you must be a fool'.
Perhaps I am a fool, I've no riches in the banks,
I often contemplate this world and offer up my thanks.
I find the world a really wondrous place,
Its problems I lay squarely on us, the human race.

The glory of the setting sun - the dawn ablaze with colour,
Forests pierced with shafts of sunlight fill my heart with wonder,
Soft twilight and the peace of evening, a night sky full of stars,
Surging oceans full of life, which only man has marred.
Great mountain ranges standing -peaks glistening in the light,
The grandeur of the Polar Ice, the tropics' brilliant birds in flight,
The prairies, fields and flowers, rolling hills of gentler lands,
All this glory - all this beauty, held in human hands.

The sheer beauty of a tiger, the lion with his pride,
Ancient wise old elephants, their babies at their side,
A leopard or a cheetah with its sudden burst of speed,
Or the old grey backed gorilla, with his family in the trees.
All man sees is a rug for his floor, a trophy for his wall,
Ivory for trinkets, furs to hold a woman in thrall.
Nothing can escape these humans' lethal weapons,
Even the ocean's gentle whales, their very existence threatened.

Human hands and human minds, with their hatred and their greed,
The only earthly creature that kills for pleasure, not for need.
Whose idea of creation is a larger bomb, a wider road,
Or a missile that can span the earth to shed its deadly load.
A constant reaching out for wealth - the need to hold the power,
To take by force from lesser men, rejoicing as they cower.
To be human, so it seems, is to be of little worth,
It is the cause of all the trouble on this beautiful, bounteous earth,

Beryl Lee

Notes

I was born in Volo, under Mount Pelion, in Thessaly, in 19212. Educated in England; and, effectively, by the 44th battalion of the tank regiment during the second world war. I married Nora Dalton in 1942 and we rejoice in five children and six grandchildren. From 1979 we lived in the Lot, in France, where Nora painted professionally. I published in 1995, *Nora in Occitania*, poems from the Lot.

My poems have appeared in the Catholic Worker (New York) edited for many years by Dorothy Day; and in the following collections: A Penny a Copy; Where is Vietnam?; More Poems of the Second World War; the Arvon Anthology 1987; New Christian Poetry; Stand Magazine; Peace News and other journals. Author/editor of Cobbett in Ireland: A warning to England (Lawrence & Wishart 1984). I have two books of poems in preparation: River Common, and Poems for Liz.

I write poems selfishly - to clear my mind, make sense of things if I can.

This poem was inspired by a phograph featured on the front page of The Guardian, 15 July 1995. The photograph was taken by Darko Bandic.

The Tuzla Tree

A woman hangs
From a small tree,
With her hair tied back
Most carefully.

I am the woman
In that photograph,
Part of the wood,
Part of the leaf.

My hair is tidy
My legs slim,
My arms hang down
Straight and thin.

I've lost my shoes.
I have no name.
I am the woman
Who was, who was.

Let Tuzla be my name.
Black Thorn. Wild Ash.
I am the woman
Who always is.

Come to me, women
Of Srebrenica,
I call a truce.
I make a peace.

Come with your children
To sort out the quarrel
Of men and religion,
Of men and the nation.

Before we are Muslim
Before we are Christian,
We are always ourselves,
We are always women -

Or I'll hang again
From the Tuzla tree,
With my hair tied back
Most tidily.

Denis Knight

Blowing Out the Candle

Notes

I am 19 years of age and currently studying LLB Law with German law and language at UEA.

I was born and spent my childhood in Denmark, where after I spent my teens in the Isle of Man where my parents still live. Horse riding is my passion and I used to compete and school my young horse, but I had to give up horses, at least for the time being as riding for University is an expensive enterprise, so now I run for the University instead.

My interests are sport, languages and travel.

Although I am outgoing and would discuss anything, I have my box in which my dreams, fears and desires are cast and only I have the key. Through poetry it's a way to put down these innermost thoughts.

If I feel upset about something, writing a poem means concentrating on issues for a period and when finished its a release it's all let out and everything is all right again.

A friend of mine spotted the competition and was entering a piece of his own work, and persuaded me to let him have one of mine to send in as well. So I want to thank Adrian Stout, this event has encouraged me to believe that my poetry is not just my own half crazed gibberish.

Blowing out the Candle is about finding faith in your own ability from within, to carry on when the world throws obstacles in your way. Also it's possible to miss yesterday but to look forward to tomorrow at the same time.

For every knock, every rejection that shakes my soul
I think of you, a sacred place where evil did not travel
Nature's blues and greens shimmer in reminiscence,
Those days gone. I wanted independence and freedom
But, in adulthood we are still bound by rules and lies
Disappointment and rejection are here too
Just as plentiful.

Time, change, hope quashed
Oceans drink down the sun, greedily gulping,
Suckling life's red centre
Travels through cold, barren lands
Illusions, dusk's outstretched branches
Snap and break, when tested,
Drop you once more.

Hope slumps away unfulfilled
Blowing out the candle, ice let in
A naked march across ice, opened to the cold
Weapons none, hope gone
Visions of tomorrow dried out.
Dreams of yesterdays warmth forsaken
Supped from outstretched branches, like hands
Raised to the sky, they sway rhythmically with the wind
Murmuring 'Grasp what treasure you have, life's joys
Are precious, learn to indulge your dreams'

J Draskau Petersson

Love Birds

Just like a parrot
Bright and strong
I know our love belongs

Like a dove
As white as snow
I hope this love
Will never go.

Like the blackbirds
Fill up the skies
I know I'll never
Say Goodbye.

And like a seagull
Grey as can be
Together we are
Always happy

Emma Williams

Notes

Whilst I was sitting in a Paris café, a man entered wearing a bright yellow shirt. It occurred to me that appearances do not always reflect people's circumstances or feelings.

Mr Clean

Look at that man in the yellow shirt,
Spotlessly clean, not a speck of dirt,
Does he have feelings, does he get hurt?
I'm sure he does,
But you wouldn't know it,
Not from his shirt.

Nelson Jarvis

Power Games

Huge orange lantern moon
Hangs low and moodily
In vermilion tinted azure skies
Awaiting sun's demise

Sun challenges though slowly sinking
Then pierced by earth's
Jagged edge bleeds
Saturating clouds
Suddenly and swiftly dies

Moon stirs smugly
Beckoned by Venus rises
To sail triumphant silver
By stella navigation
Through cloud's sea
In the now deep purple skies

Jeanne Seymour

A Kiss can Change a Frog

Notes

History tells us that all great civilisations decline rapidly when the ruling classes begin to enjoy aberrant sexual practices; particularly the Greeks and the Romans and their interest in children.

Letters of complaint especially to; Stephen Dorrell re The Boys from St Vincent; Michael Forsyth - this poem; are ignored.

Now we have a University lecturer suggesting paedophilia is OK if the child is bright!

My reply to his suggestion will I think be with you shortly.

Bill Cumming is a physiotherapist aged 53. He recently spent some years in Africa working with disabled adults and children. Divorced, he has two grown-up children, his daughter Carmen recently presented him with his first grandchild, Scott-Nicholas.

You'd sack the gardener for neglect
'Tis well within your powers
These tender plants you must protect
The weeds will choke the flowers

I ask for those who have no vote
Should children cry in vain?
Or may we have an antidote
To take away the pain?

Yes you've tried and yes you've failed
To cure this practice vile
Although he's caught, convicted, jailed,
He's still a paedophile

And like a hibernating bear
When stirring thinks of food
The predator will leave his lair
To prey upon your brood

When Maggie gave us that vile tax
A year before the rest
We proved that we could take our whacks
On Scotland try the test

Never mind those garbled quotes
'Scots wha pay' that's tame
If you would like auld Scotia's votes
'Hang perverts' that's the game.

Look, Scotland's lost you must agree
You'll scarcely hold a seat
Why not commission system three
One question on their sheet

The question asked would need no guile
All Scotland would go wild
'Would you hang a paedophile
Caught preying on your child?'

You'd best remember Megan's law
The mice have belled the cat
He's heard wherever treads his paw
No welcome on the mat.

Much kinder then to end it all
You'd shoot a rabid dog
You know that when a child is small
A kiss can change a frog.

Bill Cumming

381

My Garden at Dusk

Notes

I am a compulsive writer. I collected my first rejection slip at the age of thirteen - from the Daily Mail!

I only write poetry occasionally, although I read it constantly. I break into verse when something moves, or amuses me.

I wrote this poem some years ago on a particularly beautiful evening.

I am now in my eighties and live alone in a very small village in Suffolk. My husband is dead, my children and grandchildren scattered, but I love my cottage and my garden, and the house overlooks the village pond. I hope to stay here until the end.

It is August, and the leaves hang heavy on the trees.
White roses, phlox and nicotiana glow like stars
Their perfume wafted to me on the evening breeze.
The birds are silent, but the blundering moths fly blindly by
In search of nectar; they brush against my face and horror
Seizes me lest they catch in my hair and mar
The loosening of daily care and that quiet peace
That dusk brings to the human soul.
The pipistrelles, with their superior radar
Pass silently by, skimming the pond for flies,
Weaving, diving, black silhouettes against the fading sunset.
Behind the trees the harvest moon begins to rise,
Ending the magic interlude of twilight
In a glow of gold.

Nina Preston

Fair Weather

Straight out of Lowry
Into reality
Bending and straining
Against the wind

Freshly-washed hair
Occluding the vision
Stray carrier bags
Sail into the sky

The people-shy sun
Shines from behind clouds
A solitary lady
Still waits for her bus

Where earlier, like lovers,
They came two by two.
She opens her handbag
To tissue her nose

Then re-reads the graffiti
Smeared over the glass
'We say raise pensions
for all with a bus pass'

Hastily glancing round
She feels quite alone
So scratches some words
With the teeth of her comb

'God bless Dame Barbara -
She really does care'

Then onto her bus
It had been worth the wait -
A traffic warden smiles and nods,
It can never be too late.

M Miller

Notes

Born in the Midlands and now living in Sussex, I was a secretary before starting my family. I have four children, the youngest of whom has multiple disabilities. My interests include painting and drawing, quizzes, family history and DIY home improvements.

I began writing poetry as a hobby ten years ago, when my marriage broke up. Six of my poems have been published in anthologies, and I contribute pieces regularly for the newsletter of a disability charity with which I am involved.

The inspiration for *Foiled Plans* was a friend's observation that I would benefit from marrying an aged millionaire!

Foiled Plans

I married the old rat for his money.
He was doddery and well past his prime,
But his offshore accounts and his assets
Made it all seem worthwhile at the time.

I thought he'd pop off within hours
Of our tying the nuptial knot.
I had visions of wealthy young widowhood,
But the devil's still not in his plot.

Twenty years I've put up with his moaning,
Twenty years I've been nursemaid and drudge,
And he's still hanging on by a whisker.
The time's ripe to give him a nudge.

The skinflint sits tight on his wallet
And I'm no better off than before,
So I've booked him a 'Fatal Attraction',
(Two quid from the video store).

With luck, the cantankerous old monster,
In his fragile state of ill-health,
Will slaver his last and snuff it,
Leaving me to inherit his wealth.

But, knowing his odd inclinations,
He'll probably giggle with glee
At a movie which should scare him rigid.
The fatality just might be me.

Linda Kingston

384

A Chief's Prayer

Notes

I was born in Birkenhead, joined the WAAF, and met my husband who was in the RAF. We have lived in Rhostyllen for 49 years.

I took a creative writing course at Drone and gained confidence to submit my poems, I have had six poems published to date.

I have always had great sympathy for the North American Indians, their culture and customs have almost been eradicated, with our modern greed. A plate painting by Chuck Ren 'Deliverance' resulted in *A Chief's Prayer*.

I cannot write to order, if I can get a line right it can flow, sadly they are few and far between.

Where the Silver Birch grows,
my heart is,
in the woods I roam
wandering free.
Listening to the wind in the Pine tree
As it blows over me.
Great Gitchie Manito
guide me.
Send my spirit forth
Give me your strength and wisdom
To lead my people north
To their home in the highlands
High in the mountains where the eagle flies,
we shall be free.
Near where the blue lake lies
We'll set our Wigwams,
cosy and warm.
Sheltered in the forest glade
Protected from the storm.

J Littlehales

Bittersweet

Notes

Whilst staying with friends in Chesterfield I noticed their use of thee and thou; next time I wrote a poem (this poem) I found myself thinking in the same dialect.

Eight years ago I was blinded during a hospital operation. Before this I was an artist. I was totally devastated and a friend, also an artist, told me 'If you can't paint with colours, paint with words.' Thank you Michael.

How do thee love me, friend of mine
As a passing thought
Soon gone with time
As a memory sweet
As a gentle kiss
As a tender word
Upon thy lips.

How do thee love me
Friend of mine
As the velvet touch
Of deep red wine.

How would I miss thee
Friend of mine
A memory sweet
In the mists of time.

Pauline Preece

Farewell

I

Where are they now,
The flowers of childhood?
All summer long
Enriching the meadows.
In every lane and lea,
On every hill.
Their names clamour
Sweet Campion, Melilot, Toadflax, Agrimony.
The herbs to heal life's wounds
Balsam, Self-Heal and Comfrey
Heart's Ease and Traveller's Joy.

Where now
The sounds of childhood?
The Skylark hovering on high
His song in tune with the dancing grass.
Joining the chorus
The crickets, with wings and strong legs rustling
Adding their tune
To the hum of bees.
Their murmur invades my dreams
Under the August sun.
The scene lit by the bright wings
Of yellow Brimstone, soft blues and meadow brown.

Where too
The sights and sounds that twilight brings?
The Barn Owl swooping silently through the field
Air full of the fluttering moths.
The white flash as rabbits hurry home.
Foxes glimpsed scavenging for their young.
The rare things, the beautiful creatures of night,
Homeless hedgehogs and hunted hares.
The Badgers rooting under the stars
Have all these too vanished into the mists of memory.

Sheila Torrington

You

You offered me a banquet
Then refused to let me eat.
You rolled out the red carpet
Then pulled the rug beneath my feet.
You almost killed me with a whisper
Revived me with a sigh
Made life not worth living
Yet too precious to die.
You made me long to write the words
I know I'll never say
You made me hurt
You made me feel
You (please)
Take the pain away

D Ingram

My Lilliputians

Notes

For my daughters.

I am a married mother in my early thirties, have five children, for which I am grateful. I had been married six years and lost two children before I was awarded with my first child (a son). On his second birthday I gave birth to a set of twin girls, the following year I lost another child and the year after that I had been told I was expecting another set of twins. Sadly one died and I went on to give birth to another daughter her twin would have been a girl. The following year I had another daughter, then a hysterectomy after her birth. Every pregnancy had complications, they were all premature. They are all fine and really healthy. I am a housewife and had been employed as a cook. My husband in an unemployed joiner.

I started writing for sanity about two years ago. I have been published in local magazines and also read on the radio a few times. I write short stories and my family love to listen to them. Life inspires me to write, I have written a lot of social history, both in poetry and short stories. I have written over 100 poems and 30 short stories.

The reason I named the poem, *Lilliputians*, is because the babies were premature, every vein in their bodies had been visible through their skin.

It is dedicated to my first set of twins. It had been a hard birth but worth it in the end.

Eight months I nestled you as one
six long hours of loving tolerant
pain which brought it's rewards
A beautiful daughter who's eyes and hair
resemble the colour of the earth that is moulded
on the surface of our globe
The very same earth
which she shall tread upon.
Our first meeting lasted but seconds
for there was more pain to endure
At my feet a commotion of white coats
busied on a vinyl floor.
Soothing words, an anxious face
as your father bends to kiss my brow.
Seven long minutes later
relief could be seen on all faces
as I was presented with my second reward
Just as beautiful as the first.
Another daughter with
hair the colour of wheat on a harvest day
and corn flower blue eyes
which focused when I said
'Hello.'
No more anxiousness
four eyes deliriously happy
stare into an incubator
At two translucent Lilliputians
one at the top, one at the bottom.
Silently I thought as tiredness won,
Ah . . . my Twins,
Megan and Claire.

Dolores Craig

Christmas

Notes

I am a wife and mother and work on a job share basis as a senior administrative officer for the Birmingham local Education Authority. I am currently in the 4th year of an Arts degree, studying with the Open University. I am also studying music, both in theory and practice, and play the piano whenever time allows.

I wrote the poem *Christmas* some years ago when I felt saddened at the way we were allowing the beautiful celebration of this holy season to be marred by the commercialism of the world in which we live.

O Lord where is the peace you came to bring?
Where is the song you came to sing?
The peace that you promised to men of good will;
Is it lost now, in our hearts cold and chill?
Your song that was hopeful, joyful and true;
Is it drowned now in the echo of a song we once knew?

How busy, how rushed, how laboured is the day;
Have we lost sight of life's purpose along the way?
The violence, the enmity, the struggles that we face;
Are we all contestants in that never-ending race?

No Lord, in our hearts we are men of good will;
We long to see, to listen, to be still.
Silent night, holy night, all is calm, all is bright;
For out of the darkness is born the Light.

Patricia Greene

?

Notes

I am a 17 year old student currently studying for a *GNVQ* Advance qualification, which I hope will eventually lead to a career in teaching or medicine, if possible both.

I have had one other poem published in 'Jewels of the Imagination' and titled *'The Meaning'*. *I* have also gained an Editors Choice Award certificate for my poetry.

My family are very supportive of my poetry as are my friends. I would like to take this opportunity to thank them for all they have done for me throughout the years.

Why do we work hard and strive to achieve,
why do some people find things hard to believe.
How do we handle the violence and pain,
how do we prevent things from happening again.
Should people in life be honest and forgive,
should some people in this world, take away people's right to live.
Can people be trusting, honest and loyal, and
can everyone nice have an exact foil.
Maybe one day we may have the perfect world,
but until that day comes, children's future we build.

Gail J Thornton

Camping by the Moselle

Notes

When I was a district nursing sister I met many people (in council houses and a castle) who recited and wrote poetry.

Since halving my working hours I have started to encourage myself (and others) to submit poems for publication. This is my first try.

I have always written 'poems' - my poetry books started with Palgrave's Golden Treasury when I was at school.

Writing helps me to recall a mood or moment especially of my travels. Camping keeps me in touch (literally) with the earth's energy and satisfies my wish to wander.

Like a curtain the shadows
are pulled back by the sun
The green lines of vines are
reflected in the water
Magnified by the ripples in the wake
of the tugs as they chug by.
Willows, silver birch and poplars
form a canopy,
below we sleep framed by red
cannas and daisies in profusion.
Sounds are many like the hum of bees,
then the campsite is still
Except for the chiming of a clock
And a few pairs of feet carrying
Sleep-filled faces.
The moon, pale, reluctant
to leave the valley,
climbs higher in the sky and
slowly fades away.
From the top of the poplar
A raucous crow sets an early alarm
swooping low to the water's edge
then up to the birch, to perch -
Muttering and trilling to himself
a loveless sound.
Swans with necks like snakes
preen each other.
And the bell tolls.

Pauline Rogers

In My Garden

Notes

I am 84 years of age and over the past few years have found a new interest in writing poetry and in verse, which I have loved since my childhood.

Being semi-housebound my outlook from my window is my world, with all its creature activities.

The robin with a wary eye
Began to scoff the food -
the rat with shining, furry coat
Came slowly from the wood;
'this is my food,' the robin said,
the rat said 'understood.'
He waited then for robin
To take his morning meal
And when the robin flew away
He, too, did take his fill.
The robin came back later
Again began to feed -
the rat just sat and waited
'til he could quaff his need
And this went on for ages:
It fascinated me,
to think two creatures could
Behave so amicably.

Elsa Norman

Notes

I am a 20 year old factory
worker from Porth, Rhondda,
Mid Glamorgan.

My hobbies are learning
guitar, growing my hair,
thinking and socialising.

I started writing poems/lyrics
about 2 years ago when I
started to go to a writing
class in Ponty.

I wanted to write down my
feelings and thoughts so
other people could familiarise
with them.

One of my first poems I wrote
at writing class, I actually
had to read out on television
as part of a poetry section of
Artyfax.

This poem was inspired by a
lot of people, but mainly my
sister, who is eighteen years
of age, who I could see had
no direction to turn to in life
and gave up hope in herself
and everybody around her.
Also the lack of ambition and
purpose and facilities to make
things happen is a downfall
for most young people my
way.

Lost

What's lost!
Routine is not
Factory line for most, the grotesque basic routine.
Then get wrecked, drive in nice cars
to the same place every night, few miles from your house, bed, work,
get (wrecked.) Small options in-between.
Lost
What's lost!
Maybe money, but what do you
want from it.
Maybe girl, but what do you want
From her.
Lost
What's lost
Ambition
Something to look forward to
Something to look for beyond the countless
years of monotonous silence
Wouldn't you like to think for yourself
Memories of the different kind around here
Memories of places they'd like to have gone
Things they should and could have done
Never realised ambitions fulfilled
We don't want memories of factories,
how much drugs we took, our so called friends, too soon for the end.
Lost
What's lost
Hope
Hope of a generation
                    Lost Hope

Scott

Notes

I am a 29 year old woman from Brentwood Essex and have enjoyed writing poetry for some years.

I had my first poem published in December 1996, it appeared in Between a Laugh and a Tear, and was entitled Riverside.

This poem *Silent Thief* was inspired out of losing my mother 8 years ago. I would like to think all the poems I write express emotion, and would ultimately like to have my own book of poems published.

Silent Thief

Calm, gentle, swaying,
reflection on things that were
once so secure, so true,
the warmth of a mother's arms.
calm on the surface,
so tempting, luring, unsuspecting
of the current which would
take her to the depths of its being.
surrounding her, drawing every breath
it could possibly take from her.
it showed no relent
to the mother it was taking,
nor of the children it was leaving
in an empty, cold world full of confusion.
The sea has no conscience
only a need to satisfy its hunger.

S A Charles

Skinny Love

Notes

I am 18 years old and live in Newcastle-upon-Tyne. I've been writing poems now and again for a couple of years, but never seriously, only really when things happen that are strange enough to colour in, or if I'm bored and need something to do, I'm generally too lazy.

This poem is probably about love, but I'm not really sure.

Why did I say that
I'd forget you,
When you're a light bulb in my head
on a string around my neck, welded to my finger
keeping warm.
So now, you can lie if you want to
because I know you lie to stay alive,
and it's not easy
when your living on a life-line
it's a fine-line
and time's a vulture
I'm your alibi
here on standby, if you need me
for a skin-graft, or a new hand
when you touch the sky again
and break your fist again.

You make me twitch all night,
twisting in my soul
with noise in your hair
but that's OK,
it's almost real again
and I can breath again
in your pockets
doing time with you, watching clouds
and wasting space.

Jessica Matthews

Anamorphia

You stand so strong
Secure in what you do
All the people that know
You like you
You are so open
Honest and happy
Everyone says you are
A blatant success.

Jamie Treby

Paper Chain

Notes

I was born in Crickhowell, Powys in September 1943. At the age of three my family returned to Essex where I was educated in Seven Kings and Chadwell Heath. I became a legal secretary but am now a housewife.

I have written poetry since my teens for my own amusement. Paper Chain is my first published poem although I have written an article for a local newspaper.

I live with my husband, two dogs and five cats in Hawkwell, Essex and have one married daughter.

My hobbies are writing, reading, gardening, genealogy, music and knitting.

I made a paper chain tonight,
The first for forty years,
And I had such a sense of fun
And such a glow of cheer.
My mind went back so long ago
And then it seemed to me
I saw, once more, the family
All gathered round the tree
And glimpsed a tiny golden child
I realised was me.
Chestnuts were roasting on the fire
And Holly hung on walls,
The Christmas lights, in colours bright
Reflected on glass balls.
Lifted high in Father's arms
I felt the surge of glee
As he helped me place the shining star
Atop the mighty tree.
My Mother, brightly smiling
With joy quite undisguised
Gazed upon the happy scene with
Lovelight in her eyes.
My Brothers' happy banter
resounded round the room
As they vied with one another at
Blowing up balloons.
I felt that I would break with love
For all that Christmas cheer
Then the glorious bubble burst
And I was lonely here.
But deep I know this is not lost
Folk never really part,
While we hold memories in our minds-
Christmas is in our hearts.

Jeannette Ferguson-Oatley

J'accuse

Notes

J'accuse is taken from a selection of poems and prose entitled 'From Picadilly on a clear clear night you can see forever - scribblings of a male hooker' by Tim Coleman, 22 years.

This rose is near to death,
but wilting as I might be,
it's time to tell the truth
of a Homosexual that is me.

We shall look at your defence
for it is you that is the accused.
Is it my femininity?
Or the children I'm supposed to have abused?

Perhaps its the way we fornicate
that makes you point the gun.
I know I'm so disgusting
. . . You have halo's like a nun.

Oh and of course there is religion
which is a favourite of yours to say . . .
A male bachelor called Jesus
. . . You're telling me he wasn't gay?
Mary Magdalene . . . a hooker as his closest friend
I bet there wasn't a Roman
to whom Jesus didn't bend

Yes we live in a lonely underworld
that you did push us under
you wanted us hidden and quiet
Well you're wrong, we scream like thunder

Pain is not a feeling, for us, it's a way of life
Balloons, parties and outrageous
is the way we hide our strife

Now a plague it is amongst us
and bitch us you do the more
Do you get a sick sensation
seeing a young man die premature?

Our pride is never stronger
we'll fight even if we lose
You know who you are I'm talking to
You know who you are . . . J'accuse!

Tim Coleman

When the Sun Shines 4 the Real Me

The fierceness of the yellow
is already shining through,
piercing from my eyes, transforming the colour blue.

My body stretching over, realising
this was not another of those days
where shadows fill the sky with dismay.

My eyes take a glimpse and open wide
the brightness falls around my head
and sprinkles in my eyes.

All I see is the beautiful tranquillity
coming through my soul, giving a
reflection filling the sky with the
most beautiful of sun-rays, reaching
out over the clear, most pure coloured
blue sky.

My soul fills with ecstasy
rushing 2 my toes.

I shiver with pure love
and realise it's time 2
lift my soul.

A smile lifts my face away, as it
appears from ear 2 ear.

I suddenly feel the excitement and
playful day ahead,
flying through with wings aspread
the ecstasy of the sun air.

My soul is taken 2 a land, where
no plans r planned.
I'm here 2 get the injection for love
and happiness 2 share all around.

I wish 4 people 2 realise the beauty
of these rays!

Sian Donovan

Untitled

Notes

I was born 31 July 1970 in Hackney, London.

This poem is dedicated to my grandfathers; Albert S Rider was my paternal grandfather who died during WW1, Frederick E Wood was my maternal grandfather, who also died before I was born. Frederick J Ealey was my paternal step-grandfather and the only one I knew. Though I always wished I had known them all.

There is a pleasure few may get
unless you are blessed,
there is only one true purity,
Pure and Eternal love

But does it really exist?
How could we know if we have eternal love?

We don't

Is it better to trust the heart,
which will make us fools,
or the mind that deceives us?

Would it be better to have bad love
Or no love at all

Love, is it good?
Is it bad?
Or is it both?

The truth of life is that we strive for love,
To be loved
To have loved.

Before the love is gone.

Michael Frederick Rider

First Love

Notes

Written as a tribute to Sir John Betjeman, probably one of this century's most prominent poets.

Inspired by my memory of a Christmas party from my childhood where I first realised the world did not revolve around *me!*

Dedicated to the memory of my grandfather Dick Phillips whom I love more than the teddy bear.

They say that first love is the one
we always keep alive,
it's fresh and sweet and full of fun,
but I was only five.

It was the first time that I'd been
allowed to stay up late,
and when I saw you, fresh and clean,
I knew it must be fate.

I sat and looked in secret glee
with thoughts of love and joy,
I knew you would not talk to me,
my lovely darling boy.

I felt with childish confidence
that you were mine alone,
and so with wide-eyed innocence
I went to take you home.

But just as I got hold of you,
Alas! You were waylaid,
and left me feeling sad and blue,
as though I'd been betrayed.

For you were whisked away from there
and held by someone new,
who could not love you, teddy bear,
as much as I loved you.

Victoria Kaye

A Mermaid

A mermaid swims just like a fish
And lives below the sea.
She's friends with all the creatures there
They're happy and they're free.

She sits in the sun to comb her hair
While she gazes out to sea.
And then she dives right in again.
And goes home for her tea.

Julie Oyediran (12)

Seasons

Notes

I am 52 years of age, married with two sons, aged 21 and 14, and a daughter aged 12. We live in London.

I love reading, entering competitions and writing - I've just started writing.

This poem was inspired by my love of God and all his creations.

I look around me at the earth
I feel the sun and showers
I see the miracle of birth
The plants, the trees and flowers.

Every spring time brings new life
To keep our earth from dying
It frees us from thoughts of gloom and strife
And helps us keep on trying.

Summer bursts upon the scene
With warmth and glowing colour.
We start to think of holidays
Our lives are now much fuller.

Autumn comes with falling leaves
From yellow through to brown.
A brand new carpet for our feet
In countryside and town.

Then, again, it's winter-time.
For spring we then do yearn
But we know we must remember
All seasons take their turn.

K M Oyediran

What Would You Say?

Why is it I must suffer for the way I have to be
But this is how I was born, how nature has made me
People do not comprehend and cannot understand
The turmoil of a woman's thoughts in the body of a man

Feelings that must be curtailed because you shouldn't show
What you really are inside, what emotions grow
It must be very difficult because I'm not like you
I often feel down hearted and don't know what to do

It wasn't what I wanted, but I could not live a lie
So I have chosen loneliness until the day I die
I could no longer hide the fact that I was not the same
So all my life I've been cast out and this has caused me pain

There is one thing I wonder - what exactly would you say
If the son you loved so dearly came and told you *he* was gay

Letitia Snow

Notes

I am 56 years old and live in Old Romney in Kent. I have three children and three grandchildren. I am a distinguished member of the International Society of Poets. I started sending poetry to competitions about 2 years ago and so far have had eight published and 2 put on tapes. My ambition is to one day have a book of my own poems published.